Let the People Decide

Let the People Decide

Black Freedom and
White Resistance Movements in
Sunflower County, Mississippi,
1945–1986

J. TODD MOYE

The University of North Carolina Press

Chapel Hill and London

© 2004 The University of North Carolina Press
All rights reserved
Manufactured in the United States of America

Designed by Jacquline Johnson
Set in Charter
by Keystone Typesetting, Inc.

The paper in this book meets the guidelines
for permanence and durability of the Committee
on Production Guidelines for Book Longevity
of the Council on Library Resources.

Library of Congress Cataloging-in-Publication Data
Moye, J. Todd.
Let the people decide : Black freedom and White
resistance movements in Sunflower County,
Mississippi, 1945–1986 / J. Todd Moye.
p. cm.
Includes bibliographical references and index.
ISBN 0-8078-2895-5 (alk. paper)
ISBN 0-8078-5561-8 (pbk. : alk. paper)
1. African Americans—Civil rights—Mississippi—
Sunflower County—History—20th century.
2. African Americans—Segregation—Mississippi—
Sunflower County—History—20th century. 3. Civil
rights movements—Mississippi—Sunflower
County—History—20th century. 4. Sunflower
County (Miss.)—Race relations. 5. Racism—
Mississippi—Sunflower County—History—20th
century. 6. Social change—Mississippi—Sunflower
County—History—20th century. 7. Sunflower
County (Miss.)—Biography. I. Title.
F347.S9M695 2004
305.8′96073′076247—dc22
2004007424

cloth   08 07 06 05 04   5 4 3 2 1
paper   08 07 06 05 04   5 4 3 2 1

For Rachel

This is Mississippi . . . the heart of the South. . . .
In some sections of the state, there is a preponderance of
colored citizens. In these counties, there is a Negro majority.
And in these counties, there is a ratio of two and even three colored
citizens to each white citizen. The situation has brought problems. It has
created challenges. But most important of all, it has inspired a social system
to meet the challenge—a social system under which both races retain their
identities and achieve their own destinies without either race forcing itself
upon the other. . . .
Such problems are best solved by those closest to the situation,
those who have an intimate and thorough knowledge of the facts. It
is for them to work out according to ethical and moral standards.
The Message from Mississippi *(film), produced by the Public
Relations Department of the Mississippi State
Sovereignty Commission, 1960*

LET THE PEOPLE DECIDE.
Motto of the Student Non-violent Coordinating Committee

Contents

Illustrations, Tables, and Map

Abbreviations

AFSC : American Friends Service Committee
BAWI : Balance Agriculture with Industry
COFO : Council of Federated Organizations
CORE : Congress of Racial Equality
HEW : Health, Education, and Welfare
MFDP : Mississippi Freedom Democratic Party
MFLU : Mississippi Freedom Labor Union
NAACP : National Association for the Advancement
of Colored People
RCNL : Regional Council of Negro Leadership
SCLC : Southern Christian Leadership Conference
SNCC : Student Non-violent Coordinating Committee
VEP : Voter Education Project

Let the
People
Decide

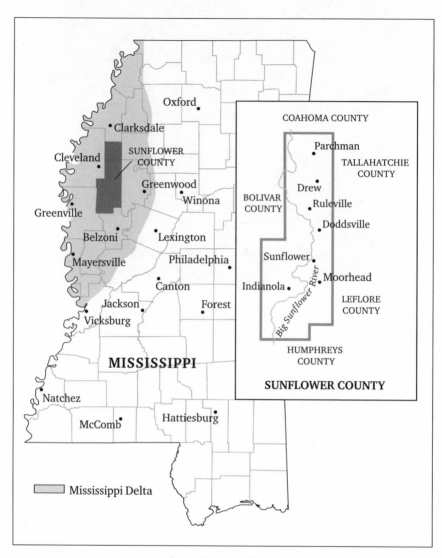

Sunflower County, Mississippi

At the Hands of Parties Known

*The Social Force of Racialized Justice
in the Mississippi Delta*

Charles McLaurin moved to Sunflower County in 1962, one of a handful of college-age staff members for the Student Non-violent Coordinating Committee (SNCC) who went into the Mississippi Delta to register African American voters. When SNCC organized a massive summer project in Mississippi two years later, McLaurin prepared a report on local conditions for the white college students who had volunteered to register voters and teach in Sunflower County's "Freedom Schools." His description of Doddsville, a small plantation community in the center of the county—and the home of U.S. senator James O. Eastland, one of the most powerful men in Mississippi—was striking. Doddsville, McLaurin reported, was a "strange little place" with only "five or six buildings old and run down from the years when cotton was King and the Negroes were even more plentiful than they are today." He reported that local people knew Doddsville as the place where "many years ago the burning of Negroes was a Sunday spectacle where whites young and old delighted at this evil which killed the spirit of the old Negroes and set the stage for the place-fixing of young ones not yet born."[1]

The deserted buildings that the civil rights worker described were empty because farm mechanization had made black laborers "redundant" (in the cold lexicon of social scientists), not because the "burning of Negroes" in Doddsville had scared others off. But the lynching to which McLaurin referred did have a brutal effect on African Americans' lives in Sunflower County. Contemporary reports from 1904 tell us so.

At first glance, the premeditated murder of Luther Holbert and a woman who may have been his wife was only one example of the racialized lawlessness and utter disregard for due process that had reached epidemic proportions in the area by the turn of the twentieth century. Perhaps as many as 200 lynchings took place in the Mississippi Delta between 1890 and 1910. Unfortunately, it is impossible to reconstruct fully Luther Holbert's life and the events that led to his lynching. The few remaining sources of evidence of this life and its grisly end conflict with one another to such a degree that any effort to reconcile them must be speculative. However, these same sources paint a detailed portrait of a biracial Mississippi Delta society in which opportunities for African Americans were strictly limited and whites upheld their positions of power with all the means at their disposal.[2]

The lynching was as monstrous as it was orchestrated, and for Holbert's contemporaries in the Delta and throughout the nation it was much more significant than one statistic among many. Journalists, novelists, "race men," progressives, and even Booker T. Washington portrayed the Holbert lynching as an unusually significant outrage. It was that. Beyond the element of inhuman savagery that was so evident in the lynching lay a less apparent, though completely deliberate, effort to quash African Americans' attempts to fashion a degree of autonomy in the Delta, an effort that continued well through the century. Everyone in the Mississippi Delta knew who killed Luther and "Mary" Holbert, but the man who choreographed the lynching remained free. His son became a leader in the local, regional, and national movements to deny African Americans the full rights of citizenship.

Luther Holbert was, according to the people whose opinion carried the most weight in the Mississippi Delta and in their parlance, a "good nigger." According to his Sunflower County neighbors, though Holbert was new to the Delta in 1903, he was "generally considered a harmless and fairly well disposed negro." Holbert had won this faint but valuable praise from the white people of Doddsville by working hard for a plantation owner, avoiding trouble, and doing what he was told. Holbert was a well-known employee of James Eastland, a twenty-one-year-old planter. He had moved with the wealthy young white farmer from Forest, Mississippi, in the central part of the state, when Eastland and his brother, Woods, inherited their father's 2,300-acre Sunflower County plantation in 1903. Holbert found the Eastlands likable enough employers; he followed them from Forest into the unknown and largely uncivilized Delta, and no evidence remains to suggest that Holbert had led anything but an uneventful life until then. But late in 1903, Luther Holbert began to have serious problems. The consequences of those problems provide a vivid snapshot of a Mississippi Delta society in which violence and race consciousness were entwined at the center of every social interaction.[3]

According to contemporary local newspaper accounts, a woman who may have been Luther Holbert's wife, whom most of the newspapers did not bother to name, had become entangled with another man, another of the Eastlands' trusted employees—another "good nigger." This other man's name has been lost to history, but he interfered with the union of what would seem to have been an unusually devoted couple. It is unclear whether Holbert and the other man sharecropped for the Eastlands or were farm laborers who worked for wages. According to these reports, the Holberts did live in a one-family home on the Eastland plantation, which indicates that the couple sharecropped for the Eastlands and received housing as part of their arrangement. Almost half of the Eastland plantation was still in the process of being cleared of cane and forest, however; this task would have required a mass of wage laborers or perhaps sharecroppers who worked for wages either within or outside of their cropping arrangements. Holbert and the other man could have been either semi-dependent sharecroppers or wage laborers whose livelihoods depended entirely upon the goodwill of James Eastland.

According to local newspaper accounts, Eastland was concerned enough by the dispute between his two employees that he went to the trouble of visiting the Holbert cabin on at least one occasion to warn Luther Holbert against molesting the other, favored plantation worker over the affair. In taking sides in the argument, Eastland designated his unnamed employee the "good nigger" of the two, leaving Holbert without the protection or favor of his employer. For an African American farmworker in Mississippi in 1903, to have lost the favor of one's white protector was to have lost everything.[4]

The dispute reportedly went on for several months, and on a cold Wednesday afternoon, February 3, 1904, Eastland rode on horseback with a black employee named Albert Carr to Holbert's home on the plantation to issue a final warning. (It is possible, but far from certain, that Carr was the man who had become involved with the woman identified as Mrs. Holbert.) Eastland apparently told the unruly Luther Holbert that he could either stop harassing the favored laborer or leave the plantation. Holbert refused to obey the order.

Luther Holbert's fate was sealed as soon as James Eastland took sides in the dispute. Mississippi's legal system in the early twentieth century had two standards of justice, one for African Americans and one for whites. A contemporary Sunflower County legal theorist labeled the state's standard for African Americans "negro law"—an "important branch of the law here in Mississippi . . . composed partly of the common law, statutory law, and unwritten law."[5] "Negro law," according to historian Neil McMillen, "determined who was punished for what," and under the system "the gravity of any crime was determined in large part by its impact on whites."[6] When Luther Holbert threatened his fellow employee and James Eastland decided that the latter was more valuable than Holbert to him, Holbert became another victim of the formalization of an everyday social system that divided all African Americans into "good niggers" and "bad niggers." The inferior party in a "negro law" conflict, Holbert lost all control over his relationship with his employer, over his ability to live a life of his own choosing.

Having failed to convince his rival to leave the woman alone, Luther could have tried to solve his problem with violence, by killing the rival or running him off of the plantation. With Eastland squarely on the side of his opponent, however, Holbert knew that to do so would have been dangerous, even though black-on-black violence did not always elicit a white response within the "negro law" system. A later observer of Sunflower County described this fact as "one result of the system which treats the Negro as sub-human and therefore places less value on his life . . . and exacts less punishment for destroying it."[7]

"Negro law" did prohibit African Americans from molesting other African Americans whom whites favored, and Eastland had clearly decided by now that Holbert's rival was untouchable. In a similar case, an African American man was tried for murder in 1911 in neighboring Humphreys County. The prosecuting attorney simplified the case for an all-white jury by explaining, "This bad nigger killed a good nigger. The dead nigger was a white man's nigger, and these bad niggers like to kill that kind." Predictably, the jury found the accused guilty and sentenced the man to death by hanging. The defendant's lawyer complained, "The average white jury would take it for granted that the killing of a white man's nigger is a more serious offense than the killing of a plain, every-day black man."[8] Luther Holbert must have known of several similar cases, most of which would have been settled outside the courtroom. Holbert knew that with Eastland on the side of his rival, he had two choices: obey his white employer's demands or do something drastic.

When Eastland visited Holbert's home on February 3 and told him to submit to the other man or leave the plantation, Luther Holbert must have felt betrayed. According to several newspaper accounts of what happened next, Holbert had been a "faithful servant" to James Eastland for a number of years. Now he had nowhere to turn. Holbert could not vote, so entreaties to elected officials were not an option. The courts obviously provided no redress. Holbert could not even have swallowed his pride, worked hard, and held out hope that things would get better; the Delta's racialized economic system offered people like Holbert no prospect of working their way to riches and power. He couldn't even dream that conditions would improve for his children—Mississippi's education system would only train them to be unskilled farm laborers. For Luther Holbert and the thousands of men and women like him in Sunflower County, only the black church offered hope for a brighter tomorrow. Unfortunately, as an institution it was as vulnerable to white power as its individual members.

Even so, no one could have predicted Luther Holbert's response to Eastland's demand, a response that went far beyond the pale of Mississippi's racialized standards of acceptable behavior. When James Eastland descended from his horse and entered Holbert's cabin to deliver his ultimatum, Luther reportedly met the powerful white man with a single rifle shot to the forehead. (Eastland was later found dead in what may have been an ironically appropriate place, on the Holberts' bed.) Holbert then allegedly shot Albert Carr, the man who had accompanied Eastland to the Holbert home, and left him dead on the front porch.

Holbert's actions set into motion a predictable series of events. In Sunflower County in the early part of the twentieth century, according to anthropologist Hortense Powdermaker, "when a white man kills a Negro, it is hardly considered murder. When a Negro kills a white man, conviction is assured, provided the case is not settled immediately by lynch law."[9] Sidney Fant Davis, the Sunflower County judge who apparently coined the phrase "negro law," described its application for black homicide suspects:

> If [a black man] kills a white man, and is caught, he suffers death in some form or another, the time, place and manner of his execution depending on who caught him, the sheriff's posse or the friends of the deceased. If the sheriff's posse are the first to get him, he is hanged the first Friday after court adjourns, but if the friends of the deceased are the first to get possession of him, he is executed at once, at or near the place where the homicide occurred; the matter of his death being always a matter of [the] individual taste of the parties conducting the ceremonies.[10]

If "negro law," which Davis identified as equal parts "common law, statutory law, and unwritten law," called for some but not all African Americans accused of murder to be lynched, then lynching in this context was not extralegal per se. Lynching in turn-of-the-century Mississippi Delta society was something closer to a social norm than an extralegal aberration.

In any case, when Woods Eastland learned of his brother's murder, he raised a posse. Holbert got off to a head start, however, allegedly with the

assistance of his brothers in a fraternal lodge that met at a black church on
the Eastland plantation. In 1904, moreover, the Mississippi Delta would
have been a good place to lose oneself. Little of the swamp, canebrake, and
forest that covered the broad alluvial floodplain in its native state had as
yet been cleared; on the Eastland plantation, the most prosperous in central Sunflower County, 1,000 out of a total 2,300 acres were still wilderness. In all of Sunflower County, fewer than 74,000 acres (out of a total of
449,920) had been cleared by 1904, which meant that more than 80 percent of the county was still heavily wooded.[11]

  Contemporary newspaper accounts and autobiographies describe a
daunting array of wildlife with which a fugitive running through the
swamp and virgin forest would have had to contend, including wolves,
bears, wildcats, snakes, and wild hogs. Mary Hamilton, a white woman
who lived in northern Sunflower County at the time, remembered, "I
never could get used to hearing a panther scream, nor wolves howl,
though it was an every-night occurrence." (Hamilton also described a way
of life in the Sunflower County timber camps that tops anything the my-
thologists of the Old West have ever concocted, complete with frequent
lynchings and train shootouts. A timberman told her that in the Tallahatchie County town of Webb, just northeast of Doddsville, "they have a
killing or a lynching on dull days between paydays and fights or some kind
of amusement like that every Saturday night.")[12]

  Knowing full well what kind of beasts lived in the swamps and what
kind of men would pursue him, Holbert could not have made the decision
to flee into the Delta wilderness lightly. He did steal away, however, and
the woman identified as Mrs. Holbert fled with him. Somewhere along the
way she cut her hair and affected men's clothing and a masculine hat.
Luther shaved his distinctive mustache and side-whiskers. They headed
south and east through the woods and swamps of the Mississippi Delta. As
Leon Litwack reminds us, flights like this gave a terrible, deep resonance
to the lyrics of the Delta bluesman Robert Johnson, who sang:

  I got to keep movin'
  I got to keep movin'
    Blues fallin' down like hail
    Blues fallin' down like hail . . .
  And the days keep on worryin' me
  There's a hellhound on my trail
    Hellhound on my trail
    Hellhound on my trail.[13]

James Eastland died on a Wednesday morning. By that evening, his brother, Woods, had raised an army of fifty armed men at Doddsville. Before setting off after the Holberts, Eastland shot and killed an unarmed man named Winters whom he suspected of aiding the Holberts' escape. In an incident that was described as an accidental discharge from a vigilante's gun, the posse also killed a woman in Doddsville before beginning the hunt.

On Thursday morning, Woods Eastland received a tip that the Holberts were hiding out at a plantation owned by the Mahoney family, several miles to the east of Doddsville. A contingent of the posse took a train from Blaine, just south of the Eastland plantation, toward the town of Itta Bena in neighboring Leflore County, hoping to head the Holberts off in what an informer told them was an easterly escape route. They missed their prey, however, and speculated that a black messenger must have tipped the couple off. This suspicion must have wreaked havoc on innocent blacks along the way, though evidence of only one incident survives. While the vigilantes milled around Itta Bena, what was described as another accidental discharge killed another African American woman.

The hunt continued, now with bloodhounds on loan from adventure-hungry locals and from Parchman Farm, the brand-new state prison complex in northern Sunflower County. As many as 250 men across four counties were on the lookout for the Holberts by Friday. When an armed white mob converged on a group of blacks working in a field near Belzoni (roughly fifty miles to the south of Doddsville), one couple made a break for it. They were ordered to stop, did not, and were shot down. That these two were not the Holberts but instead a pair of frightened farm laborers did little to dampen the mob's bloodlust. The excuse of the Holberts' escape had given the mob carte blanche to open fire on African Americans, at least five of whom now lay dead.[14]

On Saturday morning, a black boy near Sheppardton told two white men, V. H. Lavender and E. L. O'Neal, about a strange couple he had just seen sleeping in the woods. (The town of Sheppardton no longer exists, but it was about twelve miles southwest of Greenwood, in Leflore County, not far from where the lynch mob had originally suspected the Holberts were hiding.)[15] Lavender and O'Neal, who knew about the ongoing manhunt, headed for the woods and surprised the couple as they slept. This pair turned out to be the Holberts. The exhausted Luther did not initially put up a fight, allowing himself to be led away from the Winchester rifle (the murder weapon, perhaps?) that lay next to the spot where he had fallen asleep. When one of the men let slip the word "Doddsville," however, Luther tried a final escape. He was subdued, and the woman with him surrendered. The Holberts' captors found the rifle and a pistol, along with a gold pocket watch and $285 cash. (There was no report of Eastland having been robbed during or after the altercation at Luther Holbert's cabin; the guns, watch, and cash may have represented Holbert's life savings.) The woman had two razors hidden on her person. Woods Eastland later paid Lavender and O'Neal $1,200 between them as a reward for their exploits; they generously passed along $30 to the boy whose tip had led to the capture.

Lavender and O'Neal handed the couple over to the deputy sheriff of Sunflower County in Itta Bena. J. A. Richardson, a newsman from the Sunflower County seat of Indianola, reported breathlessly, "The deputy made a stout effort to hold the murderers but the pressure was too great and he being overpowered yielded to superior numbers and the prisoners were taken in charge by this mob who quickly placed them in a spring wagon and drove hurriedly through the country toward Doddsville."[16]

The deputy sheriff's attempt to uphold the law was not as uncommon as it may seem in light of the number of extralegal executions that did occur in Mississippi.[17] Later in March, another Mississippi sheriff, "single handed and armed only with a small pistol," foiled a mob that was set on lynching a different African American man.[18] A study of a similar Mississippi lynching finds that feeble as their efforts may have been at times, law officers and political officials did make concerted efforts to bring accused African American criminals to trial. They reasoned that if the state could at least go through the motions of convicting black criminals in kangaroo courts and *then* execute them, Mississippi would bolster its law-and-order image.[19] However, if Governor Andrew Longino was concerned about law and order in the Holbert case, no documentary evidence of that concern remains. Longino was a lame duck serving out the last few days of his administration, awaiting the inauguration of James K. Vardaman, the self-proclaimed "White Chief" who had whipped up a wave of racist hatred and ridden it to victory in the campaign of the previous fall.[20] Sunflower County's law officer did not have the support of higher elected officials, nor the support of the white community he served, and his attempt to protect the couple from the mob proved futile.

By early Sunday afternoon, the lynch mob had returned the couple to the highly symbolic spot in Doddsville that Woods Eastland had picked for their execution, the front yard of the black church across the road from Luther Holbert's home. The Indianola newsman who reported on the lynching for the *New York Herald* maintained that "there was no effort to terrorise other negroes, several of whom were present." Yet the choice of the site, "near the negro church, which has [also] served as a lodge room," could hardly have been coincidental. It had to have been chosen to set an example for Holbert's friends and neighbors.[21]

The two were to be killed within sight of their home and the scene of the crime, on the grounds of their church. The church was the one institution in turn-of-the-century Mississippi that allowed African Americans spiritual release, autonomy over their own affairs, and the faith that justice would someday prevail over the inequitable system under which they labored. Eastland forced the lynch mob to wait until midafternoon, the time when rural black churches have traditionally met in the Delta, to begin the execution—most likely in the hope that as many blacks as possible would witness the grisly spectacle and learn a lesson from it. He may have hoped to give the lynching the appearance of moral sanction by placing it where he did, or he may have hoped to send a different message: *You have nowhere to turn.* In any case, the choice for the site was fraught with meaning, though the reporter for the *Greenwood Enterprise* also insisted, "[T]here was no effort at the terrorization of innocent negroes."[22] But terror was precisely the point.

As the *Greenwood Commonwealth* reported, "It had already been announced that the negroes were to be burned at the stake, hence the news spread rapidly that the event was to take place." An estimated 1,000 people, black and white, had gathered there by midafternoon.[23] However, "[s]everal citizens who realized the enormity of the offense which was about to be committed mounted a stump and tried to dissuade the mob from its purpose." Among these men was Sunflower County's Sheriff Anderson, who "did all in his power to prevent the burning of the murderers[,] but he was absolutely powerless in face of the determined citizens that opposed him. . . . [T]he [words] of the orators were drowned [out by the] frenzied cries of the spectators. Burn them! Burn them! [was all] that could be heard."[24]

"The mob went about its work in an orderly manner," wrote yet another local reporter. "Several wagon loads of inflammable [*sic*] wood had been prepared and a roaring fire was soon kindled. Holbert and the woman were dragged to the scene." But before they were burned to death, Luther Holbert and his "wife" were subjected to a gauntlet of cruelties:

[W]hile the funeral pyres were being prepared they were forced to hold out their hands while one finger at a time was chopped off. The fingers were distributed as souvenirs. The ears of the murderers were cut off.

Holbert was severely beaten, his skull was fractured, and one of his eyes[,] knocked out with a stick, hung by a shred from the socket. . . . When the executioners came forward to lop off fingers Holbert extended his hand without being asked. The most excruciating form of punishment consisted in the use of a large corkscrew in the hands of some of the mob. This instrument was bored into the flesh of the man and the woman, in the arms, legs and body, and then pulled out, the spirals tearing out big pieces of raw, quivering flesh every time it was withdrawn. Even this devilish torture did not make the brutes cry out. When finally they were thrown on the fire and allowed to be burned to death, this came as a relief to the maimed and suffering victims.[25]

After receiving the nod from Woods Eastland, the leaders of the mob huddled and decided to burn the woman first. She asked to pray with her sisters from the congregation, but Eastland denied her request. "She was then bound in chains and cast into the flames," according to one report. "She tugged at the chains for a few seconds, then swooned. It was all over with her."[26]

Luther Holbert then met his fate with a stoicism that stunned the spectators. Both victims went to their death "with out repenting their crime or complaining of their crime's avengers," the reporter from Indianola marveled.[27] Another newsman described Holbert's final minutes:

Bruised and battered almost beyond recognition; bleeding from a hundred tortures, with ears shorn from his head; with palsied limbs and fingerless hands—more dead than alive—Holbert was then lead [sic] to his doom. A chain was placed around his body, at either end of which was two strong negroes, who knew that failure to obey the instructions of the mob meant death. Passing two on either side of the fire, they dragged the murderer into the flames and tried to hold him. Several times he succeeded in getting clear of the blaze, but each time he was dragged back. At first he shrieked pitifully, but his throat was soon parched by the flames and he only struggled and writhed.

"It was a scene," wrote the reporter from the *Greenwood Commonwealth*, "such as a man wants to witness only once in a lifetime."[28]

Concerned that two black people on the run could stay hidden for three days and nights, local whites cracked down on their employees in the immediate wake of the Holbert escape. Woods Eastland had already murdered one Doddsville black man who was suspected of aiding the Holberts' escape. The two women who were shot "by accident" may have been suspected of aiding the Holberts in flight, or they may have been victims of the mob's "sport." One local newsman wrote in the lynching's aftermath, "The fact that the [Holberts] were sheltered and piloted throughout the whole hunt by other negroes has had a great effect on sentiment in the entire section of the State." He concluded, "Especially have the negroes who belonged to the same lodge furnished aid. This has been established beyond all doubt, and the matter is generally recognized as being a most serious one for the whites and a problem requiring earliest considerations and drastic action."[29] Little evidence appears to exist to prove that lodge members had assisted in the couple's escape, but the conspiracy apparently seemed real enough at the time to the white minority of Sunflower County, and the mob did take pointed action to punish possible conspirators. Four unnamed "strong negroes, who knew that failure to obey the instructions of the mob meant death," were forced to restrain the Holberts as they perished in the flames. The men were probably employees of the Eastlands and might have been members of the fraternal lodge. They may have been chosen to participate in the horrible, choreographed spectacle as a way of demonstrating what could happen to them if they followed Luther Holbert's example.

The fact that the woman identified as Mrs. Holbert had fled with Luther amazed the journalists who would later describe with perverse relish the couple's end. It did not, however, prevent them from labeling her as a woman of loose morals whose attention toward the "good nigger" had gotten Luther into trouble in the first place. There is also confusion as to whether or not whites recognized the Holberts as man and wife, even though the couple may have had a sixteen-year-old son; local newspapers referred to her alternately as "Mrs. Holbert," "Holbert's paramour," and "the woman with whom Holbert was living." This may tell us more about the attitudes of local white newspaper reporters toward the institution of marriage among African Americans at the time than it does about the couple's union. Considering the ordeal that the pair went through together, there can be little doubt that they were deeply committed to each other. Conceivably the woman could have remained in her home in relative safety after Luther killed James Eastland and Albert Carr and ran off; she could even have run off in another direction to get help for "Mr. Jim." She instead chose to risk her life in flight with Holbert. Given the chance to renounce him and perhaps escape execution after their capture, she instead remained steadfast and silent.

Considerable confusion remains over the circumstances that led to Eastland's murder. The Sunflower County newsman who covered the lynching for the *New York Herald* reported that "[t]he woman with whom Holbert was living brought on the trouble between the two negroes" and that this was the altercation that had precipitated Eastland's involvement in the first place.[30] Newspaper reporters from nearby towns based their accounts on the same story. It is conceivable that they did so after consulting only with the Indianola newsman. It is possible, too, that the story was accurate. It is also plausible that white people in the Delta who were amused by what they perceived as black hypersexuality wanted to believe that a love triangle was behind the entire saga, whether it was or not.

It is almost certain that the woman who fled into the swamps with Holbert was not his wife. The 1900 U.S. census listed a "Luther Halbert" in Scott County, Mississippi, town of Forest, where James and Woods Eastland had lived before taking over the Doddsville plantation. The forty-eight-year-old had been born in Mississippi and had been married to Anna Halbert for sixteen years. A day laborer, he could read, write, and speak English, although the census taker listed no level of education attained, and he owned a home (as opposed to a farm) free of a mortgage. He and his wife had four daughters, aged six to twelve. The 1910 census recorded a widowed "Anne Halburt" living in Forest with four daughters, three of whose names corresponded with the family's 1900 entry, and a fourteen-year-old son.

This is speculation, but Luther Holbert may have left his wife and family in Forest in 1903 to work for the Eastlands on their Sunflower County plantation. Who, then, was the woman who fled with Holbert into the wilds of the Delta if she was not his wife? The census may provide another clue. The 1900 version found Albert Carr, a twenty-seven-year-old Mississippi native, living in Scott County with his wife of ten years, Emma, and two sons. Carr was murdered in 1904, so his absence from the 1910 census makes sense. Why, though, is there no 1910 record of Emma Carr? Is it possible that she was the woman identified as Luther Holbert's wife? Might Holbert have interfered with Albert Carr's marriage, and not the other way around? We can never know with any certainty. And in truth, love may have had nothing to do with it.

The *Voice of the Negro*, a news magazine for African Americans published in Atlanta, told a drastically different story of resistance to debt peonage. The *Voice* based its account on a statement from "a prominent and reliable white man" who had been in the Delta at the time of the manhunt and who had talked to members of the mob. On this evidence, the journal reported that "Holbert had persuaded a Negro whom Eastland held in involuntary servitude to leave the white planter, telling him that no man could make him work for him against his will." According to this version, Eastland claimed that the man owed him a large sum of money and planned to have him work it off. When Eastland went to Holbert's home to retrieve the man, the white planter "started to give Holbert a lesson about how to keep quiet and allow white men to do what they pleased." An altercation ensued, Holbert shot Eastland, and then, according to this version of the story, Holbert accidentally shot Albert Carr.[31]

There are several important discrepancies between the *Voice*'s story and local news accounts—for example, in this account Holbert lives outside the Eastland plantation, and there is no mention of the previous connection between Holbert and Eastland—and it is certainly full of wishful thinking, but it cannot be dismissed entirely as groundless propaganda. If Holbert really had tried to assist another black man in escaping "involuntary servitude," it would help to explain why he was executed in such a ritualistic fashion before such a large crowd. Perhaps only a recognized leader in Doddsville's African American community would have taken such a step and then debated it with a white man. If Holbert was indeed a leader, his skills would likely have manifested themselves in both the black church and the black fraternal lodge.

If this version of the story is accurate, it may explain the decision to lynch Holbert on the site of those two institutions rather than at the spot where he and the woman were captured. If the Holberts were black leaders who questioned the right of white planters to do as they pleased, the object lesson of their lynching was that much more powerful for the African Americans of Sunflower County. There is ample reason to believe that the lynching included what we might call a "political" element such as this. Mississippi whites had used organized violence and premeditated murder to "redeem" the state from Republican rule in the 1870s, to disfranchise African Americans in the decades since, and to rout the Delta's incipient Colored Farmers' Alliance.[32]

The full truth of the Holbert saga is elusive, but at its core lies one apparent verity. Whether Eastland and Holbert were arguing about a woman or about involuntary servitude and the rights of black laborers, James Eastland (in the words of the *Voice of the Negro*) attempted to give Luther Holbert "a lesson about how to keep quiet and allow white men to do what they pleased," and Holbert shot him dead in response. As payment, a white mob hunted down and executed Holbert and his companion in a highly ritualistic fashion. On at least one level, it does not matter why

Holbert killed Eastland, because at base the two men disagreed over what a white employer could force a black man to do—no matter which version of the story is accurate. To at least some degree, it does not matter where or how gruesomely the pair was lynched, because every lynching denied an American citizen equal protection before the law, destabilizing and degrading the society in which it took place.

In light of the Holbert lynching, the *Voice of the Negro* concluded that "[t]here is a growing feeling among Negroes [in the Mississippi Delta] that something must be done. Almost anything is preferable to the shameless, bare-faced humiliations that are heaped upon the race." Such beliefs may have squared with the feelings of Atlanta's black bourgeoisie, whose members published and read the *Voice*, but in the Mississippi Delta such resolve was unlikely to have existed, at least in public, in 1904. Middle-class African Americans in Atlanta who refused to accept the "shameless, bare-faced humiliations" of southern life could surround themselves in a supportive community of other middle-class African Americans. Delta blacks like the Holberts did not have that option. Nonetheless, the *Voice* predicted that there would be either "a general higira [*sic*] of black men from that sin-stricken section, a determined stand for right, or a surrender to serfdom."[33] What would develop over the next century was in fact a combination of the three.

The graphic accounts of the Holberts' lynching that the Delta's newspapers provided met the public appetite that Jacquelyn Dowd Hall has named "the late-Victorian relish in the details of death."[34] As if to assert that such perversity was not confined to the Delta, however, the final mention of the Holberts in the local press described an obscene export. Harry Williams of Cleveland, Mississippi, a farmer who had lent his bloodhounds to the Holbert hunt, received as a souvenir for his participation one of Luther Holbert's ears. He mailed it—in pickled form—to a friend in Arcola, Illinois. According to the *Greenville (Mississippi) Times*, a Mr. Cox, also of Arcola, was in the Delta on business at the time of the lynching and was "lucky" enough to receive a two-inch-square piece of Luther Holbert's skull, which he took home with him.[35] "While stating that these relics are handled very gingerly in that part of the country," wrote the editor of the *Times*, "the Arcolan gives a very impartial account of the burning, and leaves of all severe arraignment of Southern methods of dealing with the negro. . . . [T]he citizens of Arcola have no use for Mr. Nigger, and he has not been allowed to make his home in Arcola for the past several years."[36]

Having made its way to Illinois, the Holberts' story later found a national audience. The most well known African American figure of the day,

Booker T. Washington, wrote to the *Birmingham Age Herald* (and made sure his letter was reprinted in the *New York Tribune*) in February 1904 to decry the Holbert lynching. Three black southerners had been burned at the stake in the last fortnight, he wrote. Not one of them had been accused of the one crime that everyone—Washington included—agreed would have justified a lynching, the rape of a white woman. Worst of all, two of the victims, the Sunflower County couple, had been burned on the sacred grounds of a church. "In the midst of the nation's busy and prosperous life," Washington warned, "few, I fear, take time to consider whither these brutal and inhuman practices are leading. . . . These burnings without trial are in the deepest sense unjust to my race. But it is not this injustice alone which stirs my heart. These barbarous scenes are more disgraceful and degrading to the people who inflict the punishment than to those who receive it." The rule of mob, Washington lamented, threatened to destroy "the friendly relations which should exist between the races" upon which his program of racial uplift depended.[37] The Sunflower County couple became a symbol of the racial violence that retarded the South's progress.

The Holbert story reached another audience via a best-selling novel. *The Hindered Hand: Or, the Reign of the Repressionist*, by Sutton Griggs, was one of the most popular novels of the early twentieth century among African American readers, and it is a corker. The similarities between newspaper reports of the Holberts' experiences and the fictional experiences of Bud and Foresta Harper are too significant to be coincidental; Bud Harper's proud behavior, for instance, is especially similar to the *Voice of the Negro*'s characterization of Luther Holbert. Literary critic Trudier Harris has concluded that Griggs's graphic description of the torture inflicted upon Bud and Foresta Harper had to have been based on an account of the Holbert lynching from the *Vicksburg Evening Post*. Griggs himself tells his readers in an afterword that "[t]he details of the Maulville burning were given the author by an eyewitness of the [Doddsville] tragedy, a man of national reputation among the Negroes." (Perhaps this was the same man who gave his story to the *Voice*?) Griggs's account of the torture event is terribly graphic, but he claims to have "suppressed for decency's sake" some of the more revolting aspects of the scene. "We would have been glad, to eliminate all of the details," Griggs claims, "but they have entered into the thought-life of the Negroes, and their influence must be taken into account."[38] The novelist apparently found in the Holbert lynching what was already a staple of black Delta folk tradition, and he transformed the story of the ritualistic execution into an American archetype. Griggs's novel, the *Voice*'s reporting, and the necrophiliac interstate trade of Luther

Holbert's body parts nationalized the tragedy and raised the story of the murders to the level of folklore.

As difficult as it is to reconstruct the lives of Luther Holbert and the woman who was lynched alongside him, we know exactly what became of the Eastlands. The sheriff of Sunflower County arrested Woods Eastland in September 1904 and charged him with "having caused Luther Holbert and wife to be burned at the stake." The state hinted that it would prosecute the case vigorously, and Eastland assembled a team of attorneys led by Anselm J. McLaurin. McLaurin, a U.S. senator and former governor of Mississippi, announced before the trial began that should the state produce evidence of Eastland's guilt, he would endorse "lynching [of African Americans] as being the only reasonable atonement for murders [of] and assaults [on whites] in the South." The strategy would have worked. Any jury in Mississippi—which would necessarily have been lily-white, because African Americans had been purged from the voter rolls—would have agreed with him. But McLaurin never even had to mount a defense. As soon as the prosecution finished presenting its case, McLaurin moved to dismiss the charges "on the ground that not a scintilla of evidence had been introduced tending to prove that Eastland had been in any way a party to the crime." "The Judges granted the motion," according to a report in the *New York Times*, "and the big crowd applauded" as a lyncher went free.[39]

Eastland returned with his wife to the family's previous home in Forest, Mississippi, although he retained his Doddsville plantation. Within the year his wife gave birth to a son whom Eastland named for his slain brother. James Oliver Eastland, the nephew of the murdered James Eastland, was raised in Forest and represented the town's district in the state legislature from 1928 to 1932. He made a name for himself in the state capitol as one of the most ardent supporters of the cartoonish Governor Theodore Bilbo. In 1932, the domineering Woods Eastland demanded that his son retire temporarily from politics in order to manage the family's growing plantation in Doddsville. Young James did just that, and in short order he was able to turn the family operation into a small empire.[40]

James O. Eastland returned to the political arena in 1941 when Mississippi governor Paul Johnson Sr. named him to fill a vacant seat in the U.S. Senate. (Johnson had first offered the seat to Woods Eastland.) Jim Eastland won the seat in the regular election of 1942 by capitalizing on his connections with the small-farm central region of the state and the Bilbo statewide machine. Had he not spent his youth in Forest, it is unlikely that the poor whites who made up the bulk of Mississippi's voting populace in

1942 would have favored the Delta planter in any statewide election. Conventional political wisdom holds that small farmers would never vote for a lordly Delta planter, and Mississippi's electoral history generally bears this out. Delta candidates have not fared well throughout the twentieth century in statewide elections, though they have traditionally wielded disproportionate power in the state legislature.[41] Had Woods Eastland not returned to Forest after orchestrating the lynching and raised young James there, it would have been comparatively difficult for his son to win a later statewide election. As it turned out, Jim Eastland won several statewide elections; he remained in the U.S. Senate until 1978.

Eastland embraced white supremacy and positioned himself as spokesman for a beleaguered white South. His 1942 campaign literature barked: "We of the South are the purest strain of Anglo-Saxon blood. It was [white] southern brains which founded this Government, and which gave to the world democracy. We demand only that we be treated fairly; that this discrimination cease; that we not be impoverished to enrich other sections of the country; that we sit as partners and on an equal basis at the counsel tables of the Nation; and that as partners and economic equals we take America forward to her great destiny as the leader in a world civilization of justice and economic equality."[42]

After his colleagues in the Senate censured Joe McCarthy, Eastland became the leader in that body for the forces of hysterical anti-Communism. The senator conducted witchhunts throughout his career against interracial groups whom he accused of acting as Communist patsies if not outright insurrectionists, and his racist, anti-Communist rhetoric played to strong reviews among whites in Mississippi. He organized southerners' resistance to the Supreme Court's *Brown v. Board of Education of Topeka* decision in the Senate. When seniority elevated him to the chairmanship of the Senate Judiciary Committee, Eastland blocked a series of civil rights bills throughout the 1950s and 1960s. He went so far as to boast to white Mississippi audiences that he had had his tailor sew special, deep pockets in his suit coats: the place where civil rights bills went to die. Seniority eventually elevated Eastland to the position of president pro tem of the Senate, placing him third in the line of succession to Presidents Nixon, Ford, and Carter. He waged a running battle throughout his career against federal welfare payments to poor black people. In this sense, Eastland can be seen as an important transitional figure between the unabashed racists who fought the New Deal and the *Brown* decision in the 1940s and 1950s and the more media-savvy southern conservatives who have fought similar battles in recent decades.[43]

While it is difficult to quantify Eastland's direct involvement in the civic life of Sunflower County—he did his most important work in back rooms over cigars and Scotch whiskey—there can be little doubt that he wielded a heavy hand during the decades covered in this study. It is indisputable that Eastland helped to turn public reaction in Sunflower County and throughout the South against the Supreme Court's *Brown* decision. Eastland told one crowd, "You are not required to obey any court which passes out such a ruling. In fact, you are obligated to defy it." For good measure, he also labeled the Fourteenth Amendment to the U.S. Constitution, which on paper extended the rights of full American citizenship to African Americans, "tyrannous" and "illegal."[44] When a group of Indianola town leaders created the first Citizens' Council, they did so with Eastland's full support.

In his career as a public servant, James Eastland fought a defensive battle against the individuals and social forces that threatened his empire in the Delta. In the aftermath of the Second World War, in the wake of *Brown,* in his struggles in the U.S. Senate to curb civil rights legislation, "Big Jim" fought to make his world more like the world his father, Woods Eastland, had known. In this world, a white minority knew what was best for a black majority and acted on it, and resistance on the part of African Americans elicited swift and violent corrective measures.

For a time, Eastland was successful in turning back the clock. For a time, Eastland and those who thought like him were able to contain African American agency in the Mississippi Delta through selective terrorism. Their means were for the most part much more subtle and civilized than those that had been employed by Eastland's father, but they were no less effective. Woods and Jim Eastland both understood the power of one careful act of terror against a powerless people, and Senator Eastland knew that overt violence made for bad public relations.

Charles McLaurin, the civil rights worker whose report on Sunflower County referred to Doddsville as the place where "many years ago the burning of Negroes was a Sunday spectacle," moved to Sunflower County in 1962 explicitly to bring attention to injustices in Eastland's backyard. The people who joined McLaurin in the Sunflower County civil rights movement sought to dismantle a system of fear and control and to create in its place one in which the rule of law predominated. They had good reason to perceive Senator Eastland as the symbol of everything wrong with Sunflower County, which they called "the worst county in the worst state," as far as racial discrimination was concerned. The Eastlands were not the only planters to treat their community as their own personal fiefdom, to be ruled as they saw fit, but the planters' opponents—who by 1964 knew the story of the lynching and the Eastland family's role in the outrageous affair—had reason to portray Senator James Eastland as an emblem of planter domination.[45]

They fought the atmosphere of fear and domination that Woods Eastland had helped to create, and they fought the policies that Jim Eastland supported as a U.S. senator with the same goals in sight. In a very real sense, the fight for civil rights in the Mississippi Delta was an effort to dismantle the world the Eastlands had made.

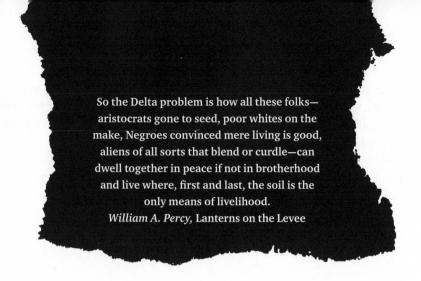

So the Delta problem is how all these folks—
aristocrats gone to seed, poor whites on the
make, Negroes convinced mere living is good,
aliens of all sorts that blend or curdle—can
dwell together in peace if not in brotherhood
and live where, first and last, the soil is the
only means of livelihood.
William A. Percy, Lanterns on the Levee

CHAPTER ONE

Introduction

The modern American civil rights movement was the accumulation of
thousands of community-sized movements for social, political, and economic justice in thousands of urban and rural areas throughout the United
States, particularly in the former Confederacy. In communities throughout the South where whites and African Americans had coexisted for
decades, if not centuries, a range of personalities, circumstances, and
concerns coalesced in the decades following the Second World War. African Americans worked together in these years to establish their rights as
American citizens and concerned members of local communities, building
on decades-long local traditions of activism. As this organization proceeded, so too did white southerners' collective efforts to preserve a hierarchical society that benefited them in a myriad of economic, political, and
psychological ways.

This study examines African American civil rights organizing and white
resistance to it in the rural community of Sunflower County, Mississippi, in

the forty years following the end of World War II. By studying organic biracial communities like those of Sunflower County over long periods of time, historians can better understand and explain the dynamics of power that have been at the center of the most important social movement in this nation's history. I share the conviction that "more attention must be concentrated on the origins, process, and outcome of the civil rights struggles in local communities before the movement and its consequences can be fully understood."[1] A major goal of this work is to examine the ways that the men and women of Sunflower County shaped and reacted to events on the local level, operated within a political culture unique to the state of Mississippi, and altered their goals and strategies in response to "national" civil rights events and policies over time.

Students of American history make a critical mistake if they believe there to have been *one* civil rights movement. This examination of the movements that developed in one southern community demonstrates that the class differences that developed in African American communities over time profoundly affected the goals and strategies of the movements they created, as did varying forms of white resistance and long-term changes in the community's economic system. These and other variables make it difficult to generalize about *the* civil rights movement in one southern community, much less the region or nation as a whole. By the same token, white reactions to change were not of one piece over time.

Community studies deepen our understanding of the mid–twentieth century's struggles for civil rights. They help to explain how and why thousands of Americans felt compelled to join movements for social change throughout the country in the decades following the end of World War II. How and why did thousands of black and white Americans organize, and in some cases risk their lives and livelihoods, for the cause of equal rights for African Americans? How and why did thousands of white southerners organize to maintain the status quo of racial segregation and inequality? How did these movements change American society and politics, and in what ways did the nation resist change? This examination of the movements that emerged from a Mississippi Delta community suggests a few answers to these questions.

Sunflower County lies flat in the middle of the Yazoo-Mississippi Delta in the northwestern corner of the state of Mississippi. Throughout its modern history, Sunflower County has had more African American than white residents. The county was established as a political entity only in 1844, which meant that the white farmers who first came to Sunflower County's fertile soil intending to organize large plantations with large servile labor forces were allowed no more than a few years of legalized slavery.

Even so, the planters who established dominion over giant tracts of Sunflower County land also found ways to control huge pools of labor after emancipation. The exact demographics of that labor force have varied throughout the years, but the county's total population remained more than 60 percent African American throughout the period covered in this study. Until 1964 or thereabout, these planters maintained control of the majority within a sociopolitical system that supported their uncontested control of local government and vital resources. Yet while Sunflower County was the site of an oppressive racial regime, it was also the birthplace of a powerful resistance culture.

The experience of Sunflower County may not have been normative for the South as a whole, but biracial communities throughout the region had much in common with Sunflower County during this period. In many rural communities throughout the South, the formation of a black middle class was effectively hindered until after the civil rights movement's heyday. This was certainly true of Sunflower County, where in 1960 more than two-thirds of the total population was black and the average income of an African American was lower than the federal poverty line. Not a single black lawyer or doctor lived in the county seat of Indianola between 1956 and 1973. The model of community organization that middle-class blacks employed to change other towns and cities in the South in this period could not have existed in rural areas like Sunflower County.[2]

Sunflower's traditional one-crop plantation economy hindered the development of an African American middle class. Before the late 1960s, in the unlikely event that a black male attended school through more than a few primary grades, he could hope to become a teacher or a minister (or an emigrant). No other career paths existed for black men in the Mississippi Delta, and the possibilities were even more limited for women. The absence of an established African American middle class made civil rights organizing in Sunflower County more perilous than it might have been otherwise. An African American middle class could have provided a buffer, an economic safety net, to civil rights activists in the 1950s and 1960s, even if the members of this hypothetical group had not participated in the movement directly.

Just as important, a black middle class could have broken down racial stereotypes and white expectations of black behavior by example alone. Whites' expectations of blacks' behavior—coupled with whites' assumption that they knew what was best for both communities and that they alone deserved to act on their assumptions—was the essence of what whites characterized as a "paternalist" social order.[3] This system barred more than half the county's citizens and taxpayers from voting, defined them as unequal in the eyes of the law, and denied them the ability to participate on an equal basis in the region's economic life. When African Americans acted in ways other than those that had been prescribed by whites, the system sanctioned—even encouraged—violent reprisal.

When a small handful of black professionals, teachers, and farm owners asserted themselves as American citizens who deserved equal rights of citizenship in the early 1950s, whites in the county seat of Indianola formed what they called the Citizens' Council. The name they chose is significant on more than a rhetorical level. Throughout the period studied here, black civil rights organizers and white segregationists appropriated and reappropriated a claim to *good citizenship*. The Citizens' Council movement matched black organizing stride for stride. Chapters modeled after Indianola's Citizens' Council cropped up across Mississippi and, indeed, throughout all of the former states of the Confederacy and beyond.[4] Contemporaries referred to the Citizens' Councils as "white-collar Klans," groups of respectable leaders of communities who came together to defend what they would have called the Delta's "paternalist" social system even as they crushed black civil rights activities through outright domination. The Citizens' Council movement had several unintended consequences, however. Among other things, by reminding African Americans of how economically vulnerable they were, the council made it more likely that if a civil rights movement was to take root in Sunflower County, it would first be a radical, poor peoples' movement and not a moderate, middle-class movement.

At least three distinct though interconnected civil rights movements developed in Sunflower County between 1945 and 1986. A movement led by the county's tiny group of black professionals and farm owners materialized in the years surrounding the *Brown* decision of 1954. It was quickly beaten back by white segregationists who used any and every form of intimidation available. The second movement, the major challenge to the hegemony of white planters in the Delta's socioeconomic system, was organized by young African American and white idealists in the mid-1960s and revolved around the charismatic personality of a farm worker named Fannie Lou Hamer. This was a poor people's movement, and its participants defined it as a human rights struggle as much as a civil rights movement. A third, cross-class movement coalesced in the 1980s around the issue of leadership in Indianola's public school system.

The Setting

For eons, during rainy seasons the Mississippi and Yazoo Rivers and their tributaries spilled into a forested, diamond-shaped plain in the north-western corner of what is now the state of Mississippi. Bounded by bluffs at present-day Memphis, Tennessee, to the north and Vicksburg, Mississippi, to the south, by the Mississippi River to the west, and by a line of hills to the east, the Yazoo-Mississippi Delta formed a basin that collected those flood-waters. In the places where the first white settlers could scratch clearings in the forests and keep the rivers under control, they found improbably fertile soil. The floods had deposited much of the topsoil of what is now the midwestern United States into this basin. (In fact, some whites in the region still say, "That's one thing those damn Yankees can't take back from us—all that topsoil." Some of them are joking.) In a few places, this loam reaches a depth of dozens of feet, and many heavily farmed patches of the region have never had to be fertilized. This diamond-shaped plain is technically known as the Yazoo-Mississippi Delta, not to be confused with the alluvial delta at the mouth of the Mississippi River south of New Orleans. But to all Mississippians, many southerners, and generations of African Americans throughout the United States, the northwestern corner of Mississippi is simply "the Delta," with no further specification needed.

Sunflower County is in the center of the Delta. It stretches approximately sixty miles from its northern to southern border and appears on a map to be tall and thin. Along the area's dry riverbeds and creek beds lie the most productive and expensive farmlands, where the sandy deposits from cen-turies of floods are deepest. The rich deposits drain water easily and are ideal for the cultivation of cotton, traditionally the Delta's cash crop. Where swamps have been cleared, the soil is closer to a thick clay, known locally as "gumbo." For decades, marginal cotton operations scraped by on gumbo plots, but in recent years, entrepreneurial Delta farmers have begun to utilize the clayey soil to better purposes: the quality of water retention that makes gumbo marginal at best for cotton production makes it perfect for large-scale catfish farming. There are countless gradations of soil in be-tween sandy loam and gumbo. Sunflower County encompasses all of these soil types and includes several microclimates. As a saying in local farming circles puts it, "As Sunflower County goes, so goes the Delta." Historically, when conditions have been good enough that most of Sunflower County's farms prospered, the rest of the Delta could count on flush times; but in the years in which a majority of the county's microregions produced bad crops, the Delta as a whole faced economic catastrophe.[5]

The political entity of Sunflower County has a relatively short history. The 1850 U.S. census, the first to canvass the people of a delineated Sunflower County, counted 348 white men, women, and children, and 754 black slaves. Most of the whites had come from the hill country of Mississippi; a few others hailed from Virginia, the Carolinas, Alabama, Georgia, Tennessee, and Louisiana. Of the 102 white heads of families, 11 came from the northern United States, and 4 heads of household were foreign-born. Together, these whites brought the majority of the population, enslaved African Americans, with them. Aaron Forrest, the brother of the Confederate cavalry general and Ku Klux Klan founder Nathan Bedford Forrest, cleared one of the first tracts in the county with the labor of slaves, whom he reportedly kept locked up at night in cages.[6]

One of the first white settlers in the northern part of the county described a wilderness that rivaled the wildest products of Joseph Conrad's or William Faulkner's imaginations and a justice system that probably met the myth of the "Wild, Wild West" as well as or better than any parts of the American West ever did. In 1886, a farmer in the central part of the county reported that a wildcat had killed fifty of his pigs, and another farmer killed a nine-foot-long panther. The editor of a local newspaper called for a bounty on bear hides. Sunflower County's earliest white inhabitants weren't much more civilized than the native fauna, either. Contemporary sources tell us that lynching was horrifically common, and as soon as the Yazoo Delta Railroad extended into new towns, those municipalities had to pass ordinances that prohibited shooting firearms from trains.[7]

For centuries, Sunflower County was heavily forested; much of its land was covered by swamps and canebreak. The heavy cover meant that enormous amounts of capital and labor—and millions of dollars in government assistance—would be required to make the county farming country. Its geographic features have ensured that only the men who could obtain the massive amounts of credit and control of labor that it would take to clear the wilds of the Delta would reap the land's vast potential for profit. That simple fact created a rigid, racist social system and has social consequences even today.

Gigantic tracts of land, some of them so flat that they seem to the naked eye to defy the curvature of the earth, had been cleared for cultivation by the middle of the twentieth century. But even at the turn of the twenty-first century, the woods at the edges of clearings are dense. Looking at them from the far end of a cultivated field, one still has the sense that if the workers and their machines whose job it is to keep the fields clear for farming were to take a few years off, the forests would retake the land.

Sunflower County has always been overwhelmingly rural; by the end of the twentieth century, it had only four main towns of any size. Indianola, the county seat, is one of the last economically viable small towns in the Delta, in part because of its strategically important location. It may be in the middle of nowhere, as local teenagers have invariably complained, but at least Indianola sits at the intersection of two major roads, U.S. Highways 82 and 49 West, that go someplace else. In the 1980s and 1990s, Indianola took advantage of the juncture, enticing a major retailer to build a regional distribution center near the crossroads, creating semiskilled jobs and infusing cash into the local economy. Even so, life in Indianola still moves at a pace established by its distinguishing characteristic, the picturesque and languid Indian Bayou that winds through downtown. To Indianola's east along U.S. Highway 82 lies the smaller town of Moorhead, where the Southern and Yazoo Delta Railroads intersect—"where the Southern crosses the Dog," one of the most famous place names in American music.

A poor people's movement emerged to the north of Indianola up U.S. Highway 49 West just past the towns of Sunflower and Doddsville in Ruleville, the county's second-largest town, due in part to the force of personality of a farmworker named Fannie Lou Hamer. Farther to the north of Ruleville is Drew, whose whites have traditionally been regarded as the most recalcitrant in the county on racial matters. When civil rights workers attempted to spread the Ruleville movement into Drew, they faced stiff resistance, but from Drew emerged another stalwart of the movement, Mae Bertha Carter. Farther north on the highway, just within Sunflower County's northern border, sits Parchman Penitentiary, the notorious Mississippi state prison farm. The image of Parchman was never far from any civil rights worker's mind.

The System

It was not a simple process, but in the late nineteenth century, Delta planters adjusted to a new world without slave labor. In the decades following the Civil War, thousands of black families migrated *to* the Delta, anxious to create lives for themselves as free men and women on what may well have been the richest, most productive land in the United States. The African American population of Sunflower County rose from 3,243 in 1870 to 12,070 (75 percent of the county's total population) in 1900, and then nearly tripled again between 1900 and 1920. For the most part, the black immigrants were unable to buy pieces of the land; only 171 of those

12,070 African Americans owned farms in 1900. Instead, these farmers cooperated in creating a compromise system, "sharecropping," which (in theory, at least) held advantages for both black laborers and white land-owners.[8]

For southern blacks without capital or marketable skills who hoped one day to own land and exercise some measure of control over their families' lives and labor, sharecropping promised a means toward the accumulation of capital and autonomy. For whites who controlled vast fields of productive earth but too little labor to farm it, sharecropping provided the massive labor force necessary for large-scale cotton culture. Share tenancy, an arrangement whereby the renter provided all of the tools and kept more of the harvest, was a less common arrangement in Sunflower County, at least among African American farmers. In Sunflower County, the arrangement that came to predominate within the sharecropping system was "halving," whereby a landowner provided a plot of land, seed, housing, cash advances, and credit at the plantation commissary to a sharecropper and his family. In return, the family turned over half of its cotton crop to the landowner.[9]

In theory, the arrangement had much to offer sharecroppers. In addition to housing and the land loaned to sharecropping families for cotton cultivation, owners also frequently allotted a patch of land for a vegetable garden and a livestock pen and allowed sharecroppers to hunt on their plantations. In an economic system that allowed, even encouraged, them to grow or kill their own food, sharecropping families almost never went hungry. Vulnerable black sharecroppers also came to rely on white landowners for what might be called the "political" protection afforded in this reciprocal, though unequal, relationship. At times, this protection proved extremely valuable.

If this socioeconomic system held attractions for landless laborers in its ideal form, in practice sharecropping proved disastrous for the descendants of the African Americans who had migrated to the Delta with hopes of establishing self-sufficient farms. Landowners insisted that sharecroppers on their land sell cotton harvests through their own brokers, which allowed for unfair practices. Croppers had to weigh their harvests on the owners' scales, which all too often meant that a given crop weighed whatever a given planter said it weighed. Croppers also had to use owners' cotton gins, which almost always meant that owners kept the cotton seed that the gins separated from the cotton fibers of the picked bolls. Cotton seed has value of its own—it can be resold as seed, ground into meal, and pressed for its oil—but it was unusual for sharecroppers to know that they deserved any payment for the seed they grew, much less to receive that payment.[10]

Landowners kept ledgers detailing how much seed, fertilizer, tools, and cash they had advanced to sharecroppers, then refused to let croppers check their arithmetic. Planters controlled the local government and made sure that schools for African Americans were inadequate. Sharecroppers who could not read, write, or figure could not very well challenge landowners' balance sheets. All too often, this translated into landowners taking advantage of their dominant positions. Finally, planters sold cotton harvests at prices that they frequently kept hidden from their sharecroppers. Coercion, violence, illiteracy, debt, and the law tied sharecroppers to the land and "gave landowners and merchants increasing control over rural workers" throughout the South.[11] In Sunflower County, a system that held attractions for African Americans in its ideal form all too often cheated black sharecropper families out of a fair price for their labor in reality.

It would be difficult to overestimate the role large-scale cotton culture played in the life of Sunflower County's people. It dictated social relations and ruled the calendar. Cotton culture was labor-intensive, at least until all of its phases were mechanized, and it shaped nearly every aspect of Sunflower County society well into the twentieth century, if not beyond. For the first half of the century, armies of men, women, and children went into the fields each year in the late winter to break the soil, plow rows, and sow cotton seeds. After the plants sprouted in the spring, the workforce passed through the fields again to thin the plants and chop weeds. Summer was "lay-by," a period when the workers could spend their time on other things. (Schools for African American children, for instance, were in session only during lay-by and deepest winter.) In September or October, bolls began to open, and the armies descended on the fields again to pick the cotton and transport it to the gin. Each phase of the process involved backbreaking physical labor.[12]

In the 1930s and 1940s, landowners bought tractors, which made furrowing and planting easier and reduced the need for a large labor force for that phase of cultivation. In the 1940s and 1950s, they invested in mechanical cotton pickers, which further reduced the need for farmworkers. By the 1960s, the use of chemical pesticides had driven unskilled farmworkers from even the weeding phase of the crop cycle. On large farms in the Delta where economy of scale was greater, these changes advanced even more quickly than they did in other parts of the South. Each advance marginalized sharecroppers and endangered their way of life. By the late

1960s, the thousands of African Americans who remained in Sunflower County and who had been trained only for menial farm labor worked as seasonal employees, and most of them depended on government assistance for their survival.

Delta planters resisted persistent calls to diversify Mississippi's economy throughout this period.[13] Certainly prior to the Second World War, and to a decreasing extent in the four decades following it, the people of the Delta simply did not have any way to make a living separate from the production of cotton. Before the economic boom that accompanied the war effort in the 1940s opened up jobs for African Americans in the cities of the North, Midwest, and West, black Sunflower County residents sharecropped because they had no other choice. When economic opportunities became available outside of Mississippi, a majority of blacks voted with their feet, expressing their displeasure with the socioeconomic system by moving elsewhere.[14]

Between 1940 and 1980, the total African American population of Sunflower County dropped from 43,477 to 21,591. The social movement at the center of this study must therefore be seen against the backdrop of sharecropping as a declining economic system (but an enduring social system), a mechanizing agricultural economy that increasingly marginalized undereducated African American farmworkers, and massive out-migration.[15]

This tectonic shift was well under way by the early 1950s, the point at which an organized African American movement for civil rights became discernible in Sunflower County. By 1962, when SNCC workers arrived in Sunflower to register voters and initiated the most intense civil rights activity in the county's history, mechanization of Sunflower County farms was already in full force, and black sharecroppers' economic fate was sealed. If sharecropping as an economic arrangement was waning, however, the effects of sharecropping as the basis for social arrangements, particularly between the races, lingered. Although (or, perhaps, because) the labor of sharecroppers was largely redundant by 1962, the racialized attitudes that buttressed the sharecropping system lived on. Generations of white Sunflower Countians based their expectations of how African Americans should behave on sharecropping etiquette, and the slow death of sharecropping as an economic system did nothing to alter those expectations.

White supremacy was the core concept that informed every aspect of Mississippi society during this period. Many Mississippi whites believed deeply in the value of racial segregation, and they defended it at great cost. But massive resistance to integration had to be manufactured in

"We in Mississippi know how to treat our niggers." A Mississippi Delta plantation owner behind the wheel of his new tractor, 1937. The civil rights movement in the Delta occurred within the context of a white-supremacist social order and a mechanizing agricultural economy that increasingly marginalized undereducated African American farmworkers. (Dorothea Lange, FSA/OWI Collection, Library of Congress Prints & Photographs Division [LC-USF34-017138-C])

Sunflower County.[16] Before the U.S. Supreme Court delivered its *Brown* decision in 1954, segregation in Sunflower County was total, but it was not inevitable; there was at least room for moderates to soften the edges of the Jim Crow system. However, increased militancy on the part of Sunflower County blacks and the perceived threat of the *Brown* decision nipped any possibility for a moderate movement in the bud. Indianolans formed what they called the Citizens' Council, an effort on the part of the white middle and planter classes to stop integration through economic intimidation. The members of the Citizens' Council proudly disassociated themselves from the Ku Klux Klan, but both organizations were indispensable wings of a phalanx that created massive resistance to integration throughout the South. They quickly made it impossible for dissenters to argue against what became very close to a prosegregation unanimity on the part of whites.[17] White conservatives demanded conformity to their segregationist social order in the years following *Brown* and were able to create a social atmosphere that made alternative ideological positions untenable.

The Citizens' Council movement spread to most of the southern states, many of which also passed legislation to enforce segregation for as long as possible. The Mississippi state legislature went farthest in this effort. In 1956, the legislature created the Mississippi State Sovereignty Commission, an agency modeled roughly on J. Edgar Hoover's Federal Bureau of Investigation (FBI). The Sovereignty Commission was given broad powers to carry out its mandate, which was to "do and perform any and all acts and things deemed necessary and proper to protect the sovereignty of the [segregation] laws of Mississippi" against "encroachment thereon by the Federal Government or any branch, department, or agency thereof."[18] For the next seventeen years, the Sovereignty Commission spied on Mississippi citizens.

The Sovereignty Commission helped to make Mississippi sui generis in the heady days of the civil rights revolution. The struggle for civil rights that was constructed in Mississippi in the 1950s and 1960s was therefore different from the movements in other southern states. The Magnolia State became, in the famous words of University of Mississippi historian James Silver, the "closed society," precisely because the Sovereignty Commission and the Citizens' Councils, among other institutions, made it dangerous for African Americans and moderate-to-progressive whites to disagree with them publicly. Fundamentally, as one observer has noted, "[T]he struggle for integration in Mississippi was not just a struggle against racism or a struggle for the rights of one oppressed race. It was a struggle for democracy."[19]

Massive resistance to the *Brown* decision in Mississippi crystallized white prosegregation opinion and placed a formidable obstacle before African Americans who longed for the rights and responsibilities of American citizenship. To surmount that obstacle, Sunflower County blacks had to reject a culture that defined them as inferior human beings who did not deserve, for instance, the right to vote for those who would represent them in government. They needed to create what historian Lawrence Goodwyn has identified in another context as a "movement culture . . . a new way of looking at things."[20]

Goodwyn's Populists of the late nineteenth century created "a new culture . . . that attempted to shelter its participants from sundry indoctrinations emanating from the larger culture." By developing a "radically altered perspective" on American society, the Populists gave themselves "a

place to think in . . . [and] something to think about—a massive cooperative vision of a new way to live" and "a new democratic language."[21]
Participants in Sunflower County's civil rights movements—and the people who identified with civil rights movements throughout the United
States in this period—did precisely the same thing. Blacks in Sunflower
County were active politically and socially in the years before the period of
this study, but they lacked the vocabulary of full citizenship. In the middle
and latter decades of the twentieth century, they created this vocabulary.
They launched mass movements to change their society and its gover-
nance and in the process claimed for themselves the rights and responsibilities of citizenship.

Goodwyn identified "individual respect and mass aspiration" as the critical building blocks of mass movements.[22] In an atmosphere where African
Americans were actively taught that they were not worth educating, that
they were incapable of selecting their own political representatives, that
they were low-down, lazy, and no-account in general, simply developing
individual respect and identifying mass aspiration was a much more difficult task than it may seem at first glance. SNCC workers in Sunflower
County labored to create this atmosphere so that local people could create
their lives anew.

A SNCC voter registration worker in the Delta spoke to the group's organizing tactics and to the importance of self-esteem in the formation of this
movement culture: "We have been working on the theory that if you can
make a man feel like a whole person and realize his own worth and dignity
and if you make him understand his plight better, he will want to vote on
his own account."[23] SNCC organizers helped local people in Sunflower
County and throughout the South transform themselves so that they could
then transform society.

To that end, SNCC organizers helped African Americans in Sunflower
County construct a social movement that challenged the foundations of
Delta social relations. This movement defined what participants were
against—segregated facilities, an unjust legal system, racist institutions,
constrained economic opportunities—but it also defined what they were
for.

They were not all for the same thing. Indeed, one of the purposes of this
study is to examine differences within the African American community
and to determine how they affected movement goals. But they had much
in common. For the most part, Sunflower County's black middle-class
movement aimed to end restrictions on black voting rights and demanded
that black citizens be recognized as equal citizens with equal political

rights by local government and by individual whites. The poor people's movement shared these goals, but it also proposed an alternative vision for society that owed much to the teachings of the black Christian church. This was a human rights movement, which posited that all human beings were entitled to decent housing, good jobs, and plenty of food to eat, in addition to the right to vote and the opportunity to earn a decent education. Both groups wanted a seat at the table where the decisions that affected them were made. Middle-class blacks in Sunflower County and in other communities where the organization was active did not always appreciate SNCC workers, but on at least one level they would have agreed that their common goal was, in the words of SNCC's motto, to "let the people decide."

According to Fannie Lou Hamer, the homegrown leader of the Sunflower County poor people's movement, "Ninety per cent of Negro people in Mississippi have gone to church all their lives. They have lived with the hope that if they kept 'standing up' in a Christian manner, things would change." In the initial phase of Hamer's movement, participants did just that: they bore witness to injustice, believing that witness would itself spur change. Freedom Summer, the 1964 project that brought hundreds of college students to Mississippi to register voters and teach in alternative schools, was an act of bearing witness. But Freedom Summer did not bring about widespread social change or concrete economic change, and Hamer began to search for new alternatives.

After 1964, Hamer, having won the right to vote but no one worth voting for, waged a struggle for economic development, decent housing, and a just, peaceful society. She never strayed from the teachings of her church. Hamer's vision for America defined a fundamentally fair and democratic society that clearly had a genesis in what Hamer had learned in Sunday school. Yet while Hamer's struggle was a Christian struggle, as she herself defined it, it was not necessarily a church struggle. She wrote in 1966, "[I]f I had to choose between the church and these young people [the civil rights workers who came into the Delta for Freedom Summer]—and I was brought up in the church and I'm not against the church—I'd choose the young people."[24]

Black ministers did not lead the civil rights crusade in Sunflower County; black Christians did. Some pastors were just as economically vulnerable as the members of their flocks, if not more so, and in many cases they simply decided that they could not afford to be perceived as agitators by the Citizens' Council. In many cases, pastors with comfortable lifestyles chose not to risk their livelihoods. On occasion, however, they were forced by their own congregants to support, if not lead, the civil rights crusade. When the women of a Ruleville church pushed their pastor to open the church's doors to civil rights workers in 1963, they "threatened his fried chicken" (in the words of one activist) and forced him to act. Ministers in Indianola made a church building available to civil rights workers in 1964 only after sncc workers and local church people applied a great deal of pressure.[25]

Journalist Tracy Sugarman watched Fannie Lou Hamer as she applied this treatment to an unsuspecting minister during a 1964 service at a rural Sunflower County church. Hamer and Sugarman interrupted a Bible lesson on the exodus story as they entered the pastor's small church. The unsuspecting preacher invited Hamer to say a few words. She complied, dramatically. "Pharaoh was in Sunflower County!" she announced. "Israel's children were building bricks without straw—at three dollars a day [the going wage for a Sunflower County farm laborer]! They're tired! And they're tired of being tired!" Hamer paused, and according to Sugarman, "Her finger trembled as she pointed to the shaken minister, and every eye [in the church] fastened on the man in the pulpit." Hamer continued, "And you, Reverend Tyler, must be Moses! Leadin' your flock out of the chains and fetters of Egypt—takin' them *yourself* to register—*tomorra*—in Indianola!" Whether or not Reverend Tyler ever attempted to register is largely irrelevant. Hamer and her allies had to force their traditionally defined leaders to lead, if they led at all. In so doing, they redefined the notion of community leadership itself. They injected a vigorous notion of citizenship into a fundamentally undemocratic society.[26]

The hydra-headed federal government was another reluctant partner to the civil rights movement in the years considered here. Washington began to play a major role in the Delta after a string of climatic and economic disasters beset the Delta in the late 1920s and early 1930s. However, the response to these calamities consolidated power in the hands of white elites just as the federal government was beginning to intervene in the Delta's economic affairs to an unprecedented extent.

Federal agricultural policy during the decades of the 1930s and 1940s arguably did more than any other institution to entrench the social and economic power of Delta planters. Franklin D. Roosevelt's New Deal agricultural policies paid farm owners to reduce cotton acreage, and those federal dollars seldom trickled down to the sharecroppers and wage laborers whose livelihoods were destroyed by agricultural contraction. Rather, the steady flow of federal monies encouraged planters to invest in farm machines that made it possible for a few tractor drivers to do the work that had once required several sharecropping families. Acreage reduction doubled as a sharecropper reduction program. By the late 1960s, the trend begun as New Deal agricultural policy had culminated in the unemployment of thousands of black farmworkers.[27]

At the same time, however, the Roosevelt administration gave new hope to a generation of African Americans—who were hit harder than any other group by the Great Depression—and to progressive white southerners. Roosevelt did not support needed national civil rights and antilynching legislation, and his economic programs actively worked against the interests of rural black workers. But the New Deal did bring relief to at least a fraction of the total black population—it was better than nothing, which was what the Republicans offered—and Roosevelt did spend a good deal of political capital on a doomed campaign to defeat some of the most conservative southerners in Congress. Black Americans perceived him as an ally, and those outside of Mississippi who could vote rewarded him with millions of ballots in 1936 and 1940.[28] Ironically, the planters who most benefited from Roosevelt's farm programs found little of merit in the ethos of the New Deal. They saw it as unnecessary interference with their particular vision of the social order. "As long as men live some will be in want, and all shall live in some sort of fear," wrote Walter Sillers, a Bolivar County planter and the Speaker of the Mississippi House of Representatives. "To attempt to provide otherwise . . . is against nature and cannot be done—not even by the New Deal and its horde of crack-pot professors and communistic theorists."[29]

Beginning with the U.S. Supreme Court's 1954 *Brown* decision, the three branches of the federal government came reluctantly and gradually to promote equal rights across racial lines in the Mississippi Delta and throughout the United States. At key moments in the struggle, when representatives of the federal government made at least a rhetorical commitment to racial equality, black Sunflower County residents took greater risks in opposing the planter regime, hoping that the power of the federal government would buttress them.

At times, the strategy encouraged blacks to take risks but disappointed them when the federal government could not or would not protect them. To take one example, a National Association for the Advancement of Colored People (NAACP) chapter gained strength in the county following the initial *Brown* decision, only to be crushed by white segregationists while the Eisenhower administration stood by silently. At other times, the strategy paid dividends. When the volunteers and local people who risked their lives to support Freedom Summer won over the hearts and minds of Americans in other parts of the country, their struggle won stronger federal statutes banning the segregation of public facilities and increasing black voter registration.

But even the benefits that accrued from the Civil Rights Act of 1964 and the Voting Rights Act of 1965 came only gradually after local people, at great personal expense and risk, forced the federal government to commit itself to enforcing the laws. Indeed, an analysis of federal policies in the Delta in this period reveals "the difficulties that are likely to accompany [the federal government's] attempts to promote economic, social and political reform in a society without altering that society's traditional power and status relationships." The federal government proved time and again that it was unwilling to favor the human rights of poor African Americans in Sunflower County over the property rights of white planters. As such, the national government must be seen as an ambivalent friend to civil rights movements in the Mississippi Delta at best, a negligent and hypocritical caretaker at worst.[30]

The paradox of Sunflower County boils down to the fact that its two most famous citizens made their homes about ten miles and a world apart. Civil rights workers moved into Sunflower County in 1962 explicitly to draw attention to U.S. senator James O. Eastland's home base. In short order, they uncovered a farmworker, Fannie Lou Hamer, who had a unique ability to define the problems that affected African Americans in the Delta in their own vernacular. Hamer was a leader waiting for a movement, and she soon settled into the role of what one magazine termed the "Prophet of Hope for the Sick and Tired." Hamer believed equally deeply in the promise of the Bible and in the promise of the United States of America.[31]

At base, Hamer demanded that black Deltans receive what they had been guaranteed by the U.S. Constitution. Her movement was something more than a civil rights movement, however; it was a poor people's movement that demanded human rights as well as voting rights for all Americans. Hamer came to distrust the black middle class deeply. She dismissed the NAACP as "the National Association for the Advancement of Certain People" and deplored the organization's reluctance to work with poor, rural people like herself. The movement she led from Ruleville, therefore, differed in important respects from the civil rights movement we have come to know from much of the literature on the struggle for black equality.

It is difficult to assess how successful this movement has been. Hamer died a dispirited woman in 1977, bitter in the belief that her fellow men and women had failed to make any progress toward the creation of a beloved community in her lifetime. But in a span of years that extended just past Hamer's death, the "closed society" was transformed: Mississippi went from the state in the Union where it was most difficult for blacks to vote to the state with the most black elected officials.

There are, moreover, ways of measuring progress other than counting elected officials. For many African Americans in Sunflower County, the journey of their civil rights work was much more important than any destination they may have reached. Through their work in the movement, thousands found in themselves and each other strengths and talents they had not recognized before. In a handful of cases, these strengths translated to election to political office or economic success. In thousands of others, the realization produced results that might not have been tangible to outsiders but made it possible for the transformed to lead more meaningful lives—either in Sunflower County or somewhere else.

Perhaps most important, by 1986 the African Americans of Sunflower County had at least begun to dismantle the foundations of the sharecropping social system that had determined their inferior status for a century. It is admittedly difficult to quantify changes in face-to-face relations, but at the very least, the black citizens of Sunflower County had made it impossible for their white neighbors to expect them to behave as they had been forced to behave during the years before 1964. They had won the power to make some of the decisions that affected their lives. That was no small accomplishment, but neither was it cause for great celebration.

What happened in Sunflower County was not a "turning point" in the American civil rights movement, but the experience was illustrative in many ways of the wrenching social changes that southerners precipitated and endured in the four decades following the Second World War. The county's experience illuminates southern African Americans' long, sustained, and at times highly organized campaigns for equal citizenship rights, economic opportunity, and basic human dignity and proves that the modern civil rights movement drew on long-standing patterns of black community organization and activism. White movements to maintain an inequitable society likewise drew on past efforts, and their organizing strategies and rhetoric continue to inform contemporary southern conservatives. It is my hope that by turning our attention to civil rights and resistance movements over long periods of time in communities like Sunflower County, we can deepen our understanding of what American civil rights movements have and have not accomplished.

If you had a negro mammy take care of you and keep
you from eating dirt; if you played with negro boys when
a boy; if you have worked with and among them, laughed at
their ribald humor; if you have been stunned by their abysmal
vulgarity and profanity; if you can find it in your heart to
overlook their obscenity and depravity; if you can respect
and love their deep religious fervor; if you can cherish
their loyalty and devotion to you, then you are beginning
to understand the negro. . . . And unless you have, to
some degree, approximated this relationship, then
you do not and cannot understand or know the negro
and his problems. As a matter of fact, you are quite
ignorant on this question.
Mississippi circuit judge Thomas P. Brady, Black Monday

You will have to see the mass of disfranchised,
frightened Negroes in the Mississippi Delta to
understand what it is to be without freedom.
Clinton C. Battle, address to an NAACP "freedom rally," 1958

CHAPTER TWO

What It Is to Be without Freedom, 1945–1955

There is no liberal tradition in Mississippi politics. Not entirely without
reason, Americans traditionally have regarded Mississippi as the most
backward state in America's most retrograde region—the state that, in the
words of V. O. Key, "manifests in accentuated form the darker political
strains that run throughout the South."[1] In the context of Mississippi, and
particularly in the literally black-and-white world of the Mississippi Delta,
relative terms like "moderate" and "liberal" do not carry the meanings
they carry in the politics of the South, to say nothing of the nation. Mississippi had its share of economic liberals during the New Deal years, the
"progressive" demagogue and Klansman Theodore Bilbo chief among
them. The Magnolia State was desperately poor, and economic liberals
welcomed government intervention in and aid to the state's economy. But
even New Dealism in Mississippi remained viciously racist. This continued

to be the case in the years between the end of the Second World War and the U.S. Supreme Court's 1954 *Brown* decision.

Yet even in the heart of the Delta in this period, there were racial "moderates" in the region's black and white communities: citizens who favored an increase in opportunities for African Americans within the Jim Crow system but stopped short of challenging the Delta's racialized social structure directly. (Their contemporaries used terms other than "moderate" to describe those who went further and defied Jim Crow head-on: "Communist," "subversive," "mongrelizer.") The radical changes in southern society that accompanied the Second World War exposed rank injustices inherent in the Jim Crow sociopolitical system. They provided a small window of opportunity for moderates to move Mississippi closer to the ideals of a one-man-one-vote polity that had been expressed in the U.S. Constitution and its Reconstruction-era amendments. By the mid-1940s, a substantial number of whites in the Delta even began to think that it might be in their own interests to provide blacks with a rudimentary educational system.[2]

At the end of the Second World War, whites enjoyed uncontested social, political, and economic dominance in the Mississippi Delta. African Americans had carried their share of the load in the war against fascism, and white moderates began to contemplate the possibility of allowing some "good Negroes" the privilege of voting. Blacks had not voted since the "Mississippi Plan" disfranchised them at the turn of the century.[3] Many whites in the Delta and beyond began to favor a slight increase in black political participation and increased spending on black schools. In very few cases, however, did any Mississippians, black or white, advocate a full-scale assault on Jim Crow before the Supreme Court's 1954 *Brown* decision.

Until 1950, even the NAACP's official policy in Mississippi was, in the words of one historian, "separate-but-*really*-equal."[4] The nation's leading civil rights organization would eventually attack the legality of Jim Crow directly. But at the end of World War II, even the bravest and most radical Mississippians chose, in all but a small number of cases, not to speak out publicly against segregation. This did not change until the 1954 Supreme Court decision created room for maneuvering.

Nevertheless, the period between democracy's victory over the Axis powers and the Supreme Court's watershed verdict presented Mississippi moderates of both races the best chance they had in the twentieth century to soften Jim Crow and, perhaps, to dismember it peacefully, deliberately, and gradually. Between 1945 and 1954, white Mississippi moderates encouraged unprecedented spending on black schools throughout the state.

White moderates embarked on a program to improve material conditions for the African Americans of Sunflower County and allowed limited numbers of African Americans to register to vote. However, the moderate program—if an organized "program" as such ever really existed—did not mollify the African Americans who grew increasingly dissatisfied with inferior schools and the limited economic opportunities available in Mississippi.

When the actions of a generation of Sunflower County blacks showed that they were prepared to demand their equal political rights as American citizens, another faction of Delta whites slammed shut the moderates' window of opportunity. As cotton markets faltered and the modernization of cotton production threatened traditional white elites throughout the rural South, a white movement to keep blacks separate and their living conditions inferior in Sunflower County rallied around resistance to the U.S. Supreme Court's decision outlawing segregated school systems.

"This Great Democracy for Which So Many of Us Risked Our Lives Freely"

The image of the black soldier who returned from World War II to fight for his civil rights at home has become a staple of southern history. Some black World War II veterans—Aaron Henry from Clarksdale, just to the north of Sunflower County; Amzie Moore of Cleveland, in neighboring Bolivar County; and Medgar Evers of Jackson, to name the three who would become most influential in Mississippi—did return to the state energized and determined to claim the rights they felt they had earned by fighting for their country. They did not, however, have direct counterparts in Sunflower County.[5]

Most black soldiers from Mississippi did not fool themselves into thinking that their status as veterans would change their inferior social status at home. "Some reported that they expected nothing when they went to war," Neil McMillen writes, "and, so well schooled were they then in Jim Crow's ways, that they were neither surprised nor even particularly disappointed to learn upon their return that nothing had changed." For many if not most black veterans, finding a decent job—not claiming voting rights—was the primary concern upon return to the Magnolia State. "I didn't know much about the right to vote," said one returning soldier, "but I did know that I deserved the right to have a job." In the Jim Crow era, even this modest claim represented a shift in African Americans' publicly expressed expectations.[6]

Black veterans were not the only ones to have felt the war's deep impact.

Mississippi's white veterans who had seen blacks in combat were in some cases persuaded that their service in the war had won blacks the right to become full American citizens. Jack Harper Jr., a lifelong white resident of Sunflower County who served in the Marine Corps in World War II and as a National Guardsman in an integrated unit in Korea, claimed in a 1997 interview to have been impressed by the sacrifices black soldiers made for their country. Harper remembered that after seeing black soldiers in action, he had concluded that "they were indeed entitled to full citizenship."[7] Others, though, agreed with James Eastland, who claimed in a 1945 speech on the floor of the U.S. Senate that "the negro soldier was a dismal and utter failure. He was a disgrace to the flag of his country. . . . He will not fight, he will not work."[8] Eastland was lying. All available evidence showed that black soldiers fought as hard and as bravely during the war as their white counterparts, under worse conditions. He and other white supremacists in the Delta had to assimilate contrary evidence into their ingrained expectations of how African Americans should behave.

One of the true white moderates of the Delta in this era was the region's congressman in the U.S. House of Representatives, Frank Smith. During the battle over segregation that followed the 1954 *Brown* decision, a young white Mississippi farmer surprised Smith when he told the congressman, "Fight integration? Why, I've just begun to fight. When I was on a beach in the South Pacific I was fighting and I didn't know why. Now we know what we are fighting for, and nothing is going to hold us back." He implied that a vigorous defense of Jim Crow was the highest form of American patriotism.[9] To a large degree, a discourse in Mississippi over the war's meanings lay at the heart of the disagreements that characterized the two decades following its end. Medgar Evers may have been a proud and patriotic World War II veteran, but so was his murderer, Byron De La Beckwith.

George Jordan, a Ruleville sharecropper, was among the most radical of Sunflower County's returning black veterans, and he did not attempt to register to vote until 1953. He was lucky enough to rent land from a white man who considered Jordan's voting none of his business—a quality that made the landlord extremely unusual among Sunflower County whites of his time. Jordan first voted in 1954, after he was able to convince the county registrar that the taxes he paid for his pickup truck, coupled with his service in the army, earned him the right to vote. Jordan reasoned, "I went and fought for my country, so I ought to have a break somewhere." An original member of the county's NAACP chapter, Jordan distinguished himself in the 1950s by making the rounds of local African American churches, encouraging members of the congregations to pay their poll

taxes and attempt to register. He was largely unsuccessful. As more people
learned what Jordan was saying at those meetings, fewer people came to
listen to him. Jordan estimated in 1997 that no more than ten or fifteen
people came to an average Ruleville voter registration rally in the 1950s,
an indication that his message was considered dangerous. Only twenty-
one blacks in the Ruleville precinct registered to vote between 1952 and
1962.[10]

But the impact of voter registration work for George Jordan could not be
measured in mere numbers. "I had to do it for me," Jordan said in 1997. "It
was important to me just to have one vote." Asked to describe what he had
hoped to accomplish with his vote, Jordan answered by referring to the
Old Testament book of Obadiah ("We have heard tidings from the Lord,
and a messenger has been sent among the nations: 'Rise up! Let us rise
against her for battle!' Behold, I will make you small among the nations,
you shall be utterly despised").[11]

The right to vote held psychological benefits that were more valuable
for Jordan than any practical electoral consequences his single ballot
might have produced. He had no illusions that his vote would by itself
change the balance of power in Sunflower County, but the very possession
of it gave him at least a psychological civic power. He used it, but he was
one of very few Sunflower County blacks to register to vote in the 1950s.[12]

"At the time I returned [from the war] we couldn't vote and we were not
given the opportunity to run for office," said Reverend David Matthews, a
longtime Indianola resident and World War II veteran. "We couldn't even
register. Our first [voter] registration [drive] was in 1952, and I was dis-
charged in 1945, so for that time I was unable even to register. Certainly I
felt that as a citizen and as one who had gone into combat for his country I
should have that right." But disfranchisement was only one aspect of Jim
Crow life in Sunflower County. "We faced *so* many obstacles," Matthews
said. Like hundreds of other returning veterans in Sunflower County, he
decided that immediate agitation over voter registration would be counterproductive and possibly dangerous. He chose to bide his time.[13] This
cautious veteran, and not the firebrand of the Medgar Evers type, was
closer to the norm among the returning soldiers of Sunflower County.

African American veterans, and African American residents of Sunflower County in general, waited patiently for an appropriate time to act, a
time when a critical mass of committed blacks could make possible the
kind of actions that were otherwise too dangerous for individuals to un-
dertake. That time came in a 1952–54 voter registration campaign. Led by
the county's lone black professional, Clinton Battle, a native of Indianola

and a medical doctor, 104 black citizens of Sunflower County—ten teachers (six men and four women), thirty-three housewives, twenty-eight male farmers, eighteen small businessmen or skilled laborers, nine male farm laborers, and five preachers—and Battle successfully registered to vote between the reorganization of Indianola's NAACP branch in late 1952 and the Supreme Court's decision banning public school segregation in May 1954. In contrast, only four Sunflower County blacks were allowed to register to vote in the eight-year period following *Brown*.[14]

"Two Identical Systems Neither of Which Is Good Enough for Anybody"

Sunflower County's racial moderates focused their attention in the immediate postwar period on creating truly equal segregated schools that improved facilities for African Americans but did not challenge segregation. As Table 2.1 demonstrates, providing merely adequate schools for Sunflower County blacks was challenge enough. The white citizens who met at the request of County Schools Superintendent Sam L. Jones in February 1949 were concerned about the fate of the black majority in Sunflower's mechanizing agricultural economy. The black schools trained students—by barely training them at all—to participate as unskilled laborers in a backward economy that was in the process of being revolutionized by tractor farming. It became increasingly clear in one-crop Sunflower County that African American students could either be trained to participate in the new, mechanized agricultural economy, or they could go onto the county welfare rolls. There was no third alternative. For Sunflower County's white moderates, the decision was an easy one for financial reasons alone. Still, in an atmosphere where less than 1 percent of all African American children even made it to the final year of high school, simply improving black facilities had the potential to create revolutionary change. If African Americans were worth equal school facilities, went the unspoken logic, it might be possible to train them to be something other than servile farm laborers.[15]

The integrated group of Sunflower County residents who began to address the problem of a catastrophically inadequate black school system in February 1949 was part of a statewide groundswell. African American teachers throughout the state had begun to push for pay equalization, and from the late 1940s through the mid-1950s, whites began to think that equalization of school facilities "might be prudent if segregation were to be preserved." The (white) supervisor of black schools for the Mississippi

Table 2.1. Enrollment in Sunflower County Schools for
African Americans, December 1949

Grade	Number of African American Students	Percentage of Total Number of African American Students
1	2,501	32.4
2	1,000	13.0
3	925	12.0
4	937	12.2
5	690	9.0
6	549	7.1
7	418	5.4
8	253	3.3
9	262	3.3
10	100	1.3
11	46	0.5
12	28	0.3
1–6	6,602	85.6
7–12	1,107	14.4
Total	7,709	100.00

Source: Adapted from University of Mississippi Bureau of Educational Research,
"The Report of a Study of the Education for Negroes in Sunflower County, Mississippi"
(Oxford: University of Mississippi, 1950), 40, table 7,
University of Mississippi Special Collections.

Note: Includes Drew, Indianola, and Ruleville school districts.

Department of Education sounded exactly this theme when he addressed the Indianola Rotary Club in 1946. He declared that "black educational advances benefited whites, and he also suggested that segregation could only be preserved if whites made a sustained attempt to address long-ignored black educational needs." Like the eventual desegregation of Mississippi's public schools decades later, the equalization program proceeded on whites' terms only. Moreover, because the state was so poor, "educational equalization was never a viable alternative." But the equalization program represented an important initiative for moderates in Sunflower County.[16]

Fifty white educators, elected leaders, and private citizens first met to investigate the problem of black education in Sunflower County. They chose seven whites and three African Americans to delve into the problem more deeply. Their work had an immediate impact. For the first time, in the 1949–50 school year, Sunflower County spent as much on the black school system as it did on white schools, up from the one-to-two ratio the county had spent in 1940 on black and white schools, respectively. But the expenditures were far from racially balanced, as the total population of Sunflower County at the time was nearly 70 percent African American.[17]

The Citizens' Committee, as the group of ten called itself, turned to the University of Mississippi's Bureau of Educational Research for an extensive report on the county's facilities for African American education. The committee decided from the outset that the report should deal only with black schools, for an examination of white schools "might jeopardize any recommendations [and funds] for the Negro [school improvement] plan." In other words, the committee knew that white public schools were lacking, too, but the black schools were so inadequate as to jeopardize the entire system of segregated education. John E. Phay, head of the Bureau of Educational Research, undertook the investigation himself and ran immediately into skepticism on the part of black teachers. His specific questions "drew vague, guarded answers" at first, but Phay personally visited every one of the ninety-four black schools in Sunflower County. He photographed each school and, when the study ran into financial problems, subsidized the investigation out of his own pocket. Phay eventually overcame the initial skepticism black teachers held of the white-sponsored investigations, and African Americans ultimately provided valuable assistance to the study.[18]

The investigators found that the county's black students were serviced by only two rickety, hand-me-down school buses, which happened to be two more than had been available the previous year. The county estimated that there were 20,473 African Americans between the ages of six and twenty-one, but only 7,709 of them were enrolled in schools as of December 1949, and of those only a very few attended school regularly.[19] Sixty-nine of the ninety-four schools met in black churches, an arrangement that gave local communities control over their schools but that was hardly conducive to education. Phay learned that in these schools, funerals took precedence over instruction.

The investigators tried to test black schoolchildren, but the shortage of desks in their schoolrooms and the novelty of standardized testing for the ultra-rural pupils made the task all but impossible. Students in the lower grades were simply unable to "recognize printed words, phrases, or sentences, [or] to associate them with pictures of objects, or accompanying

"If you miss me at the back of the bus . . . " Students gather in front of one of the two buses available for black Sunflower County schoolchildren, 1949. (John E. Phay Collection, Special Collections, University of Mississippi)

thought." Nor could many of them spell their names or remember their birthdays for the researchers.[20] After examiners attempted testing in five schools and realized the obstacles that faced them, they jettisoned plans to test children in all of the ninety-four black schools throughout the county. Nonetheless, the examiners tentatively concluded that Sunflower County's black schoolchildren, on average, performed in six subjects at a grade level two years below the average southern white student and more than one grade level below the average southern black pupil, despite the fact that Sunflower County's black students were on average more than two years older than white children in their grades and more than a year older than the black average for comparable grades throughout the South.[21]

Of the 181 teachers Phay and his investigators found working in the black schools, only 26, or 14 percent, had spent four years in college. Fewer than half had even one year's worth of college credits. Ten percent of the 181 teachers had not taught the year before, but more than two-thirds had taught for six or more years, which suggests that what many lacked in formalized training they made up for with experience. Their average yearly salary was $730.82, though nearly half made less than $600.[22]

Phay learned that black students had to pay a fee of $1 to $6 for heating costs in the winter months, but he visited schools that were no more than "badly lighted shacks overventilated by holes in the roofs, cracks in the walls, and doorless doorways." The bureau's report recommended a concentration of black schools, in the form of two new high schools, one each in the southern and northern parts of the county; eight new elementary schools throughout the entire county; and an increased effort to hire college graduates with state teaching certificates. Estimates for the cost of Phay's plan, which also included smaller class sizes, a renewed stress on vocational education, the purchase of a minimum of twenty-five school buses, and a nine-month school session that would not have interfered with the cotton season, totaled $2,493,745. Sunflower County had never shown a willingness to spend that kind of money on the education of its black residents, but Phay promised that the new schools would pay for themselves by creating productive members of the community. "[I]f educational opportunities are not made available so that the Negro can be self-sustaining," he and the other authors of the report warned, "the mechanical revolution in cotton production may soon force the displaced Negro workers on unemployment relief. An education aimed at teaching the Negro to become self-sustaining is the best and cheapest answer."[23]

In return for increased spending on black schools, Phay's plan would have taken control of the schools away from black communities. The schools offered African Americans in the Delta a rare area of jurisdiction. However, surrendering this autonomy may not have been too great a price to pay. Desperately poor black families bore the brunt of their schools' expenses, and they got even less than what they paid for. In too many cases, that meant classrooms without heat, inadequate furniture, and few or no books. When black schools were constructed or renovated, Sunflower County blacks had to throw themselves on the mercy of white planters and merchants, perpetuating paternalist practices by begging for money from white benefactors. In several cases, black school principals even rented out the labor of their students at cotton-picking time to raise funds for their schools.[24] In the end, white Sunflower County voters refused to pay for the improvements to African American schools but consolidated them anyway, transferring control of the schools from decentralized black communities to white bureaucrats beholden only to white voters.[25]

Hodding Carter III of nearby Greenville, whose Pulitzer Prize–winning father edited the Delta's best newspaper, the *Delta Democrat-Times*, insisted in a 1959 book that other moderate whites in the Delta shifted their views toward African American education in the early 1950s. Carter per-

"You know, as well as we know[,] that we have had the Separate all right but in very few cases have we had the Equal." Exterior and interior views of the Williams School, southeast of Ruleville, 1949. (John E. Phay Collection, Special Collections, University of Mississippi)

ceived a "widening acceptance, in theory, at least, of the concept that the 'separate but equal' doctrine . . . should be applied as strenuously toward providing equal facilities and opportunities as toward insuring that those facilities and opportunities should be separate."[26] Carter would become famous outside of Mississippi precisely because he was out of step with the Delta's prevailing racial mores, but a widening skepticism toward knee-jerk defenses of white supremacy on the part of many white Mississippians did exist before 1954. White Mississippians who began to question the logic, to say nothing of the business sense, of strict and virulent segregationist practices did have an opportunity in the early 1950s to open the doors of "the closed society." When Governor Hugh White traveled to Indianola in 1953 for the dedication of Gentry High School for Negroes, he identified finding enough money to support two school systems as the main financial problem that his administration faced.[27]

While Mississippi anticipated the likelihood of a head-on assault of its segregated society, the state government maneuvered to shore up the bulwarks of Jim Crow. The poorest state in the Union actually began to make an honest effort to create two legitimate school systems. During the period between Thurgood Marshall's *Brown* arguments before the Supreme Court in December 1952 and the Court's decision in May 1954, the Mississippi legislature contrived explicitly to influence the Court's verdict. Governor White called the legislature into special session in November 1953 and authorized an unprecedented equalization program. The main provisions of White's plan were equalization of salaries for black and white teachers, equalization of transportation and building facilities for black and white students, and mandatory eight-month school terms for the students of each race.

Under White's plan, precedence would have been given to spending on black school facilities until they could be considered reasonably equal to the state's white schools. White hoped the program would show good faith on Mississippi's part to provide separate and truly equal educational facilities and would, in turn, influence the Supreme Court's decision. The state legislature passed White's ambitious plan in December, the governor signed it into law, and Mississippi waited for a verdict. The state could not begin to implement the new plan, however, for the newfound commitment to equalization had been passed into law without funding. Mississippi's equalization program would have spent an additional $6 million on African American education, but spending was contingent upon a favorable Supreme Court ruling.[28] As Table 2.2 shows, the state had a long way to go before it could even pretend to provide school facilities that

Table 2.2. Mississippi Public School Expenditures by Race, 1952–1953

Race	Number of School-Age Children (% Enrolled in Schools)	Transportation Expenditures ($ per School-Age Child per Year)	Classroom Education Expenditures ($ per School-Age Child per Year)	Average Teacher Salary
White	398,866	$4,476,753	$23,536,022	$2,109
	(68%)	($11.22)	($59.00)	
Black	496,913	$1,179,826	$8,816,670	$1,153
	(55%)	($2.37)	($17.74)	

Source: Mississippi Department of Education figures, reported in *Southern School News*, September 3, 1954, 8, 16.

were both equal and separate. And the Court's May 17 decision would, of course, be far from agreeable to Mississippi's segregationists.

Mississippi's leading man of letters, William Faulkner, who considered himself a moderate on the race question, responded to the equalization plan with characteristic sardonicism in a letter to a Memphis newspaper:

> Our present schools are not even good enough for white folks. So what do we do? Make them good enough, improve them to the best possible? No. We beat the bushes, rake and scrape to raise additional taxes to establish another system at best only equal to that which is already not good enough, which therefore won't be good enough for Negroes either; we will have two identical systems neither of which is good enough for anybody. The question is not how foolish can people get, because apparently there is no limit to that. The question is, how foolish in simple dollars and cents, let alone in wasted men and women, can we afford to be?[29]

"We Have Every Reason to Expect Some Fine Things from Indianola"

In 1948, Reverend H. M. Foster organized a branch of the NAACP in Indianola. Foster signed up sixty-three dues-paying members in his first weeks of organizing and claimed to have sixty more waiting to pay the NAACP membership. There was obviously interest in civil rights organizing in the county seat, but the chapter was quickly driven underground by white pressure and, it appears, ineffective leadership.

Of the thirty-two original members who listed an occupation, seven were pastors, five were teachers, nine were merchants, ten were skilled laborers, and one was a farmer. (Five listed themselves as housewives.) When the president of the NAACP's Mississippi Conference of Branches visited Indianola in 1948, he reported back to national headquarters, "In my opinion, we have every reason to expect some fine things from Indianola." The branch was still adding members at a healthy clip in March 1949 when Foster asked the national office for additional membership cards so that "the Boys going off to the army" could have their proof of membership before they left for basic training. The branch achieved its first concrete success in February 1949. Responding to requests from the NAACP chapter, the Indianola police force hired Nathaniel "Slim" Jack, a charter member of the Indianola branch and the first African American police officer in the entire state.[30]

Within a year, however, the Indianola branch of the NAACP was dormant, apparently as a result of whites' financial pressure. Foster reported that so many members had been forced to move "on account of the farm program, and they had nothing to do"—that is, no land to farm—that he had stopped holding meetings. Enough of Foster's members were share-croppers or renters—the most vulnerable agents in the Delta's economy—that economic pressure from white landowners and creditors seems to have destroyed the incipient organization by April 1950. It lay dormant for roughly a year.[31]

Robert Love, a native of Itta Bena, Mississippi, was home for vacation from a factory job in Cleveland, Ohio, in 1951 when a Sunflower County principal asked him to teach a class in rural Stephensville during a summertime "split session." (The split session was a semester for black students that met in the weeks between cotton-chopping time and the harvest season.) Love planned to return to Ohio after the summer but instead stayed in Sunflower County for forty-six years. He befriended the physician Clinton Battle and began working with him to reorganize the Indianola branch of the NAACP. Love convened a meeting of eight men at Indianola's Club Ebony in 1951; the group elected a Ruleville house painter named Gentry Black its chapter president and Battle the secretary-treasurer. The members of the cadre covered "the full strata," according to Love, and consisted of a black professional, laborers, schoolteachers, small business owners, and farm owners.[32]

Battle was a native of Indianola who had been educated at the state of Mississippi's expense at Fisk University's Meharry Medical School in Nashville. (During the Jim Crow era, the state paid for gifted and fortunate black Mississippians to attend out-of-state graduate programs that were not available through historically black colleges in Mississippi.) He returned to the Delta and opened practices in Indianola and Belzoni that served the black sharecroppers of the surrounding plantation communities.

Battle held exactly the kind of position that made it possible for him to organize blacks for civil rights activity. As a physician in a segregated society, Battle was as independent of whites as he could have been, but he never achieved complete financial self-reliance, and he would ultimately pay for his economic vulnerability. Under the Delta's racialized health system, when a black farmworker became ill, the owner of the plantation on which he sharecropped gave him or her a "scrip" authorizing a specific doctor to treat the patient in return for a guarantee of future payment from the plantation owner. The owner would then deduct the cost of medical treatment from the cropper's harvest or the laborer's wages. Battle had been authorized to treat black patients for local plantation owners. The arrangement was a comfortable one for Battle at first; it guaranteed him a steady flow of patients but ultimately left him at the mercy of white plantation owners. Still, Battle's occupation gave him something of a cushion against financial hardship and a great deal of prestige in Sunflower County's African American community.

Battle's youthful self-confidence—he had already graduated from medical school, established a successful practice, and resurrected the Sunflower County NAACP chapter by the age of twenty-five—translated to a charisma that drew others to the civil rights organization. The doctor's home became a place for young black men to hang out and shoot the bull; conversations there invariably turned toward civil rights activity. Meanwhile, Battle's reputation as an excellent physician spread. His picture appeared in *Ebony* magazine alongside a story about his delivery of live conjoined twins, which at the time was something of a medical miracle, at South Sunflower Hospital in September 1955. According to Indianola lore, Battle also treated ill white men and women who waited for cover of darkness to visit the black physician whose skills were considered superior to those of Indianola's white doctors.[33]

When Battle wanted to schedule a second NAACP meeting, he sent postcards through the mail announcing the time and location to members. This horrified the cards' recipients. According to Love, the addressees were "real offended because the white citizens of Indianola were now aware of [the new NAACP branch] being organized." They knew that this information could be used to harm them. A U.S. Postal Service employee in Sunflower County intercepted and read NAACP correspondence, and those who received mail from the organization began to get unwanted attention from powerful whites. Accordingly, turnover in the branch's officer positions was high. Louie Walker, a former secretary of the Indianola NAACP branch, wrote in 1954 to national headquarters in New York, "It is imperative that I no longer receive mail from the N.A.A.C.P. Please, please, discontinue from sending me mail from there and take my name from your mailing list. This is of importance to me." Branch president Theodore Keenan told field secretary Medgar Evers in 1955, "I have been personally contacted and told to cease my activity with the N.A.A.C.P. and stop any mail from them or leave the State and go where the other people are that are pushing it. . . . Since I'm not in a position to leave the State now, I'm asking that my name be canceled [from] the mailing list."[34]

Battle's father had been a member of the original incarnation of the Indianola branch, but the new organization was not his father's NAACP. The relative ease Battle had in reorganizing the branch suggests that Reverend Foster may not have provided forceful enough leadership in the face of white pressure to encourage and reinforce his enthusiastic members. NAACP Southeastern Regional Office secretary Ruby Hurley toured Mississippi in March 1952 and commented on young Battle's exuberance and energized leadership. The branch, she reported to Gloster Current, director of branches for the national organization, "has come a long way in the months since its reorganization and shows a great potential for spreading the NAACP in this part of the Delta." Hurley found, somewhat to her surprise, that the branch was involved in a highly successful voter registration drive, "making real efforts to get more Negroes qualified and registered to vote . . . in the city as well as in the County, State, and National elections." Battle and his comrades faced huge obstacles, however: "[T]he . . . problems in the area are myriad," Hurley noted. "The majority of Negroes . . . in the county are living in virtual slavery." Hurley despaired that Sunflower County blacks had been conditioned to accept their situation without questioning it but found reason for hope. "[T]he branch leadership[,] which is young—the president a young doctor about 25, the vice president a little older and the secretary, a young veteran of World War II—are aware of the problems facing them and are attempting to build a strong Branch to cope with them." Between December 1952 and May 1954, 104 blacks registered to vote in Sunflower County, with the names of Clinton C. Battle and his wife, Millicent, at the top of the list.[35]

The statewide apparatus of the NAACP apparently agreed with Hurley's assessment of the Indianola branch, for the NAACP held its 1953 Conference of Mississippi Branches at Indianola's Bell Grove Missionary Baptist Church. From a pulpit in the heart of the Mississippi Delta, state conference president Amos O. Holmes pledged, "We will work toward the goal of full integration, full freedom and full democracy for every Mississippian, Negro and white, and see to it [that] the vicious system of segregation is challenged until it is removed and justice is done."[36] The statement was highly incendiary locally and on the statewide level.

The U.S. Supreme Court had already heard arguments in the *Brown* case. Holmes and the Mississippi NAACP anticipated a favorable ruling, but in the event the Court should decide against the NAACP, Holmes vowed, "[W]e will continue to fight segregation by every legal and legitimate means at our disposal." Roy Wilkins, assistant executive secretary of the national organization, attended the conference and launched a fund-raising campaign to finance three suits against the admissions policies of the all-white University of Mississippi School of Law.[37] The NAACP clearly hoped to parlay the momentum generated by the Indianola chapter and by the statewide conference of branches into a statewide mass movement. The conference also attracted the attention of Indianola whites, however, and accounts in large part for their decision to organize an actively pro-segregationist program when they did.

Grass-Roots White Organizing to Defend Jim Crow

In 1953, Robert "Tut" Patterson managed a Leflore County plantation and was part-owner of a Holly Ridge farm just west of the Indianola city limits. The stocky, red-haired Patterson was a veteran of both the Mississippi State College football team's Southeastern Conference campaigns, where he had served as a team captain, and the Battle of the Bulge, where he had fought as an army paratrooper. In November, he attended a meeting at his daughter's Indianola elementary school and heard Wilma Sledge, Sunflower County's representative in the state House of Representatives, explain that the U.S. Supreme Court would probably soon order southern schools to desegregate. That was a terrible proposition, she said, but there was nothing they could do about it. "I just sat there like the rest of them, like a bump on a log," Patterson later remembered. "But I couldn't sleep that night. I got up out of bed and went into the bathroom and turned on the light and started writing a letter to the editor. Then I wrote to everybody I could think of."[38]

He had one letter printed for distribution among Indianola whites. "Dear Fellow Americans," it began. "I attended a meeting the other day on the elementary school issue and when I left I was confused, mad and ashamed. It seems a great danger is hanging over the heads of our children —mongrelization." Patterson denounced "our leaders [who] cringe in confusion and await what they claim is inevitable"; he could not stand the possibility of white "children . . . being taught the Communist theme of [the equality of] all races and mongrelization."[39]

Patterson announced to his neighbors that a deceptively simple solution had occurred to him soon after hearing Sledge speak. "I gathered my children," he said, "and promised them that they would never have to go to school with children of other races against their will, and this is my solemn vow and pledge." Patterson assured them, "If every Southerner who feels as I do, and they are in the vast majority, will make this vow, we will defeat this communistic disease that is being thrust upon us. . . . [I]f we all stand together, this can be accomplished. We must not accept mongrelization as inevitable!"[40] Before long, Patterson would convince a good many of his white neighbors not only that integration was far from inevitable but that massive resistance to it was the only acceptable behavior for patriotic white southerners.

Patterson goaded his neighbors into action. In a December 1953 letter to his local newspaper, the *Indianola Enterprise*, Patterson mused, "I have often wondered how long it would take the communists, through their many tools and organizations in the country, to make some of these red-blooded Americans mad. It is a known fact that we are the most complacent and apathetic people in the world."[41] Underscoring Patterson's point about white Deltans' indifference, the editor of the *Enterprise*, who often encouraged his readers to write to the newspaper and express their opinions on the issues of the day, received only one other letter that he deemed important enough to print in the seven months between this and Patterson's next letter, which the *Enterprise* printed in June 1954. That letter encouraged other readers to support a Christian organization for high school students, and it ran on the front page of the newspaper. This span of time contained, not insignificantly, the announcement of the *Brown* decision.[42]

Patterson's 1953 letter, which presupposed the *Brown* verdict, tangled Communism and desegregation together as a matter of course. The World War II veteran claimed—erroneously—that President Truman's recent desegregation of the armed forces had put "morale at an all time low, and desertions and failures to reenlist are at an all time high," presumably putting the nation at even greater risk of Communist infiltration. The idea behind desegregation, the idea that men of all races are created equal, he wrote, "is pure communism. It's principal [*sic*] is this. . . . You pass laws and decrees making all people equal. Naturally, in doing so, you kill all individual initiative and turn us all into a mass of maggots. I don't want to be a maggot," Patterson asserted, "and I don't believe any other American, regardless of race, color, creed, education, or what, wants to be either."

As Sunflower County and the rest of Mississippi anxiously awaited the Supreme Court's decision, fears of the worst began to take hold. W. W. Chapman, the editor of Sunflower County's two newspapers, the *Indianola Enterprise* and the *Sunflower Tocsin* (the two would merge in 1955), wrote in a December 1953 column:

> We sincerely hope that all of this propaganda about the outlawing of all the SOUTH's segregation customs will not set the NEGROES back in their efforts toward betterment in their Educational Facilities. They must realize that any attempt to rush into the White Schools will not help them in their cause, that they must FIRST prove their worth, and SECOND, accept their place in Society and do their part toward the improvement of the communities in which they reside. Until this is done, they CANNOT expect too much aid. The NAACP is wrong when it seeks to FORCE the Colored people [to do] what they, themselves, know is the impossible. Let us all work together, using our heads and putting forth EVERY EFFORT to prevent any unhappiness and possibly some BLOODSHED.[43]

The stridency of Chapman's rhetoric indicates that if there had ever been a window of opportunity for Mississippi moderates, it was closing quickly.

Patterson and others in the massive resistance crowd might have feared the worst, but for the most part they remained silent while the Supreme Court considered the merits and implications of the NAACP's *Brown* case. When the Court issued its decision in May 1954 and announced that it would delay an implementation decree, Mississippi's moderates had one last chance to assert leadership and guide the state to grudging acceptance of the inevitable. But few moderates stepped forward. For that matter, however, few radical exponents of massive resistance stepped forward at first, either.

Mississippi congressman John Bell Williams quickly labeled the day of the Supreme Court's decision "Black Monday," a moniker that stuck, and Senator Eastland predicted, "The South will not abide by nor obey this legislative decision by a political court." Following that theme, Sunflower County's representative in the Mississippi House, Wilma Sledge, noted, "It seems that politicians can sit on a legal bench as well as in the halls of Congress or the White House, and that political expediency can govern the cloistered chambers as well as the cloak rooms."[44] The elected officials' defiance remained muted for the time being, however, in part because it did not represent the mood of a united white South. Many districts in the border states moved quietly and quickly toward full compliance. Senator Estes Kefauver of Tennessee urged, "While we may not agree with the decision, we must not let this disrupt our public school system." Frank Smith, Sunflower County's representative in the U.S. Congress, urged calm consideration of the issue. Significantly, there were no mass demonstrations protesting the decision in Mississippi. Neither did Mississippi blacks hail the decision publicly.[45]

To be sure, the verdict was an extremely unpopular one among whites in the state, particularly in the majority-black Delta. But few citizens and public figures rallied openly around the incendiary words of political leaders like Williams and Eastland in the first two months following "Black Monday." The abstract ruling of the nation's highest court had no immediately tangible impacts in Sunflower County. Surprisingly, the decision went all but unnoticed in the county's newspapers. Local whites had prepared themselves for the worst, and they got it. The overthrow of segregation may have seemed total, though even the most pessimistic whites had to notice that the Supreme Court had said nothing about implementing its decision. The people of Sunflower County, the state of Mississippi, and the rest of the South had no choice but to wait for the Court's implementation ruling.

The implementation ruling's delay gave moderates one last opportunity to move public opinion and pave the way for acceptance of integration. But, according to young Greenville journalist Hodding Carter III, "Suddenly, when a need arose for some kind of middle-ground action, there was none. 'Acceptance' and 'calm'; these were the words heard most often from this group, but action was rapidly becoming the order of the day." If Sunflower County's newspapers are any guide, even this gradualist message did not find an audience. No one spoke out publicly in favor of desegregation. "There had been no planning by the middle of the roaders," Carter wrote, "but the activists on both right and left either already had, or soon did have, their plan of action." That plan of action would emerge from the heart of the Mississippi Delta.[46]

The Triumph of Prosegregationist Thought

Mississippi circuit judge Thomas Pickins Brady of Brookhaven, in the southern part of the state, outlined the segregationist plan of action when he answered the Supreme Court. He titled his speech "Black Monday."

Brady, a Mississippi native and graduate of Lawrenceville and Yale, first delivered the talk to a meeting of the Sons of the American Revolution in Greenwood, where Robert Patterson was in the audience. Patterson had Brady give the speech again in Indianola, transcribed it, and asked Brady to expand on it for publication. He did, and the resulting ninety-page book included the judge's outline for a massive resistance movement and a critique of the legal logic behind *Brown* that was laced with questionable "scientific" racial theory. (According to Brady, he also received encouragement from Eastland, Strom Thurmond, and Herman Talmadge—powerful men in the U.S. Senate, in the "Dixiecrat" movement, and in *Brown* resistance—to publish "Black Monday" in book form.)[47] When Patterson released the book in 1955, it became at once the bible of the crusaders for massive resistance to desegregation.

Black Monday: Segregation or Amalgamation, America Has Its Choice contended that *Brown* was an unprecedented seizure of the states' rights to control their educational systems and that this "usurpation constitute[d] the greatest travesty of the American Constitution and jurisprudence in the history of this nation."[48] The dubious science that undergirded Brady's arguments "proving" the superiority of "Homo Caucasius" over "Homo Africanus" is fodder for another study; the best that can be said of the quality of *Black Monday*'s scientific ideas is that they were unoriginal. The treatise's simplistic racism is helpful, however, in illustrating an especially stark and white-supremacist wing of Mississippi paternalism. "The date that the Dutch ship landed on the sandy beach of Jamestown," Brady wrote in a characteristic passage, "was the greatest day in the history of the American negro." American slavery, Brady averred, brought that race into contact with another race of men whose innate genius for self-government has been unparalleled in human history; white Americans rescued Africans from an existence "only one-half step from the primordial brute. . . . These are the melancholy facts," Brady wrote, "and they cannot be disputed."[49]

Predictably (the book was, after all, written for the consumption of white supremacists), Brady provided his readers with a comparison between African Americans and chimpanzees in which neither party fared favorably and an obligatory paean to southern white womanhood. Brady even proposed that the United States buy a forty-ninth state, in Baja California, Alaska, Hawaii, or the Philippines, for the sole purpose of repatriating black southerners. Mississippi whites would return to this idea again and again, going so far as to sponsor a program encouraging black migration from the state, in the coming years.[50]

*"Southern people know that if the Supreme Court attempts to impose [desegregation]
upon them by force, stern resistance and lawlessness will inevitably result,
regardless of whether the requirement is invoked forthwith or gradually."
U.S. senator James O. Eastland. (Mississippi Department of Archives and History)*

Tom Brady and Jim Eastland were two of the best-educated men in a
poorly educated state; both were highly respected leaders of the white
community they served. Brady's book and Eastland's contemporary
speeches are valuable if they are read as the crystallization of segregationist reaction to the legal principles behind *Brown*.

Segregationists complained to the last breath that the Supreme Court had no right to coerce white southerners into sending their children to school with black children, and here Brady and Eastland joined them. But the two also put into words the segregationists' deep discomfort with the Supreme Court's jurisprudence. Brady's pseudoscientific analysis dovetailed with Eastland's criticism of the revolutionary "psychological, sociological, and anthropological" evidence that had swayed the Supreme Court in *Brown*. Could the highest court in the land really base an opinion on sociological evidence? If the Court could do that, Eastland asked ominously on the floor of the U.S. Senate, "What is to prevent the Court from citing as an authority in some future decision the works of Karl Marx?" (Eastland would later charge that Gunnar Myrdal and several of his associates, upon whose sociological research Thurgood Marshall based much of the NAACP's case, were "members of Communist and subversive organizations.") Could the Supreme Court's decision have been anything but the result of a Communist conspiracy? Eastland charged that the justices of the Court had been "indoctrinated and brainwashed."[51]

Their words were those of middle-aged white men who were used to being in charge but saw events spinning quickly out of their control—and here Brady and Eastland had much company. They sputtered at the notion that separate-but-equal, as upheld in the Supreme Court's 1896 *Plessy v. Ferguson* decision, could have been appropriate for the world in which their fathers and grandfathers had thrived but was inappropriate for their own. The justices of the Supreme Court had already ruled that separate-but-equal did not violate the Fourteenth Amendment, and, according to Eastland, "the meaning . . . of an amendment is fixed when it is adopted. It cannot conceivably have one meaning at one time, and another meaning in later years." This fear and disbelief lay at the core of white resistance to *Brown*. The Supreme Court justices who ruled that segregation was constitutional in 1896 and their successors down to the present had been perfectly good jurists, Eastland said. "They were not fawning politicians," he remembered fondly. "They were not the servants of and spokesmen for belligerent minorities." Those judicial giants considered the welfare of the country as a whole, not the squawkings of a minority pressure group. In contrast, the present justices had "substituted the shifting sands of sophistry for the solid rock of judicial integrity on which our institutions have heretofore been based."[52]

Eastland and Brady saw only one possible solution, and it did not involve accommodation. In a rambling speech to the Senate, Eastland rewrote southern history and compared the federal government to the British empire and himself to Gandhi. Eastland predicted, "Southern people know that if the Supreme Court attempts to impose [desegregation] upon them by force, stern resistance and lawlessness will inevitably result, regardless of whether the requirement is invoked forthwith or gradually. . . . We in the South have seen the tides rise before," Eastland explained. "[W]hen we refuse to be engulfed, they recede. The present campaign against segregation is based upon illegality. The South will therefore prevail."[53] Brady maintained, "To blindly submit to an erroneous decision which breaks all established rules of law is not loyalty or patriotism. It is simple folly or ignorance."[54]

Brady and Eastland needed the votes of white Mississippians to keep their jobs, and their remarks played well with constituents who expected such rhetorical flourishes. But the implications of their words were subversive. A judge and one of the highest elected officials in the state advocated outright lawlessness, and Mississippi "moderates" held their tongues. Brady and Eastland now represented the views of their white constituents faithfully, in some cases counseling caution when white Mississippians wanted blood, in other cases goading their constituents into more virulent defenses of segregation than they might otherwise have taken. Eastland, who had sworn to uphold the U.S. Constitution, broke his oath brazenly and proudly and encouraged his constituents to defy a lawfully rendered Supreme Court decision.

Black Monday inspired a massive resistance movement among middle- and upper-class Delta whites. It taught African Americans in the Delta that if there had been any reason to rely on their more powerful, better-educated white neighbors for assistance in the past, it was unwise to expect their help in the future. For the NAACP chapter emerging in Indianola, it meant that the white moderates who had allowed them to register to vote would no longer look favorably upon black efforts to claim the rights of American citizenship. Senator Eastland's appeal for massive resistance to the *Brown* decision and Judge Brady's crystallization of segregationist ideology served as a call to arms for whites in Sunflower County.

Within months after *Brown*, segregationist leaders Patterson, Eastland, and Brady had made it impossible for a centrist, moderate movement to express itself in Mississippi. Their actions ensured that Jim Crow would not be dissolved quietly in the Mississippi Delta and that African Americans would not be able to challenge it directly without reprisal. If blacks could organize to fight Jim Crow, whites could organize to save it.

> This meeting should have been held 30 years ago . . . when it was very noticeable that the Negro was organizing. Then there was a light in every Negro church, every night, regardless of the time you passed. . . . The Negro continued to meet and organize and through their concerted efforts, with the help of what I believe to be subversive groups and others, have made them a force to be reckoned with.
>
> *Herman Moore at the first meeting of the Indianola Citizens' Council, 1954*

CHAPTER THREE

Organized Aggression Must Be Met by Organized Resistance, 1954–1960

While the U.S. Supreme Court considered arguments in the *Brown* case, Robert Patterson railed against the two-headed monster of miscegenation and Communism. He portrayed himself as a modern-day Paul Revere in a desperate race to warn his neighbors of the dangers that approached. But Patterson found his community uninterested in his alarms even up to and after the Supreme Court's May 17, 1954, decision. Not until July—a full six months after he had begun predicting the coming apocalypse of integration imposed from above and two months after the *Brown* verdict was announced—could Patterson organize a meeting of fourteen Sunflower County white men who were willing to fight to preserve segregation.

They met at the home of D. H. Hawkins, the manager of a local cotton compress. Patterson's cabal was the perfect cross section of a small-town power base in the rural Jim Crow–era South, composed of the most respected and publicly active middle- and upper-class men of Indianola. The town mayor, the county sheriff, a farmer with large landholdings, a smaller farmer, the town banker, a farm manager, a dentist, a Harvard-educated lawyer, a gin operator, a farm implement dealer, two auto dealers, a druggist, and a hardware merchant pledged at the meeting to preserve segregation and called for a public meeting at the Indianola town hall one week later.

An estimated 70 to 100 white men assembled for the second gathering, where they voted to form an organization they called the Indianola Citizens' Council. Herman Moore, president of the Indianola Bank, opened the convocation: "This meeting should have been held 30 years ago . . . when it was very noticeable that the Negro was organizing." Moore warned that the new wave of black activism could only be the result of Communist subversion. African Americans *had* been organizing for social change in various ways and to various degrees throughout their history in the Delta. Civil rights organizing in the 1950s and 1960s built on a long tradition of resistance to white power. Now whites were organizing to address that resistance.[1]

There were men like Robert Patterson all over the South, and the Citizens' Council movement could have begun anywhere in the region, or at least anywhere in the Black Belt. It began in Indianola because the NAACP had held a statewide conference there the year before. Moore's argument, that African American organizing had made white organizing necessary, was one to which the council movement would return again and again over the next several years. Arthur Clark Jr., a Harvard-educated attorney, followed Moore on the program and told the crowd that Walter White (then executive secretary of the NAACP) favored mixed marriages, hitting on another emotional theme that would persist in the rhetoric of the Citizens' Councils.

Cutting to the heart of the matter, Clark told the audience that the motivating belief behind Indianola's nascent organization was "that the solution to this problem [of enforced desegregation] may become easier if various agitators and the like could be removed from the communities in which they operate. We propose to accomplish this result through the careful application of economic pressure upon those men who cannot be controlled otherwise."[2] At the risk of overstating the obvious, the Citizens' Council advocated removing those "who cannot be controlled"—in other words, those who tried to exercise their rights as American citizens—from their communities through the use of "economic pressure," which was another way of proposing what critics called white-collar terrorism.

Clark explained to the crowd that the proposed council would operate not by way of frequent mass meetings but through four committees whose outlines had been sketched by the original group at Hawkins's house. A political and election committee was "to screen all candidates for public office and eliminate anyone who favors integration or a breakdown of segregation of the races" and "those who might be seeking the Negro vote." A membership and finance committee took responsibility for screening members, raising funds, and mobilizing public opinion. An information and education committee would "secure information on the activities of the NAACP and other like organizations . . . and to anticipate other concerted action which is contrary to the actions of this group." Finally, a legal and advisory committee would take care of the "various legal questions which may arise."[3]

Nonconformity was uncomfortable most everywhere in America in the 1950s. The Citizens' Council aimed to make nonconformity to its position on the race issue painful to the extreme. The form of organization the council chose was a distillation of how Delta society worked: members of the white minority made decisions for the majority, and anyone who dared to question their authority would be crushed. The meeting's participants elected Herman Moore president of the Indianola Citizens' Council; Arthur Clark vice president; Patterson executive secretary; and Dave Hawkins, the cotton compress manager, treasurer. Judge Thomas P. Brady helped the new group write its charter and bylaws.[4]

The newly rechartered branch of the NAACP and the newly formed Citizens' Council now circled each other warily. This phase of NAACP organizing met with Citizens' Council pressure at every turn, and vice versa. When the one perceived the other gaining strength, it made new pitches to prospective members. When the local branch of the NAACP registered a large number of voters, the Citizens' Council struck back by firing the black employees of council members. The council threatened to purchase the mortgages and loans that had been made to known NAACP members and make them payable immediately. When the council put the economic squeeze on local NAACP activists, however, the national organization of the NAACP, with help from T. R. M. Howard's Regional Council of Negro Leadership (RCNL), instituted a special loan program for council victims at a black-owned Memphis bank.[5]

As Indianolan Robert Love remembered it, the Citizens' Council was formed in Indianola explicitly to counteract the formation of the local NAACP branch, and the first thing council members did was fire domestic help whom they suspected of joining the NAACP. Suspicious black Indi- anolans began warning Love not to be seen at Battle's house lest he lose his own job. Love and other NAACP members also began to notice that known council members had begun writing down license plate numbers wherever more than a few blacks congregated. "Of course, they also had some blacks who were telling them everything," Love added. "You know, there's always somebody [in the black community] who's got to get in with the people who've got the upper hand."[6]

If the window of opportunity for Sunflower County moderates had ever really opened, the formation of the Citizens' Council slammed it shut. The large number of white men who attended the original council mass meet- ing made it appear that a united community had already decided to fight desegregation tooth and nail. But there is no reason to assume that an equal or greater number of whites would not have attended a meeting to discuss less radical strategies for dealing with the *Brown* decision, in the manner of a Parent-Teacher Association meeting. Whether or not such a discussion may have been possible at that particular time, such a commu- nity conversation became unimaginable after the Citizens' Council began imposing its orthodoxy. With the emergence of organized opposition to desegregation, the possibility of gradual acceptance of the Supreme Court's decision became all but impossible. Eliminating the middle ground between acceptance of integration and massive resistance became the council's primary objective, and in that the council succeeded from the outset.

State Representative Wilma Sledge provided an unwitting example of how the middle ground became impossible to defend against the councils' attacks. Sledge's grudging acceptance of desegregation had lit a fire under Patterson in the first place in November 1953. Her speech to Indianola parents had warned them that school integration was inevitable, so they had better begin to think of ways to live with it. Sledge sniffed the political winds blowing around Indianola in the form of Patterson's written re- sponse to her November speech, however, and in January 1954 she again predicted that the Supreme Court would strike down segregation when it ruled on *Brown*. She did this, though, in a message to her constituents encouraging them to pay no mind to Governor White's school equalization program—which was especially unpopular among white taxpayers in the black-majority Delta. The coming Supreme Court ruling, she assured them, would make the program moot. When the Supreme Court announced its decision in May, Sledge criticized the justices for sacrificing the Constitution on the grounds of "political expediency."

Sledge completed her slide from moderation to militancy on September 13, when she presided over what amounted to a coming-out party for the Citizens' Councils on the floor of the Mississippi House of Representatives. Sledge introduced the council movement as "a widespread group of local organizations composed of reliable white male citizens who believe that segregation is not discrimination and are organized solely for the purpose of maintaining segregation of the races." The councils had recently come under the scrutiny of Hodding Carter II, the editor of Greenville's *Delta Democrat-Times*. After reading one of Robert Patterson's recruitment letters, Carter dared members of the councils "to come out into the open." Carter had heard that the councils were made up of responsible men, "the most respectable citizens in each community." If what he had heard was true, Carter charged, "then the only unresponsible aspect of the organizations is their secrecy."[7]

Representative Sledge answered that the Citizens' Council was anything but irresponsible. Organization activities had been kept secret thus far for tactical reasons, but "[c]ouncil leadership is composed of the most prominent, well-educated and conservative business men in each community." Sledge assured her fellow legislators, "These leaders are reliable men who have been selected because of their stability and good judgment." The councils, Sledge promised, would "maintain segregation through unity of purpose, consolidation of public opinion, and utilization of all legal means available. They do not and will not advocate violence in any form." Sledge's precarious position as a woman in a men's legislature made it all the more imperative that she fully support the council movement.[8]

Despite protests from Sledge and others, the councils' image was entrenched in the public mind outside the Delta as a "manicured" Ku Klux Klan, as the editor of the *Montgomery (Ala.) Advertiser* called it, or an "uptown Ku Klux Klan," as Carter would later charge. The councils' tactics, the two editors contended, amounted to "Economic Lynch Law" and "the Klan in spirit if not the Klan in fact." Nevertheless, Patterson maintained that the Citizens' Council phenomenon was no more than "the modern version of the old-time town meeting called to meet any crisis by expressing the will of the people."[9]

The councils spread rapidly throughout Mississippi and the Deep South. By November 1954, Citizens' Councils had been organized in 110 Mississippi towns, and by 1956, the councils claimed 80,000 members in Mississippi alone, with chapters in nine other southern states and more than a quarter of a million dues-paying members. (The councils tapped into the remnants of the Dixiecrat machine; this, in part, accounted for the groups' rapid multiplication.)[10] Patterson, Brady, and other leaders refined the councils' ideological thrust in what amounted to refighting the Civil War and Reconstruction. "The white people of the South will again stand fast and preserve an unsullied race as our forefathers did eighty years ago," Patterson predicted in 1954. "Eighty years ago our unconquerable forefathers were beaten, in poverty and degradation, unable to vote and under the heel of negro occupation troops. . . . Are we less than they?" Perhaps the council movement was possible in the first place because white men like Robert Patterson really believed that their Confederate forefathers had been "unconquerable."[11]

Judge Brady pointed out that only one southern state, Tennessee, had voted before 1868 to ratify the Fourteenth Amendment guaranteeing African Americans equal rights as American citizens and argued that only "Carpetbaggers . . . Scalawags . . . Northern troops . . . [and] negroes" were responsible for its ratification thereafter. It was illegally ratified, the jurist told an audience of Indianola council members in an interesting bit of historical revision, "and therefore, the Fourteenth Amendment has never had any moral effect in the South because our fathers knew it was illegal, and their fathers knew it. We know it."[12] Brady and Patterson connected their cause with the glorious Lost Cause of their grandfathers. It is worth noting that Brady was a state judge responsible for abiding by the Constitution of the United States, including all of its amendments and not just the ones he happened to like best.

To their appeal to the Lost Cause, the councils added a dash of anti-Soviet rhetoric. Patterson was especially incensed that northern politicians had used the context of the Cold War—*his* Cold War—to criticize Jim Crow. U.S. senator Hubert Humphrey, for example, had attacked segregation on the grounds that it hindered the United States' mission to align third-world nations with the free world rather than with the Soviet bloc. In a letter to the editor of *Time* magazine, Patterson claimed that "to impress the Asiatics [*sic*], nine misguided political appointees have decided to change the way of life of 50 million Americans in 21 states of our great nation."[13] This was misuse of Patterson's Cold War of the worst sort: trampling the rights of white southerners under the pretense of extending the benefits of free-market capitalism and democracy to people who were not even white.

Patterson remained the spokesman for the new organization. He and other council leaders were careful from the movement's outset to disassociate the Citizens' Council from groups with severe public relations problems like the Ku Klux Klan. "We don't consider ourselves hate-mongers and bigots," he later told one reporter. "We just felt like integration would utterly destroy everything that we valued." The Klan played the important role of foil for the councils. No matter how mean-spirited and racist the organization's rhetoric became, council spokesmen could point to their middle- to upper-class membership and say, "After all, we're not the Klan." Judge Brady told an Indianola audience in 1954, "None of you men look like Ku Kluxers to me. I wouldn't join a Ku Klux [Klan] . . . because they hid[e] their faces; because they [do] things you and I wouldn't approve of." Brady hedged his bets, though, and concluded, "I'm not going to find fault with anyone who did [join the Klan]. Every man looks at the same proposition not in the same way."[14] Nevertheless, fairly or not, the Citizens' Councils did come to be known as "the white-collar Klan" in the national press and in moderate southern circles. Council rhetoric constantly distanced the movement from the Klan, but Klan literature utilized a logic undeniably similar to the official council line. Robert Patterson was tactful enough not to use racial epithets, but council ideology agreed in important respects with Klan pronouncements. Both organizations espoused the line that the federal government was transferring the reins of power in the state to an ignorant, inferior race, most likely as the result of a Communist conspiracy.[15]

The Klan and the councils were not indistinguishable from one another. Differences between the two certainly were discernible, in terms of tactics and (if conventional wisdom is any guide) in terms of membership.[16] It was necessary for the Citizens' Councils to keep the Klan at arm's length if council rhetoric was to be taken seriously in the rest of the country. However, if the Klan served as the councils' foil in public pronouncements, the Klan's members also stood in lockstep alongside the councils' in the phalanx that constituted massive resistance to desegregation.

A solid South depended upon not just the physical terrorism of the Klan but also the more socially respectable economic reprisals orchestrated by the Citizens' Councils, the "legal" barriers that prevented acts of nonconformity by elected officials, and the more mundane "chilling winds of social ostracism visited upon dissenters by southern white society."[17] This is not to lump members of Citizens' Councils in with the membership of the Klan, nor to equate the firing of kitchen help with lynchings and crossburnings. But the programs of the Klan and the councils did, after all, share a lowest common denominator: a belief that blacks were not the social equal of whites—and were therefore incapable of coexistence with whites in civilized society—and a determination that no person nor institution would ever be given the chance to prove otherwise. Indeed, on at least one occasion, the richest and most respected whites in Sunflower County society found their way to the very head of a lynch mob. During some of the tensest moments in Sunflower County's troubled history of race relations, council members also participated in acts of physical intimidation that differed little from Klan raids. Moreover, as a radical Mississippi civil rights group would point out in response to a wave of bombings in 1967, there was plenty of blame to go around. "The blame must be evenly distributed to all Mississippians . . . who prefer to be acceptable and quiet, rather than to speak out and organize" in response to heinous acts of terrorism.[18]

Patterson and his compatriots pointed with pride to the fact that their area had never been a Klan stronghold. But in an atmosphere where the local chamber of commerce crowed, as Indianola's did in March 1957, "Your chamber of commerce carries on a vigilant, positive, and determined campaign in opposition to subversive activities of every type and character," might the Klan have been redundant? "There is no need for a Ku Klux in Mississippi," Patterson argued, and in several ways he was right. The poor whites who were likely to join Klan organizations did not have the power to fire domestic help or call in mortgages. If more advantaged whites, who did have this power, used it to check black activism, there was no need for physical intimidation.[19]

The council attack was three-pronged. Like nearly every other American activist political organization in the 1950s, its message was anti-Communist. It went to great lengths to connect the NAACP and Supreme Court with a red conspiracy to subvert the rights and liberties of white Americans. Influenced by the "findings" of the Army-McCarthy hearings, Patterson conflated desegregation of elementary schools with the Soviet nuclear threat: "We long ago let Russia steal all of our atomic threats and heaven knows what else. What should be my cue for excitement? When an atomic blast levels my home?"[20]

Such a blast, in Robert Patterson's world, could as easily be delivered by the mere seating of a ten-year-old black boy next to his daughter in the school cafeteria as by an intercontinental missile. "We cannot and must not accept this scourge as inevitable," Patterson concluded. "America must call all of their resources and stand together firm against communism and mongrelization." Communism and miscegenation skip hand-in-hand through Patterson's early writings, a dual danger that together posed one dire threat to constitutional government and what Patterson and others venerated as "the Southern way of life."[21]

Second, the councils' organizing strategy exploited the urge of the small-town businessman to *join*, to be a part of an organization. More specifically, it convinced many white southerners that by joining this particular organization, they could participate in the salvation of the "Anglo-Saxon race and culture" and "the Southern way of life," though these terms were invariably (and intentionally, one suspects) left undefined and ambiguous. Surely the Citizens' Councils perverted the ideals of American citizenship.

Finally, and most generally, the council movement in the Delta represented a circling of the wagons to protect the cherished system of Delta paternalism. Delta paternalists had boasted for decades, going back at least to the 1911 Percy-Vardaman Senate contest, that their self-described benevolent system was best at providing for the needs of the people of both races. Delta paternalists lived among their employees, and that geographical proximity, they argued, allowed them a unique understanding of exactly what black people wanted and needed. Classic Delta paternalists shied away from the councils (William A. Percy and his adopted nephew, the novelist Walker Percy, both denounced the councils, as did the Hodding Carters); one historian called the movement to maintain segregation "a Snopesian perversion of the aristocratic agrarian tradition."[22] But Patterson and other council leaders clearly acted within the larger culture of Delta paternalism. They maintained throughout that they knew what was best for whites and blacks alike and implied that only they possessed the God-given talents needed to act on that knowledge. Patterson enjoyed pointing out to reporters that he lived "crammed in the middle of thirty-five Nigra families," the only white man within a mile-and-a-half radius. Who could better determine—could know innately—what was best for both races? "If I had ill will toward the black people, I surely wouldn't have lived in Sunflower County, Mississippi, with a sixty-eight per cent black population," Patterson argued. "I'm completely integrated."[23]

The coverage of the Citizens' Council provided by Indianola's weekly newspaper created an impression that the council was relatively harmless and really not all that different from Indianola's several other all-white community and service organizations. Its distinguishing characteristic throughout its history—in Indianola, at least—was a form of Babbittry particular to the Cold War era. Members of the council in Indianola were compulsive joiners of clubs. Men who were identified as leaders in the Indianola council by the *Indianola Enterprise-Tocsin* were also leaders of the Rotary and Lions Clubs; elected officials of the Delta Council; chairmen of March of Dimes campaigns; chamber of commerce presidents; sponsors of the Boy Scouts and Little League; active in the local PTA; leaders in the VFW and American Legion; elected members of the city board of aldermen, county board of supervisors, and school board; precinct-level Democratic Party chairmen; and founders of the county's modern-day Republican Party apparatus. Council leadership included Indianola's mayor and school superintendent, the county's chancery clerk and circuit clerk, bank presidents, and some of the richest merchants and planters in the area—and this list includes only the men who held positions of elected leadership in the council or sat on its board of directors; one may well imagine how far the tentacles of the rank-and-file members of the council spread into the community.[24]

The Citizens' Council may have appeared harmless on its surface, particularly when its pronouncements on race and the Communist threat were read against what passed for "moderate," to say nothing of far-right, political thought throughout the United States in the 1950s. But white Indianolans in the 1990s all but refused to acknowledge that the Citizens' Councils existed. A member of the council who had sat on its board of directors for at least eight years and who had dealt with council members regularly as an elected official of the town's chamber of commerce stated flatly in a 1997 oral history interview that he knew nothing about the council or its program.[25] Whites in modern-day Sunflower County are not proud of the organizing program that they once touted as the only way to save civilization as white Americans knew it.

The Return to Equalization

The Supreme Court's May 1954 decision on public school segregation should have relegated Governor Hugh White's equalization plan to the dustbin. Even so, White met in early July with seven men whom he considered leaders among Mississippi blacks. Among the group were the presidents of Alcorn College and Mississippi Vocational College (men whose success depended in large part upon their abilities to stay on the good side of the white legislators who controlled the colleges' budgets) and Percy Greene, a Jackson newspaper editor who denounced the NAACP and other integrationists. Governor White presented another massive equalization program and asked the men for their ratification. The seven pledged their support of the plan and encouraged the governor to present it to an even wider group of African American leaders for their stamp of approval.[26]

Armed with this affirmation, White called an emergency biracial meeting in late July. White convened the public meeting ostensibly to discuss the implications of the Court's ruling with black leaders from throughout the state, but in reality the governor simply sought the endorsement of a proposed "segregation by choice" plan for propaganda purposes. The original audience of seven had been so sure that the vast majority of black leaders would approve of the plan that they persuaded White to invite members of the state's NAACP leadership to the meeting. The governor's generous equalization program would have begun to wipe out an estimated $115 million statewide disparity between white and black school facilities and would have increased the salaries of the state's African American public school teachers substantially. On the surface, it seemed to hold attractions for Mississippi's black leadership class, which was top-heavy with schoolteachers. The governor was certain that the leaders would agree to the program.[27]

He vastly miscalculated. At the Indianola meeting of Mississippi NAACP branches, Amos O. Holmes, the state NAACP president, scored J. D. Boyd and H. H. Humes, two of the seven African American "leaders" who had supported White's equalization program. Holmes asserted that Boyd, Humes, and the other supposed leaders had shown "by their backstage doubletalk . . . that they neither have the best interest of their people at heart nor can they be trusted to represent even the people who are members of their respective organizations." Boyd was at the time the president of the Mississippi Negro Teachers' Association and Humes the president of the Mississippi Missionary Baptist Convention. "We will not accept the Negro 'Uncle Tom,' recognized by white or Negro reactionaries to lead our folk," Holmes promised.[28]

Holmes and the larger group of black leaders made good on that boast, and a new class of African American leaders emerged in the state with the *Brown* decision. Prior to their gathering with White, the ninety African American leaders who had been invited to discuss equalization huddled together at what became known as "the meeting the night before." After much heated debate, they agreed to present a united front in opposition to White's equalization program. The next day, they made a mockery of White's carefully orchestrated public meeting, which the governor was forced to adjourn abruptly. White, visibly shaken, announced that only one black leader of the ninety had approved the plan. "I am stunned," he admitted.[29] *Brown* had given the African American leaders the impetus they needed to step out and challenge segregation, but this was still a remarkable step to take. They had no political cover in opposing the governor.

T. R. M. Howard of the all-black town of Mound Bayou, in neighboring Bolivar County, emerged as the group's spokesman. Howard was the founder of the Mississippi Regional Council of Negro Leadership, an organization that was closely associated with members of the state branch of the NAACP, although regional and national NAACP leaders considered the RCNL a competitor and Howard a clownish dictator. Howard had the audacity to tell the governor at the conference that as far as segregated education was concerned, "You know, as well as we know[,] that we have had the Separate all right but in very few cases have we had the Equal." Howard lectured the governor, "We have gone to the ends of the earth to fight, bleed and die for Democracy that even today we don't know anything about in Mississippi. We have never failed to let you down. Through 250 years of slavery and 91 years of physical freedom, you have taught us that the Constitution of the United States of America was the greatest document on Earth. . . . [S]o today, when the eyes of the Democratic forces of the world are focused upon America, let us not reduce the Constitution to a mere scrap of paper by asking Negroes to help you evade the law of the land."[30]

Following the meeting, Howard announced that rather than support the governor's plans for massive spending on segregated schools, the black leaders would favor "strict observance of the Supreme Court's integration order" and the appointment of blacks to policy-making boards at state and local levels. NAACP members at the meeting backed the flamboyant Howard's call for "consolidation and integration of the present schools on all levels." The betrayed Governor White confided, "I have believed that a certain element representing a vast majority of the Negroes would go along. Now I am definitely of the conclusion that you can't put any faith in any one of them on this proposition."[31]

The catastrophe provided a revealing moment for White and other Mississippi segregationists. Historian Eugene Genovese has depicted the wrenching "moment of truth" during the Civil War in which slaveowners throughout the South discovered that they had not really understood the workings of their slaves' hearts and minds after all. Not only were the slaves not grateful for all their owners had given them over the years, but the slaves were willing to abandon their plantations for freedom, in some cases by taking up arms against their former owners and their homeland.[32] July 31, 1954, the date of White's meeting with the ninety black leaders, should have been such a moment of truth for Mississippi's Jim Crow leaders. They had believed that separate accommodations were conducive to mutual progress and had fooled themselves into thinking that African Americans agreed with them. Governor White's comments following the meeting revealed a great deal about how Mississippi whites perceived their black neighbors' reactions to the *Brown* verdict. White had found out the hard way that, in his words, "you can't put any faith in any one of them." What White should have learned was not to put any faith in what he thought African Americans believed about segregation.

The men who disabused White of the notion that black Mississippians were happy in inferior, segregated schools exposed one of the central myths of Mississippi paternalism. White Mississippians believed that they knew what was best for African Americans. They hoodwinked themselves into believing that blacks agreed with them and appreciated white efforts to protect them from having to make difficult decisions. From time to time, individual blacks emerged from the Delta's tyrannical social system to disprove what whites accepted as the gospel truth. They did so when slaves escaped from their plantations to aid Grant's army during the Vicksburg campaign. They did so when freedmen voted African Americans into political office during Reconstruction. Most spectacularly, the state's black leaders did so when they rejected Governor White's voluntary segregation plan. (In every previous instance, whites had been able to dismiss those blacks as "bad niggers," but the governor had already decided that this group of African Americans was a responsible one. It would be considerably more difficult to reject or ignore their opinions.)

We should not assume that at other times black Mississippians were somehow content with the Jim Crow social order simply because they were not risking their lives to oppose it. In between these moments of truth lay periods in which African Americans coalesced and organized, biding their time until they could safely risk speaking truth to power. When black Mississippians perceived the power of the federal government behind them, they acted forcefully to obtain their rights. When they perceived indifference on the part of the national government, they chose caution over suicide.

Forceful action in every case inspired equally forceful action on the part of white segregationists, however. Later on the same day of White's summit meeting, the governor's Legal Education Advisory Commission voted unanimously to ask White to call a special session of the legislature. The session's sole purpose would be consideration of a constitutional amendment empowering the state assembly to abolish Mississippi's public school system should the federal government decide to enforce desegregation.[33]

In September, the state legislature affirmed the constitutional amendment allowing the legislative body to abolish the public school system and sent the measure to a statewide public vote. Governor White, who before the *Brown* decision had shown as little interest in racial issues as possible, concentrating instead on bringing industries to the state, now became the amendment's most ardent defender. He claimed that Mississippi was not trying to defy the Court's verdict but was "simply exercising the same legal right to resist this most unfortunate decision that the NAACP exercised in contesting the unanimous court decisions of over half a century." Appropriating the rhetoric of Mississippi's growing crowd of rabid segregationists, the governor promised, "We will meet this threat without faltering; by our joint efforts we shall unitedly find the solution. We shall not fail our heritage."[34] White's distasteful experience with the ninety African American leaders pushed him into a more radical defense of separate-but-equal than he might otherwise have taken. The governor also felt increasing pressure from a growing crowd of Mississippi whites who vowed to defend Jim Crow with all the means at their disposal.

The Councils Strengthen

During the year between the U.S. Supreme Court's original decision in *Brown* and its 1955 implementation ruling, the Citizens' Councils organized steadily throughout Mississippi and the Deep South, but the movement met with no spectacular success. "You've got to have opposition," Robert Patterson was fond of saying, "to have a ball game." The councils needed NAACP activity to scare whites into organizing actively. To raise needed funds, Patterson asked for and received the copyright to Judge Brady's *Black Monday*, which he then printed and sold under the auspices of the Citizens' Councils of Mississippi. Patterson organized steadily in Mississippi communities and throughout the Deep South, hammering away with neat truisms that certainly caught the imagination of small-town white businessmen: "Maybe your community has no racial problems! This may be true; however, you may not have a fire, yet you maintain a fire department," one read. Patterson assured his readers, "You can depend on one thing. The NAACP (National Association for the Agitation of Colored People), aided by alien influences, bloc vote seeking politicians and left-wing do-gooders, will see that you have a problem in the near future."[35] By the time the U.S. Supreme Court returned to the issue of school desegregation in May 1955, Patterson's organization claimed 60,000 members in Mississippi alone.

Brown II, as the Court's desegregation implementation order came to be known, was a major victory for the forces of massive resistance. Supreme Court chief justice Earl Warren had insisted that the original verdict upending Jim Crow had to be unanimous. *Brown II* proved that gradualism was the high price of unanimity. Rejecting Thurgood Marshall's arguments in favor of immediate and total desegregation of public schools throughout the South and border states, the Supreme Court ruled that desegregation plans should be left to local and state school authorities. The ruling delegated the responsibility of determining the pace of integration to federal judges, which ensured that desegregation would proceed only in a slow and piecemeal fashion. All but admitting that the federal government could not compel the South to act on the Supreme Court's reading of the Constitution, Chief Justice Warren's ruling commanded only that desegregation proceed with "all deliberate speed."

Following the original *Brown* decision, the councils had pushed for and won a fight to amend the Mississippi Constitution. After the Supreme Court had struck down the legality of Jim Crow and after the councils had lobbied intensively for voting restrictions, voters had approved an amendment to raise voter qualifications by a wide margin in 1954. (A similar effort had failed in 1952.) On the heels of the "all deliberate speed" ruling, the councils pushed for and passed an amendment allowing the state legislature to abolish public schools in 1956. In Sunflower County, the heart of that movement, the electorate voted 2,465 to 78 in favor of the amendment to abolish the public schools.[36] The amendment fights established the Citizens' Councils in Mississippi as the state's most efficient political mobilization agent and a powerful force whose pronouncements had to be taken seriously.[37]

The council movement had a colorful—and powerful—champion in Indianola. W. W. Chapman, the longtime editor and publisher of the weekly *Indianola Enterprise-Tocsin*, identified himself as a member of the board of directors of the Indianola Citizens' Council, and he frequently ran stories about council membership drives on the front page of his newspaper. In a small town such as Indianola, the editorial position of the newspaper should not be underestimated as a measure of community thought. The local newspaper can be a source of pride and a source of cohesion, and in Indianola it has at times been both. But where the newspaper is the sole source of local news, its editor invariably holds a unique position of power to influence community mores and opinions. Chapman had a stage to present his views that no other person in the county enjoyed, even if his livelihood depended on keeping the opinions he expressed close to those of his neighbors.

Chapman's newspaper advocated a peculiar blend of New South economic modernism, political conservatism, prosegregation ideology, and Cold War paranoia. The editor deemed social security "Socialistic" as late as 1954, and his political idol was Mary Cain, a newspaper editor and perennial gubernatorial candidate from Summit, Mississippi, who refused to pay into the social security system. (According to journalist Curtis Wilkie, Cain "considered the program a dagger jabbed into American democracy by Communists." Many in Sunflower agreed with her.) Chapman also solicited members for the local Citizens' Council without apology and without any hint of partisanship or subjectivity.[38]

In a September 18, 1955, page-one editorial "To All White Men and Women in Indianola," Chapman urged organization in the face of the integration threat. Referring to Thurgood Marshall as "mulatto chief counsel for the NAACP," Chapman advised, "[T]here is nothing inevitable about the campaign of the NAACP . . . to accomplish the socialistic aims by desegregating us. . . . There is only one way to meet the attack of the NAACP. Organized aggression must be met by organized resistance." The Citizens' Council, he said, "ought to have 500 members, men and women, in Indianola. There is every reason to expect that it will, unless the people of Indianola have forgotten how to recognize the face of personal tyranny, and what is more vital, unless they have forgotten how to fight it." If his readers believed that segregation provided "respect and right conduct, [that it was] the only stable arrangement for mutual good will between the races," Chapman wrote, "then you owe it to yourself, to your friends and neighbors, and to your children and grandchildren, to . . . JOIN NOW."[39]

As it spread the party line of the Citizens' Council, the *Enterprise-Tocsin* enforced the community's racial orthodoxy. In an October 3, 1957, front-page editorial, Chapman warned, "If you are not now a member of the White Citizens Councils, then YOU are making a mistake if you want to preserve YOUR freedom. If you don't know where to send your application, just call [the newspaper office] and we shall be happy to tell you."[40] Chapman's newspaper actively campaigned to keep Sunflower County blacks segregated, undereducated, and ill-equipped for the modern, diversified economy his editorials advocated.

Black Organizing on the Heels of Brown

Capitalizing on the momentum his organizing generated in Indianola, Clinton Battle succeeded in organizing another local branch of the NAACP in Belzoni in January 1954. Approximately thirty miles to the south of Indianola down Highway 49, Belzoni was the seat of neighboring Humphreys County and the site of Battle's second medical clinic. Gus Courts, a local grocer who made money on the side by hauling field labor in a secondhand school bus to a Sunflower County plantation, was the first president of the Humphreys County NAACP branch, but the Belzoni Citizens' Council forced him to relinquish that position. In late summer, according to Courts, a Humphreys County planter named Percy Furee took him to the office of Paul "Junior" Townsend, a member of the Belzoni Citizens' Council (one of the first in the state to organize after Indianola) and an official in the Guaranty Bank and Trust Company. Townsend asked Courts for the list of members in the Humphreys County NAACP, and Courts refused to turn it over. Townsend threatened, "We will tie up your bus and tie up your store. We will run you out of town." Courts owed the bank for a small loan at the time, but after meeting with Townsend, he paid it off long before it came due. Nonetheless, he notified the national NAACP office of his forced removal late in 1954 and asked headquarters to send any future correspondence in a plain envelope.[41]

Reverend George Lee was Courts's best friend and one of the first African Americans to register to vote in Humphreys County. By 1955, he was a vice president in the RCNL. Members of the Belzoni Citizens' Council demanded that he tear up his poll tax receipts and remove his name from the registration rolls. C. L. Puckett, a Belzoni accountant and member of the council, bragged to a northern reporter that "level-headed businessmen" guarded the polls against African American voters on election day in Belzoni for "security purposes." The reporter later learned that one of the guardsmen had followed an African American voter home from the polls and knifed him. Numerous threats followed these incidents, and on May 7, 1955, a car pulled alongside Lee's on a Belzoni road and an unidentified party fired a shot that tore the lower half of Lee's face from his body, killing him.[42]

There were only two known witnesses to the Lee shooting. One, an NAACP investigator learned, "moved suddenly from her home during the night following the murder and has not been heard from since." The other turned up a month later in East St. Louis, Illinois, reluctant to tell his story even that far from the reach of Mississippi terrorists. Without eyewitnesses to the crime, Humphreys County sheriff Ike Shelton was bold enough to suggest that Lee had simply been in a car accident and that the metal fragments embedded in his jaw were tooth fillings. Battle and A. H. McCoy, a Jackson dentist and president of the Mississippi State Conference of NAACP Branches, performed an autopsy on Lee at the Delta's only hospital for African Americans in Mound Bayou. McCoy's gruesome, detailed postmortem compared Lee's lower face to something that had "gone through a hamburger grinder" and concluded, "It was clearly evident to me that Reverend Lee's death was caused by blasts from a shotgun. Lead is not used for filling teeth." Lead had also been found in Lee's blown-out tire.[43]

Battle returned to Indianola and told his friend Robert Love, "We got 'em now! Bullets and everything! We're gonna turn it over to the FBI." He forwarded the evidence to the FBI and expected a full investigation, trial, and conviction. Love was much less optimistic. He told Battle, "Those [agents] work with the FBI, but their sympathies are with the [white] southern people." True to form, the FBI spent parts of five weeks on a perfunctory investigation in Belzoni but did not pursue the case, and a Humphreys County coroner's jury—which the NAACP claimed was composed entirely of Citizens' Council members—refused to indict anyone for the murder.[44] Battle would later tell an audience at an NAACP fund-raiser, "I have talked to FBI agents on more than a half-dozen occasions and found them to be half-hearted and apathetic in their investigations of disfranchisement of Negroes," to say nothing of the murder of black activists. Battle himself had previously contacted the FBI with a complaint about the difficulties he had faced as a voter, but the agency sent a native white Mississippian to investigate. "These FBI men aren't going to make charges against their friends and neighbors," Battle huffed.[45] This lack of federal investigative support would severely hamper civil rights activists in the future.

NAACP executive secretary Roy Wilkins returned to the Delta to eulogize Lee, calling him "a man . . . a good citizen, a minister of the church, but one who believed not only in the life hereafter, but the life here." Reverend Lee was shot, Wilkins thundered, "because he thought he ought to vote just like other Americans." Wilkins denounced the Citizens' Councils and compared Mississippi blacks to the American colonists who had been taxed without governmental representation. He left it up to his fellow mourners to decide whether or not Mississippians should follow the violent example of their Revolutionary forefathers. Lee's murder focused attention on the Delta, on efforts of the local chapters of the NAACP to register voters and desegregate the public schools, and on the Citizens' Councils' stop-at-nothing determination to halt black political participation. Sadly, it was also the first in a long line of events that wore down the resolve of Clinton Battle and thousands of other African Americans to create a democracy in the Delta.[46]

Wilkins's presence at Lee's funeral generated national media attention, but it meant little for African Americans in the Delta. Local blacks—and whites—could not help but notice that the FBI had not taken seriously the threat to blacks who dared to speak up. This surely made it safer for whites to restrict blacks' civil rights in the most violent ways. Soon after Lee's murder, a member of the Belzoni Citizens' Council reportedly told Gus Courts, "They're planning to get rid of you. I don't know how and I don't want to know." Another white man told Courts that "the same thing [that happened to Lee] would happen to him." A Humphreys County planter convinced the Sunflower County plantation owner for whom Courts transported field labor not to hire anyone who rode Courts's bus. In November 1955, Courts's grocery wholesaler said that the Belzoni council would not allow him to sell merchandise to Courts, even for cash. (The council demanded that whites toe the line, too.) Finally, according to Courts, Hezekiah Fly, a former chairman of the Belzoni Citizens' Council, began following Courts around town, tracking his every move. Soon after the November election—in which 8 or 10 blacks voted, down from a high of 400 the previous year—an unidentified white man fired a gun through a window of Courts's store and ripped open the side of his body. (Courts and an African American customer saw an "unmistakably white" man jump into a car and speed off but did not see his face. Courts was certain that Fly was somehow involved.) Sheriff Shelton was equally certain that "some damn nigger just drove there and shot him," and the Belzoni Citizens' Council and Rotary and Kiwanis Clubs were brazen enough to offer a reward for information leading to a conviction in the shooting.[47] Battle arranged for the NAACP to hustle his friend off to Chicago à la the Underground Railroad and set him up in the grocery business.

The shooting of Gus Courts came close on the heels of a court trial that exposed to the world the violent, desperate determination of Delta whites to maintain their eroding social system. In September, Roy Bryant and J. W. Milam went on trial in Sumner, Mississippi, for the murder of Emmett Till, a black fourteen-year-old from Chicago who had been visiting relatives in the small Leflore County town of Money. The Till tragedy is a famous one, and for good reason it has been told elsewhere.[48] "Bobo," as Till was known, stepped into a small grocery store in Money with friends and encountered Carolyn Bryant, a twenty-one-year-old who had won two beauty pageants while a student at Indianola High School. There are conflicting accounts of what happened in the grocery store, but Carolyn Bryant perceived that Bobo Till had somehow stepped over the line of the Delta's highly racialized, highly gendered, and highly charged system of etiquette.

When Bryant's husband, Roy, learned of the incident, he and his half-brother, J. W. "Big" Milam, set off for the house of Mose Wright, Bobo Till's great-uncle. Brandishing pistols (Milam had brought his .45 back from the war in Europe), they demanded the boy. The three headed west in Milam's Chevrolet pickup truck at roughly 11:00 P.M. on a Saturday night. Till's body was found days later floating in the Tallahatchie River.

When Tallahatchie County prosecutors brought Bryant and Milam to trial on a murder charge, it caused a sensation the likes of which the Mississippi Delta had never seen. Dozens of out-of-town reporters covered the trial; they marveled when the prosecution's star witness, Mose Wright (who was identified in court as "Mose" or "Uncle Mose" but never as "Mr. Wright"), was asked to identify the men who had abducted his nephew. "Thar he," Wright said, pointing to Milam, "and there's Mr. Bryant." These were quite possibly the two bravest sentences ever uttered in a Mississippi courtroom. Wright's declaration was followed by testimony from a nineteen-year-old Sunflower County sharecropper's son named Willie Reed. Early in the morning following Till's abduction, Reed had seen a group of men take a black youth from a Chevrolet pickup into a barn near the town of Drew, in the northern part of Sunflower County. He then heard someone being beaten inside the barn and cries of "Mama, Lord have mercy, Lord have mercy." Reed's aunt, Amanda Bradley, also heard the cries; after they stopped abruptly, she saw a white man with a holstered pistol exit the barn and get in his truck. Bradley and Reed recognized neither the man nor the boy until they saw a picture in the newspaper of Emmett Till. They then realized that they had witnessed Till's beating and possibly his murder. Reed and Bradley both identified the white man with the pistol as Milam.[49]

Reed and Bradley had sought out Clinton Battle, who told them that the NAACP would protect them if they were willing to tell the truth in court about what they had seen. Bryant and Milam admitted that they had kidnapped Till but claimed that they had released him, unharmed, at around 3:00 A.M. Reed's testimony disputed this claim; he stated that he had seen Till at the barn—which, it turned out, sat on a farm that was managed by Milam's brother—between 6:00 and 7:00 in the morning. Following Reed's testimony, Battle helped the young man, whose family feared for his life, move to Chicago. NAACP field secretary Ruby Hurley hoped that the eyewitness accounts would be grounds for a mistrial and a change of venue to Sunflower County. During the delay, she hoped, the NAACP would be able to build public pressure for a guilty verdict.[50]

Instead, an all-white Tallahatchie County jury acquitted Milam and Bryant. (The county's overall population was 63 percent black, but its voting population was nearly all white, hence the lily-white jury: another consequence of black disfranchisement.) Condemnations rained down on the Delta. William Faulkner observed glumly that if Americans had "reached that point in our desperate culture when we must murder children, no matter for what reason or what color, we don't deserve to survive, and probably won't." Roy Wilkins charged that "the State of Mississippi has decided to maintain white supremacy by murdering children." On another occasion, he embedded the Till murder squarely in the middle of the Citizens' Councils' movement to force blacks "to forfeit their right to vote . . . and to forego their demand for civil rights." Wilkins called the murder "the logical and inevitable culmination of a reign of terror" that had been generated in Mississippi since the *Brown* verdict. "[A]ny dullard," he charged in a scathing letter to Eisenhower's Justice Department, "could understand that the authorities and the responsible people of the state were prepared to do nothing if violence occurred. The green light was given to hoodlums to demean, to persecute and to kill Negroes, with or without provocation."[51]

Milam and Bryant were not, Robert Patterson was relieved to learn, dues-paying members of the Citizens' Council. He deemed their actions "very regrettable." Yet Wilkins's charges rang true; the councils' paranoid membership pitches and the racist demagoguery Mississippi politicians used to stir up interest and votes were cut from the same cloth as the brutal beating and murder of the fourteen-year-old boy. The defense based its case on a theory that the NAACP had staged the murder. The NAACP, Milam and Bryant's lawyers said, had really hustled Till off to Detroit, and the organization was using the case for publicity. The tactic smacked of Citizens' Council propaganda. To argue it, they challenged Mamie Till, Emmett's mother, when she testified that the mutilated body she had buried in Chicago was really that of her son.[52]

"Respectable" Delta whites did not initially rush to defend Milam and Bryant, but in the face of criticism from the NAACP and the northern press, whites soon closed ranks and fought for acquittal. Attorney John Whitten, chair of the Tallahatchie Democratic Party (and first cousin of U.S. congressman Jamie Whitten), was chief counsel for Milam and Bryant. In his summation, he asked the all-white jury for an acquittal and confided in the nine men his belief that "every last Anglo-Saxon one of you has the courage to do it."[53] Not all attempts to galvanize white opinion were as blatant as this. The council movement maintained more subtle forms of intimidation, but its results were no less effective than the methods used to silence Till.

Council Pressures in the Mid-1950s

Council pressures peaked for the first time in the Delta in 1955 and 1956. Theodore Keenan, the Sunflower County farmer and former president of the Indianola NAACP branch who resigned his position after a member of the Citizens' Council began reading his mail, applied for a Federal Housing Administration loan of $5,000 after his 1955 crop failed. Previously, Keenan had been able to secure loans of amounts as high as $7,400 from his local bank without collateral. This time his application was refused.

He learned that Walter Scruggs, the director of the Bank of Ruleville, was angry because Keenan and his wife had been the only voters in the Blaine precinct to vote against "Big Jim" Eastland in the 1954 Democratic Senate primary. Eastland was reported to be equally angry. Scruggs told Keenan that the "good white folk had been good to him and he had not shown proper respect by voting against Eastland and participating in [the] NAACP." If Keenan would stop associating with the NAACP, Scruggs said, he might think about approving the much-needed loan. J. H. White, the president of Mississippi Vocational College for Negroes in nearby Itta Bena, offered to intervene on Keenan's behalf if Keenan would help him "convert" Amzie Moore, a vocal leader in neighboring Bolivar County, away from civil rights activity. Keenan believed that White, the epitome of the black leaders whom NAACP officials denounced as "Uncle Toms," was on the Citizens' Council payroll. Keenan stopped voting, resigned his NAACP membership, and received the loan that kept him from going broke.[54]

According to African American lore, a Citizens' Council leader named John Hough, one of the richest plantation owners in the Indianola area and a landlord who owned several substandard houses on the black side of Indianola, began to harass Clinton Battle. He instructed the families who rented houses from him not to patronize Battle, and he ended Battle's relationship with his plantation workers. When other planters followed suit, Battle's practice began to suffer.[55]

In September 1956, the Indianola police arrested Battle on a driving-while-intoxicated charge on his way home from a football game in Itta Bena. Battle insisted that the arrest was a frame-up, and he attributed it to "a vicious smear campaign of the Citizens' Councils." Battle, who as a rural doctor could ill afford to lose his driving privileges, figured that the police were acting on a plan hatched by the council to rescind his driver's license. The doctor was so worried that the plan would work, and thereby deprive him of his dwindling livelihood, that he asked Gloster Current and Roy Wilkins of the national NAACP office to refrain from commenting publicly on his case.[56]

The state of Mississippi had paid for Battle's medical education at Fisk University in Nashville, Tennessee, under the condition that he practice in the state for at least five years. The very month that his term expired in 1957, Battle left the Delta for a surgical residency in Kansas City. The doctor's parting shot to Indianola was a charge that the Citizens' Council had killed the NAACP in Sunflower County and that most blacks there were too terrified even "to speak out against violations of their [own] rights." Battle spoke at an NAACP rally in St. Joseph, Missouri, and told the story of the terrorist acts inflicted upon NAACP members in the Delta and the economic pressure that had driven him from the area. The *Indianola Enterprise-Tocsin* reprinted an account of his speech. Editor Chapman opined, "[I]f this is the way we abuse negroes, by giving them a good FREE Education and an opportunity to amount to something on his own, then God Pity Us All. If we had our way, we would herd up all the Clint Battles and send them back to Africa as quickly as possible, along with quite a few White Agitators."[57]

Battle's departure all but doomed the NAACP and overt black organizing in Sunflower County. After Battle left, Indianola became much less of a concern for the NAACP. Field Secretary Medgar Evers, who had made frequent visits to Indianola and stayed overnight in the Battle household, found fewer and fewer reasons to check on Sunflower County. The NAACP revoked the Indianola branch's charter in January 1958 due to inactivity. There would be no more civil rights organizing in Sunflower for another four years. When civil rights activists returned, their tactics would differ markedly from those of the NAACP.

> Politics is about *our lives*.
> It is about whether the roads are any good.
> It is about what our kids learn in school.
> It is about what the sheriff does.
> It is about whether we have work to do.
> Politics is about *who* has *power*. . . .
> We do not have money.
> Our power must come from *ourselves*.
> From our numbers.
> From us being together.
> We must have power for *us*.
> *"The Sunflower County Political Handbook," 1964*

CHAPTER FOUR

Our Power Must Come from Ourselves

Civil Rights Organizing, 1960–1964

When four students from North Carolina A&T College sat down at the segregated lunch counter of a Woolworth's store in Greensboro, North Carolina, in February 1960 and refused to leave until they were served, they initiated a new phase of the American civil rights movement. The tactic of the "sit-in," as the lunch counter protest became known, was not new, but it captured the imagination of young African Americans across the country who wanted to protest Jim Crow more directly than their elders had. Sit-ins spread to other cities across the Upper South and border states, and even to the urban North, where sympathetic students picketed the chain stores that enforced segregated seating in the South. Established civil rights organizations struggled to corral the energy of the student-led sit-ins until April, when SNCC organized under the auspices of Martin Luther King's Southern Christian Leadership Conference (SCLC).

The SCLC's embattled executive director, Ella Baker, ensured that the student movement would maintain its independence and encouraged the students to chart their own path. Baker had seen personality conflicts, hair-splitting, and leadership dilemmas diminish morale among the rank-and-file members of the NAACP and SCLC, and she vowed to prevent those organizations' problems from infecting the new student movement. Her decisive action in steering the organization's independent philosophy, in the words of a SNCC historian, marked "an important step in the transformation of a limited student movement to desegregate lunch counters into a broad and sustained movement to achieve major social reforms."[1] SNCC chapters mushroomed in several cities across the South, most prevalently in Nashville, Tennessee, and Atlanta, Georgia, cities with large populations of African American college students. They learned from experienced nonviolent resisters and then taught one another the forms of nonviolent, direct resistance to segregation and challenged the older generation of black leadership. John Lewis, an early chairman of SNCC, maintained that almost from the organization's inception its goal was "revolt . . . against this nation's traditional black leadership structure as [much] as it was against racial segregation and discrimination."[2]

Later in 1960, the U.S. Supreme Court ordered the desegregation of bus terminals and train stations that served interstate travelers. African Americans waited into the next year to see if newly elected president John F. Kennedy would enforce the edict, but many suspected he would not. James Farmer, the new executive director of the Congress of Racial Equality (CORE), decided in 1961 that his group should create a crisis that would "make it more difficult politically for the federal government *not* to enforce federal law."[3] CORE decided to test the federal government's commitment to desegregation by sponsoring interracial bus rides through the South. Farmer's strategy, the "Freedom Ride," was a reincarnation of the "Journey of Reconciliation" that CORE had attempted following a similar Supreme Court ruling in 1947. (The Journey of Reconciliation had ended with several participants arrested and sentenced to a North Carolina chain gang.) CORE recruited thirteen volunteers, many of them college students from Nashville who had participated in the SNCC sit-ins in that city. On May 4, 1961, they set out from Washington, D.C., and headed through the Deep South toward New Orleans, intending to desegregate waiting rooms and lunch counters in the bus facilities along the way.

The "Freedom Riders," as the volunteers were known, had been taught the tactics of nonviolent resistance, and when they reached Alabama they were forced to put that education to the test. A mob firebombed the Greyhound bus carrying one of two groups of Freedom Riders just outside of Anniston on May 14. On the same day, a mob attacked the other at a Trailways station in Birmingham; the Freedom Riders gave up and boarded a plane to New Orleans. The Freedom Ride had succeeded in putting the Kennedy administration's collective feet to the fire, but the experiment seemed to be over; the majority of Freedom Riders judiciously decided that their point had been made and returned home.

However, an integrated group of ten sit-in veterans from the Nashville movement decided to finish the journey from Alabama to New Orleans. They traveled to Birmingham in hopes of boarding a bus and riding it through Alabama and Mississippi; there were additional beatings and equally serious constitutional conflicts between the state of Alabama and the federal government. It seemed that even if the Freedom Riders made it through Alabama, they would never make it through Mississippi, which was by now widely considered the most viciously racist state in the Union. Finally Attorney General Robert Kennedy made a deal with Senator James Eastland, who personally guaranteed the Freedom Riders safe passage through Mississippi, and the journey continued.

Eastland's influence over violent white segregationists and Mississippi law enforcement authorities proved real. National Guardsmen protected the Freedom Riders all the way to the state capital of Jackson. When the Freedom Riders arrived at the Jackson bus terminal on May 24, there were no lawless mobs, just an overwhelming police presence. The Freedom Riders were ushered through the facility and arrested without incident. The next day, the young men and women were charged with violating state laws against segregation and trespassing and were dragged into court. While their defense attorney pled the Freedom Riders' case, the presiding judge turned his back to the courtroom and faced a wall. When he turned around to face the protesters again, he sentenced the Freedom Riders to sixty-day sentences at Parchman Penitentiary. For the first time, the young people who catalyzed the most active phase of the modern civil rights movement entered Sunflower County—in shackles.

The Freedom Riders and the other direct action protest participants of the early 1960s sparked the collective imagination of the black Delta, but the new wave of direct action did not immediately crash into the deepest of the Deep South. The surge of sit-ins and Freedom Rides certainly did not translate into a groundswell of protest against segregation on the part of Sunflower County blacks. They still had the Citizens' Council to contend with, and they remembered all too well the negative lesson of Clint Battle and his cohorts with the local chapter of the NAACP.

In 1960, an estimated 22,000 African Americans were registered to vote in the state of Mississippi, 5.2 percent of the state's total black voting age population.[4] In Sunflower County, where the names of 107 African Americans made it onto the voter rolls out of a total black population of 31,018 (3.4 percent), Citizens' Council pressure all but eliminated the number of blacks who actually voted.[5] The Citizens' Council had driven the NAACP underground in the years before 1960 in Sunflower County and throughout most of the Delta. By the advent of the Freedom Rides, outright black organizing in Sunflower County was all but nonexistent. Council pressure made direct action protests along the lines of the lunch counter sit-ins and Freedom Rides futile, if not suicidal. It was clear that if the racial order of Sunflower County was to change, it would take massive registration of African American voters.

Indigenous leadership had been forced out of the county. It therefore appeared that the same young people who had compelled the nation to acknowledge the injustice of Jim Crow through direct action would now have to assume responsibility for registering these masses of black voters in Sunflower County and throughout Mississippi. SNCC moved toward filling that role. When the young foes of Jim Crow did arrive in Sunflower County, it mattered not whether any of them had participated in the integrated bus rides: the black Deltans chose aesthetics over textbook accuracy and referred to all of the young men and women as "Freedom Riders."

"Moses Is Coming"

The thousands of young Americans who devoted their energies to civil rights crusades in the early 1960s did so for thousands of reasons. Charles McLaurin, a native of Jackson, joined for love. McLaurin and a group of friends, one of whom had attended an SCLC training session for nonviolent direct action, protested segregation at the Mississippi state fair in 1961 and were all arrested. After several days in jail, the teens received a visit from Medgar Evers, state field secretary of the NAACP. Evers offered legal assistance and bail money to McLaurin and his friends but asked that they stay in jail for a few more days so that the NAACP could publicize their case. McLaurin's friends took the bail money. McLaurin, who had met Evers earlier when McLaurin delivered newspapers for a civil rights news project Evers called the *Mississippi Free Press*, agreed to stay in jail alone for ten more days. The passionate, charismatic Evers was responsible for the involvement of most of the young civil rights workers from Mississippi who fanned out across the state in the early 1960s. Many if not most of them had joined the NAACP youth chapters that Evers had initiated in the state in the 1950s. On that day in 1961, Evers added McLaurin to this cadre of young recruits.[6]

McLaurin's family history predisposed him to civil rights activity. He remembered his grandmother, a Tuskegee Institute graduate and owner of a Jackson restaurant, receiving threats from members of the local Ku Klux Klan, and he grew up hearing stories of how the Klan had run his grandfather out of the state. McLaurin had himself spent a brief period in the U.S. Army as a teenager, and when he returned to Mississippi he was visited by a Klansman and warned not to wear his army-issued work shirt in public. McLaurin had not necessarily been "politicized" by the time of his arrest at the state fair; by his own admission he had not developed anything approaching a coherent antisegregationist ideology at the time, so much as a vague feeling of being tired with the way things were. But McLaurin did know that he was fed up with Jim Crow and ready to do something about it.[7]

When McLaurin got out of jail, he found the black community in Jackson buzzing with excitement over a visit the Reverend Martin Luther King Jr. was about to pay to the city. Two days after his release, McLaurin, now something of a minor local celebrity, attended a mass meeting at the Jackson Masonic Temple where King spoke to a rapt audience. McLaurin was awed by King, whom he knew through the newspapers and the grapevine as the man who had organized the Montgomery bus boycotts and the SCLC. But he really fell in love with Diane Nash, a Fisk University student recruiting for SNCC, who spoke to a group of young people at the temple after King finished his sermon. "I don't think I'd ever seen a person so beautiful, so *fine*," McLaurin remembered in 1997. The smitten McLaurin chatted with Nash following the meeting and agreed to attend a SNCC informational meeting to take place a few days later. He had found his act of civil disobedience at the state fair invigorating and was proud to have been able to help Medgar Evers in some way, but he was not a committed civil rights activist by any stretch. When he got to the SNCC informational meeting days later, however, "there was just plenty of beautiful women there!," and McLaurin was hooked on civil rights.[8]

At the SNCC meeting, McLaurin and the other young people of Jackson heard that "Moses is coming," and they got excited. They weren't exactly sure who "Moses" was, but he sounded interesting. "We didn't know exactly when, but he was due," McLaurin said. "Then one Saturday night, they said, 'Wait at the freedom house. Moses is coming!'" When McLaurin finally met Moses—Bob Moses, an erudite math teacher from New York City who had come to Mississippi to register voters under the auspices of SNCC—he was surprised to find a man so small of stature. The bespectacled Moses nonetheless commanded respect with a simple demeanor that betrayed his elite education. McLaurin later remembered being almost entranced by the penetrating eyes that Moses used to analyze the world around him. McLaurin signed up with SNCC and dove into voter registration.[9]

In 1962, after completing a SNCC-sponsored training session at Tougaloo College near Jackson, McLaurin was given his choice of sites around the state where he could go to register voters. He picked Sunflower County for his project because at his training sessions he had learned about Senator Eastland and the power he wielded both in the Delta and in Washington. "I thought if I could get something going in his territory, then it would make me stand out, I would get some publicity," McLaurin said. "Maybe even get the chance to have a picture made with him, you know." McLaurin had only been through the Delta once, on a hitchhiking trip to Chicago. Bob Moses had chosen Ruleville as a possible site for registration because of its proximity to the Eastland plantation and because Moses and SNCC had had some initial success organizing in nearby Greenwood. Moses and Amzie Moore, an NAACP leader and small-business owner from the Delta town of Cleveland, had canvassed Ruleville for two weeks in the early summer of 1962 and convinced six residents to travel to Indianola to attempt to register. The town seemed to provide fertile ground for civil rights organizing.[10]

Charles Cobb, a Howard University student from Massachusetts, joined McLaurin on the Ruleville project. Like McLaurin, Cobb came from a family with a long history of resistance to white supremacy. Cobb's great-grandfather had founded New Africa, an all-black community in the Delta, during Reconstruction; he also had an uncle who worked as a union organizer and an aunt who was a civil rights activist in the North, and he described his father as a "socially activist" clergyman. While at Howard, Cobb had read a magazine article about Bob Moses' activities in Mississippi and had written two letters to SNCC headquarters in Atlanta volunteering his services. After his freshman year, he received money from CORE to travel to Houston, Texas, for a workshop on sit-in tactics. From Washington he traveled by bus as far as Jackson, but he got off the bus there and found the local SNCC office. At SNCC headquarters, Lawrence Guyot, a political science student from Tougaloo College, regaled him with tales of derring-do from the Greenwood project. He challenged Cobb: "How come you're going to Texas for a civil rights conference when you're right here in Mississippi [where all the action is]?" Cobb, too, was hooked.[11]

At the appointed hour on a day in early August, Moses met McLaurin, Cobb, James Jones, Landy MacNair, and Jesse Harris—all young SNCC staffers—in Jackson. They left late in the afternoon (a time that had to have been chosen carefully because Moses' car had already been identified by Delta whites who were all too willing to use violence against him), and Moses drove the group into Sunflower County. All the way along Highway 49 up through the Delta, Moses, himself a newcomer to Mississippi, lectured about the region's history. When they passed through Belzoni, he told the young men the cautionary tale of George Lee, who had been killed for trying to register African Americans to vote, just as these young men would try to do just up the road.

The carload finally arrived in Ruleville late at night, but there was a curfew in Ruleville that said blacks had to be off the streets by midnight; Moses and the others had to drive through town without being seen. The palpable fear that hung over Ruleville impressed McLaurin, who had no doubt been frightened by the Lee story. He later remembered, "We drove through town *verrrrry* slowly, expecting any minute for the police to pop out from behind any corner, knowing that if they did we'd never be heard from again." They made it to the intersection of Highway 8 near the center of town and took a left, heading for Cleveland and Amzie Moore's house. "Man, when we made it through those city limits," McLaurin said, "we thought we were home free."[12]

When the Freedom Riders returned to Ruleville the next day, they did not quite have to start their campaign from scratch. Diane Nash, now married to Reverend James Bevel (yet another veteran of the Nashville movement), had moved with her husband to Cleveland earlier in the year. Along with Amzie Moore, the couple had begun to lay groundwork for a movement in Ruleville under the auspices of both SNCC and the SCLC. Which national civil rights group one represented mattered little in the Delta, where men like Moore and Aaron Henry subscribed members for the NAACP while they housed and worked alongside SNCC workers. Organizational conflicts raged in the state capital, where NAACP field secretary Medgar Evers had to scrounge for bail money when SNCC and CORE youngsters got themselves arrested for desegregating bus terminals, even though younger activists continued to criticize the more conservative NAACP.[13] In the Delta, however, the battle plans were too simple and the stakes too high for internecine squabbles.

On Sunday, August 9, McLaurin and the others got dressed, and Amzie Moore took them to church in Ruleville. Moore introduced them to Joe McDonald, a Ruleville sharecropper and a leader in the Williams Chapel

Missionary Baptist Church. Ruleville already had a tiny network of local civil rights activists; McDonald's niece was one of six or eight girls in Ruleville who had done voter registration work with Bevel and the SCLC. McDonald opened his house in "Sanctified Quarter"—a Ruleville neighborhood whose name harkened back to the geography of slavery days and described the religiosity of its inhabitants—to the civil rights workers.[14]

McLaurin later described this experience and explained why the McDonalds' acceptance of the civil rights workers was so vital in "Notes on Organizing," a short primer that he wrote for the benefit of SNCC volunteers who would follow him into the county. McLaurin's language was hypothetical but clearly based on his own entrance into the African American community of Ruleville:

> An invited [organizer] goes to live with person X in Y community. Mr. X carries the person to church on Sunday. He introduces him to his friends and neighbors. You are there to do a job which at this time is undefined; so you act friendly, smiling and greeting the ladies as they approach you. Then, with your warm, friendly face you say to the people, "I want to do something for this community." That afternoon you are asked out to someone's home for dinner. Go, because this is one time you will be able to talk with a family, or maybe several families. Remember, try to answer all questions asked of you, because you are on trial. You must impress, as well as express.[15]

The Freedom Riders, as local people continued to refer to them, got to work immediately. The next day, a Monday, they started canvassing the neighborhood, going door to door to try to get people to register and to publicize mass meetings. At 10 A.M., Ruleville mayor Charles Dorrough welcomed the civil rights workers to Ruleville in his own way. He drove his car into Sanctified Quarter, stopped, pulled out a gun, and said to McLaurin and the others, "You niggers get in this car." Mayor Dorrough ran Ruleville as a personal fiefdom; on another occasion, he told a civil rights worker who had asked the mayor's opinion of the U.S. Constitution, "That law hasn't come here yet."[16]

On that Monday morning, he asked the civil rights workers who were new to town, "When did you boys get in here from New York?" "We didn't get in here from New York. We got here from Jackson," they answered. "Well, when did you leave New York?" Dorrough persisted. McLaurin, the group's spokesman, insisted he had never been to New York, but Dorrough's questions continued. It was impossible for the mayor to understand that it might occur to African Americans from one part of Mississippi

(Cobb was the only non-Mississippian of the five, and he, too, had strong family ties to the state) to come to another part of the state in order to convince people to register to vote. The workers explained what they had done, how Moses had taken them to Cleveland and Moore had brought them to Ruleville. Dorrough would hear nothing of it: "Naw, you people are from New York and we're not going to have you comin' in here and stirrin' up trouble in our town!" No matter what the young men told him, Dorrough could not believe that black people from Mississippi would do that, and he left the young men in jail.[17]

Dorrough allowed the group to make one phone call. They elected McLaurin to make it, because he knew Medgar Evers personally, and if any black man in Mississippi could get them out of that jail, it was Evers. Evers was not in his office in Jackson when McLaurin called, but McLaurin did leave a message explaining his situation and asking Evers to call the Ruleville jail.

In a matter of minutes the call came; it was one of Evers's lieutenants, and he convinced a Ruleville police official that the civil rights workers would be missed if they spent much more time inside the jail. Dorrough told the men that they were free to go, and they were glad to be free of him. However, they made the mayor drive them back to the same spot where he had picked them up. "The psychology was," McLaurin explained, "the black people [of Ruleville] had seen him take us away, so now they're figuring that [Dorrough] took us away somewhere and lynched us and that was the end of us. So we [made Dorrough take us] back to that spot [where he had arrested us]. The same people there were peepin' out the windows and standing out in the yards, and we went on over and talked with them, told them what had happened to us. We told them, 'They can't run us out of town. We're gonna be here.'" Local teenage girls with voter registration training, SNCC workers' first connection to the larger community, told McLaurin that those same local people wished the SNCC workers really would leave. The activists were unpopular, not because they were stirring up trouble, but because the locals feared that the civil rights workers would get killed and the locals felt guilty that there was nothing they could do about it. Within a few days, word had spread that there would be big trouble if anyone got caught associating with McLaurin and his friends.

The civil rights workers opened a voter education school at Williams Chapel. On August 17, Mayor Dorrough asked Lenard Davis, a forty-nine-year-old Ruleville sanitation worker, what he knew about the school. Davis played dumb. Dorrough told Davis that he knew what was going on there, and he was not going to allow outside blacks to force civil rights down Ruleville's throat. "The mayor said that anyone attending the school would be given a one-way ticket out of town," Davis told the SNCC organizers, "and if that would not do it, they would use whatever [means] they had available."[18]

The civil rights workers pressed on anyway. Soon McLaurin had three elderly women willing to try to register. On August 22, he drove them to Indianola on what he later remembered as "the day that I became a man." He was at first discouraged by the small number of willing registrants who showed up to make the trip to Indianola. Several others who had previously expressed an interest in registering proved too scared to follow through and were so ashamed that they had moved from their homes rather than tell him so. However, when the time came for McLaurin to accompany the women who were willing to make the trip to Indianola, he realized "that the numbers were not important. I learned that a faithful few was better than an uncertain ten." McLaurin set off for the county seat and tried to mask the terror he felt by keeping quiet all the way to the county courthouse in Indianola. When he and the ladies got there, McLaurin enjoyed a literally transforming experience:

> As I opened the door to get out I got a feeling in my stomach that made me feel weak[;] sweat started to form on my forehead and [it] became moist. At this point I was no longer in command, the three old ladies were leading me, and I was following them. They got out of the car and went up the walk to the courthouse as if this was the long walk that [led] to the Golden Gates of Heaven, their heads held high. . . . I watched as they walked up the steps and into the building. I stepped outside the door and waited, thinking how it was that these ladies who have been victimized by white faces all of their lives would suddenly walk up to the man and say, *I want to vote*. This did something to me.

SNCC's organizing strategy was crystallized in its four-word motto, "Let the people decide." McLaurin and his cohorts were to help people learn to help themselves, not do things for them. This, of course, is more easily said than done. When McLaurin put the ideal into practice—or, more accurately, had it put into practice for him by the three ladies—on August 22, he became a believer. "[W]hen that day came I followed them. The people are the true leaders. We need only to move them, to show them. Then watch and learn."[19]

McLaurin spelled out his own theories on community organizing in "Notes on Organizing," the primer he wrote for the benefit of his fellow SNCC organizers. "A SNCC worker should never take a leadership role in the community unless he is in his own community," McLaurin wrote. "A SNCC worker should give the responsibility of leadership to the community person or persons whom he has or is building. The SNCC worker should give form and guidance [but not necessarily direction] to the peoples' organization, and/or their programs."[20] For the eager young men and women like McLaurin who marched out into Mississippi communities like Ruleville under the SNCC banner, it was often difficult to step back and let people from the communities make their own decisions. The organizers wanted to change the world, today at the latest, and their relationships with rural, illiterate sharecroppers were tense at times. Still, the instances in which SNCC workers moved into Mississippi communities and behaved as dictators are remarkably few.[21] SNCC staffers like McLaurin and Cobb were much more likely to put in sixty-hour weeks full of thankless, plodding work whose rewards could be realized only in the distant future.

After at least two weeks of persistent canvassing and small victories, the SNCC workers had enough momentum to call a mass meeting, which they held in the third week of August. The local blacks who were curious to hear from the "Freedom Riders" in their midst packed Williams Chapel. James Bevel preached a sermon based on Matthew 16:3 ("And in the morning [Jesus said], 'It will be stormy today for the sky is red and threatening.' You know how to interpret the appearance of the sky, but you cannot interpret the signs of the times") and Luke 13:54–56 ("He also said to the multitudes, 'When you see a cloud rising in the west, you say at once, "A shower is coming!"; and so it happens. . . . You hypocrites! You know how to interpret the appearance of earth and sky; but why do you not know how to interpret the present time?'"). By sermonizing on the signs of the times, Bevel dared his listeners to evaluate their position in the Delta's socioeconomic system and shamed them into doing something to try to change it.

The main thing they could do to change Delta society, Bevel said, was to register to vote. Listening to Bevel, one of the meeting's attendees thought to herself that she would like to try voting for herself: "I could just see myself votin' people outta office that I know was wrong and didn't do nothin' to help the poor."[22] Bevel and Amzie Moore convinced eighteen people to travel to Indianola and take the registration test. McLaurin ran an impromptu voter registration clinic for the eighteen volunteers. The registration test required applicants to interpret the Mississippi Constitution to the satisfaction of the county's circuit clerk, C. C. Campbell. McLaurin simply encouraged those who were literate among the would-be registrants to write their names clearly on their applications and, if they could not interpret the section of the state constitution they were shown, just to reword it if they were able. He instructed the illiterates among the group to pay close attention to what the others were doing and to put their Xs where the other applicants told them to. Soon afterward, Amzie Moore rented an old school bus from a Cleveland man who used it to transport field laborers.[23]

On August 31, McLaurin took only his second trip to Indianola, and while his charges attempted to register, he and Bob Moses wandered around the town learning the lay of the land, mingling on street corners on the south side of the railroad tracks with local blacks. Cobb waited outside the imposing Sunflower County courthouse with the small group of prospective voters. After a while they attracted a crowd of curious whites who threw water on them—which came as a relief to Cobb, because he thought they would throw acid. Circuit Clerk Campbell allowed the candidates for registration to enter his office only singly (because, according to local lore, black crowds made him nervous). Early in the afternoon, he simply closed his office doors. Every person who made the trip with the civil rights workers was denied the right to register. The entire process took around two hours, and the group headed back to Ruleville in the bus.[24]

A state highway patrol car and an Indianola police cruiser began following them at the outskirts of Indianola. After a few miles, the police pulled the bus over and ticketed the driver for driving a bus "with too much yellow on it"—in other words, for impersonating a school bus. The patrolman levied a $100 fine on the bus driver and threatened to throw him in jail if the bus riders did not produce the fine on the spot. The riders did not have $100 among them, so the eighteen applicants, Cobb, and McLaurin volunteered to go to jail with the bus driver. Instead, the policeman took the driver back to the county courthouse; Moore, Moses, and another SNCC worker followed in a car to see what they could do.

The people on the bus became restless, and to settle them a short, stout woman whom McLaurin and Cobb had not noticed previous to the trip began to sing. Someone said, "Ooh, that's Fannie Lou. She's gonna *sing*. She can *sing*." While the woman sang spirituals, "kind of [taking] away some of the fear," McLaurin noticed that pickup trucks full of armed young white men were driving slowly back and forth past the bus. Finally Moses returned and said he needed $32 to pay the driver's reduced fine. (Apparently the policeman did not want to make a bigger scene than he already had and decided that arresting twenty people for riding in a yellow school bus would bring bad publicity to Indianola.) The would-be registrants passed the hat to raise the necessary money and returned home to Ruleville. The armed whites followed them, shouting catcalls, all the way home.[25]

Nearly all the local people the civil rights workers had met lived in or around Sanctified Quarter, but the singer, Fannie Lou Hamer, lived outside of Ruleville and worked as the timekeeper on the Marlow plantation. Hamer's job in itself made her something of a leader among farm workers. As timekeeper, Hamer was responsible for tabulating the hours that each wage laborer worked on the farm and for measuring the cotton that each sharecropper and day laborer picked. The job placed Hamer in a "position of trust and honor, if there is such a thing in the plantation schema."[26] Hamer had earned the job of timekeeper by dint of her superior education: she had completed, by her recollection, six years of school, which placed her far ahead of the Marlows' other sharecroppers. In time, Hamer had developed a reputation for being fair to her coworkers at risk to her own job. When she believed that the Marlows had cheated a certain worker out of a day's labor or a seasonal settlement, Hamer reputedly used a weighted "pea" to skew the weight of cotton that the worker had picked, revising the worker's pay upward. Hamer saw to it that her employers credited an honest day's work with something closer to an honest day's pay, but for obvious reasons she could not afford to use the "pea" indiscriminately. Known in the African American community of Ruleville as someone who was concerned with justice issues even before she became involved with the civil rights movement, Hamer understood black workers and white landowners better, more deeply, than most.

Hamer had attended the first mass meeting at Williams Chapel and had been among the first to volunteer for the trip to Indianola. According to Cobb and McLaurin, however, she had never attracted attention to herself before she was the first to step off the bus in Indianola and again when the bus was stopped on the return trip to Ruleville.[27] When she did draw the civil rights workers' attention, it was for singing her favorite spiritual, "This Little Light of Mine." In the specific instance of the stopped school bus, Hamer's strong voice and calm delivery soothed the nerves of the understandably shaken voter registrants. Her contribution to the movement in Sunflower County did not end there, however. Hamer flourished in the democratic atmosphere that SNCC created, and she would go on to become the absolute personification of "Let the people decide," the archetype of SNCC's organizing strategy. Before the trip to Indianola, she had been, in the words of one biographer, "a person in search of a freedom movement." She told Charles McLaurin that "she had always wanted to get involved with something to help her people but she just didn't know exactly how or what to do." Like so many Afro-Mississippians who became involved with the civil rights struggle, Hamer had read about the Freedom Riders and caught bits and pieces of news about them through the radio and television. Like hundreds of others, she had waited for an opportunity to join in their struggle.[28]

In August, Hamer got that chance and took advantage of it. Within the year, she would travel to northern and midwestern cities to tell her story and to spread the "freedom songs," soul-nourishing spirituals like "This Little Light of Mine" that enriched and spread the movement culture, all the while raising much-needed funds for sNcC's programs in the rural South. When Hamer sang a slave spiritual such as "Go Tell It on the Mountain," with its line "Let my people go," she connected the civil rights workers' struggles with the story of Moses leading the slaves from Egypt. "Wade in the Water" was another of Hamer's favorite spirituals; in the African American oral tradition it is associated with Harriet Tubman, another figure who led her people out of bondage. Hamer did not choose these songs at random. According to the musicologist Bernice Johnson Reagon, Hamer was adept at selecting the verses from traditional arrangements "that [spoke] symbolically to the goals of the struggle at hand."[29] The freedom songs that Hamer plucked from black oral tradition and made even more relevant to the modern freedom struggle were instrumental in the creation of a movement culture in Sunflower County.

When Hamer returned home on the night of August 31, 1962, she learned that W. D. Marlow, the owner of the plantation on which she and her husband worked, had been "raising a lot of Cain" since Hamer had left on the school bus for the courthouse. When Hamer's husband, "Pap," returned home from his job at the plantation's cotton gin, he informed Hamer that Marlow had demanded that she either stop trying to register or leave the plantation. Marlow came to the family's home and told her himself: "I mean that. You'll have to go back to Indianola and withdraw, or you have to leave this place." According to Hamer, she replied, "Mr. Dee, I didn't go down there to register for you, I went down there to register for myself." Before she attempted to register, she had been a favorite employee of the Marlow family. Marlow's paternalistic affection, however, apparently did not extend to allowing Hamer to exercise the most basic right of citizenship. When his employee attempted to register, Marlow too found himself under pressure: he told Hamer that "They gon' worry me tonight. They gon' worry the hell outta me, and I'm gonna worry [the] hell outta you." Hamer did not ask who "they" were but speculated that they were either Klansmen or members of the Citizens' Council; it didn't matter which, because, in Hamer's words, "I don't think one is no worse than the other."[30]

Four days after the Ruleville group's trip to Indianola, a series of incidents in Ruleville demonstrated how widespread and concerted an effort to eliminate black voter registration activity could be. Mayor Dorrough notified Williams Chapel Missionary Baptist Church, the voter registration campaign's main meeting place, that the church's free water and tax exemptions were being cut off because the building was being used for "purposes other than worship services." The church's deacons were forced to close the building to civil rights meetings. Dorrough also fired Lenard Davis, the Ruleville sanitation worker, because he learned that Davis's wife had been attending the citizenship school. The city closed the Surney family's dry cleaning business for violating unspecified city ordinances. The Surneys had been among the first families to embrace the SNCC organizers; because their business came from black Ruleville, they had been largely immune to white economic pressures and could afford to associate with "agitators," at least until now. On the same day, Fred Hicks, who drove day workers to the plantations around Ruleville, was dismissed from his job. Hicks's employer told him, "We gonna see how tight we can make it—gonna make it just as tight as we can. Gonna be rougher and rougher than you think it is." Hicks's offense? He was the son of a woman who wanted to vote. That night, as Moses and Amzie Moore walked down a Ruleville street, they were followed by a white farmer in a pickup. The man asked, "Are you the folks getting the people to register?" Moses and Moore allowed that they were. The man asked the pair if they could come out to his plantation; the stunned Moses and Moore answered that of course they could. "I've got a shotgun waiting for you," the farmer replied. "Double-barrel."[31]

After she refused to renounce her intent to vote, Fannie Lou Hamer left the Marlow plantation and moved in with a friend, Mary Tucker, in Ruleville. Hamer soon learned that Tucker's home was in danger because whites knew where she was staying. Hamer received tips that her life might be in danger, and she moved again to a house in neighboring Tallahatchie County.[32] On the evening of September 10, night riders fired shots into the homes of Tucker, Joe McDonald, and Herman and Hattie Sisson, all in Sanctified Quarter. Charles McLaurin had been staying with the McDonalds but was with another family that night. Hattie Sisson had been one among McLaurin's group of "little old ladies." At Tucker's home, shots went through one wall at about the point where Hamer's head would have been had she still been sleeping there. At the Sissons', the blasts hit two Jackson State College coeds, one of whom, Vivian Hillet, was the Sissons' granddaughter, visiting on her way to college. Hillet was struck in the arms and legs. Her friend, Marylene Burks, was more seriously injured, absorbing shots to the head and neck. According to the Sovereignty Commission's official report, night riders fired into a total of forty-two Sunflower County homes in the nights surrounding August 10. However, the situation was not as dangerous as it sounded, according to the commission's investigator. He reminded his superiors that the night riders were only using shotgun shells. Rifle shot would have made for a different story.[33]

Bob Moses contacted the FBI but expected little or nothing from the agency. Indeed, as Charles McLaurin wrote, "The FBI men that came didn't seem to be looking for the person or persons that did the shooting. . . . The FBI did more to frighten people than to help them." Moses also urged SNCC workers to get out and ask aggressive questions to demonstrate to local people that the civil rights workers wanted to know who had done this, that they cared deeply about what happened to the people with whom they now lived, and that they demanded justice. The Sovereignty Commission's special investigator whined, "Robert Moses acted like he was some special government investigator at Ruleville," and Dorrough arrested Charles Cobb at the North Sunflower County Hospital (where the two college students were being treated) because Cobb was "asking a lot of silly questions." S. D. Milam, the brother of one of Emmett Till's murderers and a Ruleville town marshal, hauled Cobb off to jail.[34]

Dorrough claimed that the shooting was "a prefabricated incident" and told the press, "We think they did it themselves." He claimed that a "reliable source" had informed him that a civil rights worker had purchased shotgun pellets just days before the shooting and accused blacks of shooting into their own homes for the publicity. His claim was ridiculous in this instance, but guns were commonplace among Sunflower County blacks, nearly all of whom depended on game to augment their families' diets. Nor were blacks afraid or unwilling to use their guns to defend their homes. As violent as white terrorists were in Sunflower County, they would have directed even more hostility toward African Americans had they not known this to be true.

The term "un-violent," as opposed to "nonviolent," may best describe the movement in Sunflower County. Few local people made the commitment to nonviolence as a way of life that Martin Luther King Jr., John Lewis, and thousands of others in the SCLC, SNCC, and CORE had made.

(This could not have come as a surprise to SNCC organizers; McLaurin and Cobb both came from Mississippi families with long traditions of armed self-defense.) Most families in the county had guns and made conscious decisions whether or not to use them as circumstances demanded. Kwame Ture (the SNCC organizer formerly known as Stokely Carmichael), for instance, remembered in a 1994 oral history interview that Fannie Lou Hamer had handed him a pistol when he stayed at her house in Ruleville. Despite SNCC's official commitment to nonviolence, its organizers operated best in the parts of Mississippi where local people reserved the right to armed self-protection even before Freedom Summer.[35]

The civil rights workers struggled for several weeks to gain the trust of the community—not because Ruleville blacks did not want to register to vote but because they were justifiably scared of their white neighbors who did not want them to vote. The local people felt terribly guilty about what might happen to the voter registration "agitators" in Ruleville. In the weeks following the shooting, McLaurin reported to the headquarters of the Southern Regional Council's Voter Education Project (VEP) in Atlanta, "[M]ost everybody in the community was down on us and we had to do something to get them on our side." The night riders' tactics had succeeded in frightening African Americans away from attempting to register, so Cobb and McLaurin had to start over again at square one, regaining the trust of the community. "[W]e went from house to house asking people about everyday problems," McLaurin wrote. "[W]e would carry them to the store downtown[,] help pick cotton and chop wood. [A]ll this would give them a feeling of togetherness and friendship. All of September was mostly spent trying to get things going again."[36]

In classic SNCC style, McLaurin organized the least prestigious members of the community first; he called his style of organizing "running the streets." Early on in his stay in Ruleville, McLaurin began hanging out on street corners, passing the time and bottles in brown paper sacks among farm laborers. A woman whom McLaurin knew only as "Mrs. Anderson" owned a small grocery store in Ruleville, and she allowed McLaurin to sit on her front porch. While McLaurin drank soda or ate bologna on the porch, she sat just inside the front door—because she could not afford to be seen with him in broad daylight—and talked with him. She taught McLaurin local history and told him about local people: who liked whom and who didn't, who would be likely to listen to him and who would be likely to tell a white employer what the civil rights workers were trying to do. McLaurin sat on the front porch for hours at a time, learning the lay of the land.[37]

Before long, the civil rights workers had befriended Lafayette Surney, a popular young man whose father owned a dry cleaning business in Ruleville, and were using the Surneys' front yard as a meeting spot. The house was something of a meeting spot for local teens and young adults. McLaurin converted it into SNCC's base of operations. The site of the first makeshift headquarters was key, for in Ruleville "the adults were afraid [of being seen with the civil rights workers] and the younger people were not." Lafayette Surney, who had graduated from Ruleville Central High School in 1961, introduced McLaurin to friends and took the civil rights workers around to the houses of people who were likely to respond to their message. "After about two weeks of these introductions," McLaurin remembered, "we were regulars in the community."[38]

McLaurin and his group of canvassers had the misfortune of trying to convince blacks to register to vote while James Meredith was attempting to enter the University of Mississippi in Oxford. Whites perceived Meredith's personal demeanor as "uppity" and resented the Kennedy administration's interference on what truly must have seemed to be an enchanted campus. (Ole Miss coeds were crowned Miss America in 1959 and 1960, while the football team steamrolled through the Southeastern Conference.) When James Meredith and John and Robert Kennedy invaded this storybook atmosphere, it enraged excitable whites across the state, and this greatly complicated the lives of civil rights workers who already had enough to worry about in the Delta.

Governor Ross Barnett whipped white Mississippians' hatred of Meredith and the Kennedys and the cause they represented into a lather, promising that "no school will be integrated in Mississippi while I am your governor," and adding melodramatically, "We will not drink from the cup of genocide." His rhetoric resonated in Sunflower County. W. W. Chapman, editor of the *Indianola Enterprise-Tocsin*, had previously called Barnett "a wind-bloated balloon who can be swayed by the last breeze to reach him." Following Barnett's stand against the Kennedy administration, however, he wrote that "Gov. Ross Barnett has sculptured [*sic*] his shrine in American history by standing up for the principles in which the people of his state believe and the laws of his state, against the firmly entrenched dictatorship of Washington." As the public war of words between Jackson and Washington escalated, Chapman asked his Sunflower County readers, "Speaking of Governor Barnett, two weeks ago did you know anyone who would admit to voting for him? Today do you know of anyone who will not admit to voting for him?" On the night before Meredith was to enter the campus in Oxford, Barnett all but explicitly encouraged massive resistance to Meredith's enrollment. The next day, thousands of outside "toughs" streamed onto the wooded campus, which was supposed to have been sealed off by state troopers.[39]

On the afternoon of September 30, while Meredith bunkered down in his dormitory room with federal bodyguards, a hostile crowd—now estimated at 2,000 to 4,000—surrounded the 536 U.S. marshals with special riot training who had come to the campus to protect Meredith. The marshals stationed themselves at the Lyceum, the school's administration building, where Meredith was to register for classes the next morning. At sundown, the crowd began hurling bricks and bottles at the marshals, then set fire to several vehicles near the Lyceum. The state police, whom Barnett had promised would remain on campus to keep order, then withdrew. Bedlam ensued. In the "Battle of Oxford," one French journalist and one Oxford bystander died, and over 100 federal marshals were seriously injured. President Kennedy eventually had to dispatch a total of 23,000 army troops to the campus to restore order.

It is difficult to exaggerate the effect the Battle of Oxford had on segregationists. Across the state, white radicals portrayed the Kennedy administration's actions as yet another example of "federal tyranny," orchestrated to usurp the state's power to run its own educational affairs. A satirical poem, "Benedict Meredith Number One College Crasher," by Catherine C. Thelkeld, which the *Indianola Enterprise-Tocsin* printed in the Battle of Oxford's aftermath, illustrates how whites in Sunflower County perceived Meredith and his quest to obtain the best available education for himself in his native state:

Ain't no use me worrin' or workin' hard, cause
I'se gwine to school in de white folks' yard.
My colored brothers here totin' guns,
Us keeps de ball rollin'; we's sho' havin' fun. . . .

Heap o' trouble with dem colleges all 'bout de state,
Dey's liable lose creditation. Now ain't dat great?
I knows my 'ploma (when I gits it) will be good any whar
So I ain't payin' no min' nor sayin' no prayer.

That crazy bunch niggers called NAACP
Got big and loud mouth, tried to be 'portant lak me.
The Federals called a 'porter and I gives my story,
Now dey's bowin' and scrapin' and I'se got the glory.

When is I gwine feel free again, 'scape de white folks hate,
Hunt de possums, coons and rabbits in my pappy's state?
I sho' don' know 'bout the future or what lie ahead but
Lawd, I'd hate to wake up some mornin' and fin' myself dead.[40]

The voter registration workers faced an uphill battle in the best of times; in the wake of the Oxford riot, winning concessions from white Sunflower Countians was impossible. White resolve across the county and throughout the state stiffened even further.

The Ruleville shootings and the debacle in Oxford understandably scared a lot of people away from civil rights activity, but, almost counterintuitively, it also encouraged other African Americans to get involved. Now they saw what they were up against. Now they knew exactly how far whites were willing to go to keep them from voting. Several Ruleville residents who had been waiting to see whether or not it was safe to join the movement decided that organization was their only hope, whether it was safe to join or not. "Now we [had] a movement developing," McLaurin said. "Now there was something there to kind of bind the community. There was some reason to come out—we were able to get a *big* meeting following this. Now we even got a better reception from some people." Cobb remembered, "Our decision was that we couldn't really tell people that we had a way of protecting them, either from economic harassment or from physical violence. . . . [G]iven that reality, our decision was basically just to be physically present in the community, just to show people . . . that we were prepared to stay and stick it out." The determination of McLaurin and Cobb to remain visible in the community and to continue trying to register voters in the face of such blatant deterrents undoubtedly convinced many fence-straddlers to join their campaign.[41]

McLaurin and Cobb stayed in Ruleville, which at the end of 1962 remained the established movement capital of the county. For the most part, SNCC confined its organizing to Fannie Lou Hamer's hometown. After a few early swings and misses, the SNCC workers all but gave up on Indianola, the county seat, which they dismissed for the time being as a lost cause. The Citizens' Council and the police force seemed to have white Indianola too organized, too united; the blacks there seemed too timid. Besides, the civil rights workers felt, there were too many middle-class blacks in Indianola who had too many mortgages to pay off. To make matters worse, the established African American churches in Indianola were as great a hindrance to civil rights activities at the time as white racists were, precisely because council members held mortgage notes over the most finely equipped black churches, the majority of which were Baptist.

Because the Baptist denomination is decentralized to the extreme, any black congregation that wanted to build a new church building or improve on an old one either had to raise all the necessary money itself or borrow money from a local lender. Even Indianola's small but substantial black middle class could not afford to build the churches that dotted Indianola. To build, the congregations had to borrow, and the officials of all of Indianola's banks were members of the Citizens' Council. The houses of worship along Indianola's Church Street were fine structures, and the congregation of each endeavored to outdo the next in a way that struck the members of churches in the more rural parts of the county as vain and pompous. In the effort to gain social prestige, pastors put their churches and themselves at the mercy of the council by mortgaging their buildings, and when the Freedom Riders came to Indianola, black preachers told their flocks to stay calm and ignore the "agitators."

Moorhead, directly to Indianola's east, did not develop into a movement town until later in the decade; nor did Drew, just to the north of Ruleville, cultivate a movement culture. Of Sunflower County's four main population centers, only Ruleville produced a homegrown civil rights movement before 1964, and this was largely due to the contingencies of geography and personality. Ruleville was apparently chosen for a voter registration school because it was near the home of an experienced ally, Amzie Moore of Cleveland, and close to the plantation of an enemy whom SNCC hoped to embarrass, Senator James Eastland of Doddsville.

Once the base in Ruleville was established, it nourished the talents of women like Rebecca McDonald, Hattie Sisson, and, most famously, Fannie Lou Hamer, truly one of the most remarkable and most charismatic Americans of her century. Uncovering Hamer had several consequential benefits for SNCC. Her unique ability to define and explain the problems of oppression in the vernacular of the Delta attracted the minds and bodies SNCC needed to wage war against Jim Crow. Her beautiful singing voice and personal interpretation of black church standards calmed nervous civil rights troops in Mississippi during trying times and brought in money for SNCC at fund-raising events in the North. Most of all, the bristling bravery that Hamer displayed while speaking truth to power in Mississippi and throughout the nation won the hearts of people inside the state. When forces outside of Mississippi joined her crusade, they would eventually bring Mississippi officials to account for their actions. On January 14, 1963, Hamer traveled to Indianola yet again to see if she had passed the voter registration test. This time she learned that she had in fact passed, and she considered her success a major accomplishment. Yet after nearly six months of heavy organizing in Ruleville on the part of the SNCC workers, Hamer's was only the sixth application to have been approved. There was much work to be done.[42]

McLaurin and Cobb kept Ruleville as the base of SNCC's operations because Ruleville was the only community in the county with enough people who were willing to stand behind them. Williams Chapel reopened its doors to the SNCC organizers in the winter of 1962–63, responding to the demands of church deaconesses like Rebecca McDonald. According to Cobb, the church's pastor was far from enthusiastic about letting voter registration agitators use his church for citizenship training classes, but he could not face down the women of his church—because to do so, in Cobb's words, "threatened his fried chicken."[43] McLaurin, Hamer, and the women of the church continued to use the pulpit on Sundays to cajole fearful congregants into attempting to register at the county courthouse. They also utilized the church as a base of voter registration operations, opening it during weekdays as a place to teach basic literacy and citizenship and during weeknights to hold soul-nourishing mass meetings.

On a Sunday evening in January 1963, the Ruleville Christian Citizenship Movement, as the new organization called itself, sponsored the showing of a documentary on the life of Gandhi at a packed Williams Chapel. James Bevel followed the documentary with a discussion on the importance of nonviolence to the movement and then gave a sermon about why people should pay their poll tax and take the registration test. A steady trickle of people obliged through the winter, and the voter registration movement again gained steam. In February 1963 alone, 400 Ruleville residents traveled to Indianola to take the registration test, which represented the high tide of the Ruleville registration project. In the previous six months, only 52 Ruleville citizens had taken the registration test. By July, upward of 600 Ruleville residents had attempted to register, though only 11 had passed. Still, some citizens made as many as fifteen trips to the courthouse in Indianola in search of the franchise. These successes did not, however, translate to a groundswell in the rest of the county.[44]

Settlement Time

As autumn gave way to winter in 1962, McLaurin and Cobb witnessed firsthand the essence of the Delta's system of racial inequality: settlement time. Under "halving," the most prevalent sharecropping arrangement in

Sunflower County, a landowner, invariably white, furnished land, seed, fertilizer, in some cases a garden patch, and in almost all cases a home to a family who was to grow cotton. In return, the landowner then took half of the profits from the sale of the year's crop. The sharecroppers were responsible for the entire cost of raising the crop. At settlement time, the landowner totaled up the loans he had made over the previous year for rent, seed, fertilizer, doctor and food bills, cash advances, and miscellaneous expenses. In many cases, sharecroppers were required to buy staples from the landowner's commissary, which took even more money from their pockets.

Sharecroppers were strictly prohibited from taking any part whatsoever in these calculations. L. C. Dorsey, who grew up in a sharecropping family on plantations throughout the Delta, took it upon herself at the age of thirteen to keep her own ledger for her family's shares. At the time, Dorsey's family lived on the Ferguson plantation in northern Sunflower County. Dorsey's illiterate father bought her a composition book, and from "furnish" time (the initial loan of land and seed that indebted the sharecropper to the landowner) until harvest, she meticulously recorded every expense her father incurred. At harvesttime, the schoolchild listened to the radio each day to see what price cotton was selling for in the area, then calculated the price that her father's cotton bales should have brought. Dorsey figured that after the plantation owner subtracted all legitimate expenses from her father's gross, he should have earned $4,000. She predicted that the plantation owner would invent $3,000 in additional miscellaneous expenses, leaving the family with $1,000, which still would have represented a better profit than the Dorseys had ever earned before. Instead, at settlement time, Dorsey's father was forced to accept a measly $200 for his family's year of labor, a mere fraction of the money he had earned. Dorsey referred to this moment as her own "coming of age" in Mississippi; she learned that day that "people were locked into this system, and the fear and lack of control made them take" whatever the plantation owner decided to give them. "There was no protest," Dorsey wrote later. "There was no saying I'm not going to take that. There was nobody else you could appeal to. *Nobody else.*"[45]

Making their rounds as canvassers, Cobb and McLaurin heard similar stories. They learned that landowners had been "deducting" (in other words, stealing) social security payments from sharecroppers' settlements and day laborers' wages, even when those employees did not have social security numbers. Needless to say, it is highly unlikely that the federal government ever received those deductions. The sharecropping system made it simple for unscrupulous landowners to cheat sharecroppers out of hard-earned money, and it is easy to understand why they defended the arrangement with such determination. Apologists pointed out correctly that there did exist honest landowners who shared profits fairly with sharecroppers, and there have been a handful of black sharecroppers in Sunflower County's history who made enough money under the system to buy their own land and achieve financial independence. Likewise, there are examples in the local folklore of a handful of black landowners who treated their own sharecroppers fairly. Sadly, however, Willie Mae Robinson's experience was a much more common one.

McLaurin and Cobb found Robinson on a plantation near Ruleville, where her family had just picked twenty bales of cotton, in the winter of 1962. At an approximate weight of 550 pounds per bale and a selling price of 34 cents per pound, McLaurin and Cobb calculated that Robinson's crop should have grossed $3,740. Under a halving arrangement, this total should have earned Robinson $1,870, minus expenses. However, her plantation owner determined that Robinson's expenses for the year came to a grand total of $1,867, which netted Robinson and her family $3 for an entire year's work. She was forbidden from keeping her own figures and was consequently unable to challenge the landowners' arithmetic. To have complained to police authorities or the federal government would have been fruitless, if not physically dangerous, so Robinson had to rely on surplus commodities from the federal government and hope for a better crop next year. She, like thousands of other black Sunflower County sharecroppers, was totally dependent on the owner of the land she farmed.[46]

Even if there had been a landowner in the vicinity whom Robinson believed would give her a fairer share of profits in the 1963 growing season —an unlikely "if," considering the planters' hegemony—her lack of capital made it impossible for her to start over again on another farm. Robinson was forced to stay on the farm that had just stolen nearly $2,000 from her, and there was absolutely nothing she could do about it. Incredibly, she found herself in a better position than the day laborers who made up a large portion of the county's black workforce. The 1962 growing season had been a dry one, so there was little cotton for wage laborers to pick even without the introduction of the mechanical cotton picker (which began for the first time in the early 1960s to replace field laborers in Sunflower County on a large scale). McLaurin found that cotton-picking machines had done most of the work, and as a result "most of the people had nothing to do and made no money."[47]

The SNCC workers now had to assist local sharecroppers in their efforts to acquire the federal welfare dollars that were administered by local authorities. Before McLaurin and the others moved to the county, all a welfare recipient had had to do to receive a meager allotment of corn meal, rice, dry milk, and flour was to go down to Ruleville City Hall and sign up. After the voter registration project began, however, the city required recipients to fill out an application that had to be countersigned by an employer or "a responsible person," then to travel to the county relief office in Indianola to pick up the commodities. Cobb and McLaurin noted dryly that since the registration project had begun, "[T]he 'responsible [white] people' are not particularly inclined to [do] favors for the Negro."[48]

Economic assistance had first become an issue for McLaurin and Cobb when the people they convinced to take the voter registration tests began losing their jobs late in the summer. In the fall, local people began asking McLaurin and Cobb for personal loans "because the[y] think if we had not came with the Voter Registration Program these things would not be so bad."[49] McLaurin and Cobb apparently took this responsibility very seriously. Their success in keeping the commodity pipeline open became essential to the voter registration operation. Without commodities, most Sunflower County blacks could not survive from one cotton season to the next. Cobb and McLaurin wrote to SNCC headquarters in Atlanta, "If [commodities are] taken from them, they have nothing at all; and the success of our voter registration program depends on the protection we can offer the individual while he is waiting on his one small vote to become a part of a strong Negro vote." This last point cannot be overemphasized. "It doesn't take much to tide over the rural Mississippi Negro," the pair concluded, "but the commodities are *vital*." Making sure that poor, rural blacks, especially those who stuck their necks out by attempting to register, had decent clothing and adequate food would soon claim a good deal of the civil rights workers' time. By early December, they had procured a space at Williams Chapel to register local people for commodities at least three days a week.[50]

When Bessie Lee Green's application for commodities was denied in November, apparently because she had attempted to register to vote, she appealed to the civil rights workers for help. Diane Nash Bevel sent a letter to U.S. Department of Agriculture secretary Orville Freeman and received a return call from Freeman almost immediately. Freeman also called the state welfare office in Jackson and the county office in Indianola to make sure that federal commodities were not being withheld from deserving recipients just because they had tried to register to vote. The county welfare agent had previously demanded letters of recommendation from "good white bosses" as part of the commodity application process and had forced applicants to wait outside her office for hours in below-freezing temperatures. In contrast, when McLaurin drove Green to Indianola following Freeman's phone call, the county agent was "very helpful" and encouraged McLaurin to bring more people down from Ruleville. McLaurin concluded that "the call from Washington changed things in Sunflower County."[51] The short, simple phone call that placed the strength of the federal government behind poor blacks did change things in Sunflower County for a short time. Unfortunately, the act was also an exception that proved the general rule of federal inaction in the face of similar injustices. It illustrated what a powerful role the national government could play in local people's lives, even if it was seldom willing to play it in Sunflower County.

Local white grocers and landowners hated the giveaways. Every commodity that the government gave poor blacks was a commodity off of which the grocers could not make a profit and which the landowners could not use to pull sharecroppers down into further credit dependence. The merchants favored a food stamp program from which they could take a cut. As Congress debated a food stamp bill in 1964, Senator Eastland explained to President Johnson matter-of-factly, "My merchants are for [food stamps] in the nigra areas. You see, [the federal government] haul[s] commodities in there and give[s] 'em out. Now you take the niggers on my property: they got plenty of money, but every damn one of 'em will line up and get commodity. The merchants in that area want food stamps, because they get a cut out of it."[52]

White authorities clearly saw the giveaways as a dangerous and growing threat to their control. SNCC staffers traveled throughout the country to raise interest in the Mississippi project and to raise funds, and in response, for the first time in February 1964, two trucks carrying over thirty tons of donated shoes, clothing, and food arrived in Ruleville from Cambridge, Massachusetts. Fannie Lou Hamer took responsibility for distributing the goods and made no secret of the fact that she would reward only the Ruleville blacks who agreed to pay their poll tax and try to register. Reportedly, she even turned away a woman with eight children who had just lost everything when the family's home was destroyed by fire. The woman told Hamer that she did not feel qualified to vote since she could not read and would not know who she was voting for or what the duties of office were. Hamer responded in so many words that if the woman couldn't stand up for herself better than that, the clothes weren't going to help her. Hamer's approach was apparently effective in most cases; according to SNCC records, more than 300 people tried to register in the week following one shipment. McLaurin said that on top of that number, an additional 150 people wanted to make the trip to Indianola but were hindered by lack of transportation.[53]

Mayor Dorrough felt so threatened by the giveaways that he initiated a State Sovereignty Commission investigation into the private program. Dorrough took it upon himself to torpedo the program and went on the airwaves of a local radio station to announce that Hamer was giving away free food and clothing to anyone who wanted it. He apparently hoped that a flood of people would swamp Hamer and that she would give up. When over 400 blacks showed up at the Hamers' Ruleville home, however, they received a lecture on the importance of their registering to vote. If they would go down to Indianola to pay their poll tax and take the test, she told them, they could have some clothes; if they were unwilling to stand up for themselves, they could freeze for all she cared. Most chose to attempt to register. The county's circuit clerk confirmed for the Sovereignty Commission's investigator that applications for registration had risen sharply since Hamer had begun giving away goods. Still, the investigator reported, "[H]e stated they were the caliber of Negroes who were totally unqualified to pass any kind of mental test." Later in the spring another shipment arrived, and the mayor informed Ruleville's citizenry that if anyone wanted some free clothes, they could head right over to Fannie Lou Hamer's and take some. According to one reporter, Hamer marched to Dorrough's office and told him in no uncertain terms to butt out of her business. "I told him not to boss us around. 'We don't try to boss you around,' I told him."[54] Dorrough did not stop harassing Hamer, but she did win from the mayor a grudging respect.[55] Even so, white authorities continued to protest the food and clothing giveaways, stonewall federal welfare programs, and harass the civil rights workers who had become involved in commodity distribution.

Canvassing potential voters wore on Cobb and McLaurin. Cobb later remembered, "[P]eople have this romantic notion of these rugged, ragged young people, you know, sort of guerillas in the Mississippi Delta . . . [but] it was slow . . . sometimes dangerous, but [more often] boring work." Their task was mainly just to be visible, to let people know they were there as members of the community for the long term, allowing people to observe and come to their own conclusions about them and the cause they represented. The two young men—neither of whom was yet old enough to vote—spent their days sitting on porches and talking to people their parents' age and older. Worse, they knew that most of the people they met could not or would not take the radical step of attempting to register.

"[T]hey had all kinds of excuses," according to Cobb. "General excuses: 'That's white folks' business,' or 'I intend to make this crop on Mr. So-an-so's land,'" or a hundred others.[56] Trying to change the minds of people like this day after day was tedious work, but it eventually paid off in spades, if only because the persistence eventually convinced Ruleville blacks that voting was not just white folks' business. McLaurin and Cobb's voter registration work through 1962 and 1963 laid the foundation upon which Sunflower County's movement culture was built.

Unfortunately, their work went all but unnoticed outside the county and outside of SNCC. The Sunflower County project received funding from the VEP, and McLaurin and Cobb wrote up dozens of pages worth of reports for that organization. Whether or not anyone read them was another matter. Cobb later remembered, "[N]obody outside of the counties you were working in was particularly interested in what you were doing. . . . I mean, largely, we were doing this and kind of being ignored by everybody."[57] Southern Regional Council director Wiley Branton eventually decided that the VEP would have to either pour much more money into Mississippi to have an effect or cut its losses. At the end of 1963, the VEP pulled its funding from the state, believing that the project was not registering enough voters to justify the money being spent.[58] For the voter registration projects in the state to have a widespread and long-lasting effect, it began to appear, SNCC would have to do something drastic to get the rest of the country interested in Mississippi.

Freedom Voting

Stymied at registrars' offices across Mississippi, the Council of Federated Organizations (COFO) tried something novel in the fall of 1963, running a shadow ticket for governor and lieutenant governor.[59] Aaron Henry, an African American World War II veteran and independent pharmacist from Clarksdale, headed the ticket, while Ed King, a white chaplain at predominantly black Tougaloo College, ran for lieutenant governor. The Freedom Vote would give African Americans who had been refused the franchise by white authorities an opportunity to cast ballots for the first time. Allard Lowenstein, a liberal Democratic Party operative from New York City, had gotten the idea for the mock election after observing one in South Africa, where he had worked as a staff member and political observer for Hubert Humphrey in the late 1950s. After a number of brainstorming sessions with Bob Moses and the COFO staff, Lowenstein received the go-ahead for the Freedom Vote, and he singlehandedly recruited more than seventy white college students from Stanford and Yale to canvass potential voters and to staff the polls from September through November.[60] On the day after their arrival, fourteen of the volunteers were arrested in downtown Indianola for passing out leaflets without a permit.[61]

The Henry/King literature encouraged blacks to vote at the makeshift polls around the state as a way of striking back against the Citizens' Councils. Their pamphlets spelled out the need for a democratic movement in Mississippi in simple terms. The vote would give black Mississippians the "[f]reedom to choose the men you want to govern you and the laws you need for a good society *without fear* of losing your jobs or endangering your family."[62] COFO expected 200,000 black Mississippians (40 percent of the state's black voting age population) to respond to the message and cast their ballots. Because the idea for the vote was not even hatched until late summer, it was organized on a nearly ad hoc basis. SNCC workers already in the state thought that they could have handled the vote themselves, but Moses and COFO hoped to use the election to spread COFO's influence into areas the movement had not yet reached, particularly in the southern part of Mississippi. To do so, COFO needed outside assistance. Still, for the first time, black activists openly questioned the wisdom of a plan that would send white canvassers into black Mississippi for a brief period of time, let them run the show, and then allow them to leave.

The Freedom Vote gathered more than 83,000 ballots, many of them through the mail from voters who could not afford to be seen in public at the Freedom Polls. The figure fell well short of COFO's goal, but it did generate some needed publicity and momentum. COFO used the vote to spread its project into all five of Mississippi's congressional districts for the first time, and the vote itself was a powerful educational tool. Timid blacks could no longer tell canvassers that voting was white folks' business, because a substantial number of their comrades had just voted. Those who did vote learned that there was nothing magical about the act of voting itself. As John Dittmer has noted, the experience may also have led many to the realization that neither of the national political parties truly had the interests of poor, rural blacks at the top of its agenda. The vote was an important first step toward "encourag[ing] local people to develop their own political institutions designed to address problems they identified" themselves. SNCC fieldworkers learned yet another lesson from the experience: Lawrence Guyot noticed that FBI agents followed the white students wherever they went in Mississippi, keeping them out of harm's way. Bob Moses realized, "This election also makes it clear that the Negroes of Mississippi will not get the vote until the equivalent of an army is sent here."[63]

The results of the vote gave COFO a renewed sense of optimism. The organizers of the vote sent Senator Eastland a telegram in which they crowed that the Freedom Vote "demonstrate[d] that Mississippi Negroes have an urgent desire to vote. . . . We conclude that Negroes would vote if they were able to register, and that they would vote for candidates who stand for freedom. We believe that you have had continuing influence in preventing Negroes in Mississippi from registering to vote."[64] On April 2, Eastland had stood on the floor of the U.S. Senate with a straight face and stated that African Americans had not been prevented in any way from registering or voting in Mississippi.[65]

To capitalize on the momentum they had gained from the vote, COFO's leaders began discussing a major project for the following summer. One possibility was to bring an even larger group of white college students into the state for a similar program to get out the vote in the 1964 national and statewide elections. A week after the Freedom Vote, COFO's staffers met for a workshop in Greenville to discuss the movement's next move. Moses seems to have taken it for granted that the movement should recruit more white volunteers for an increased push the following summer, but he had little support among the rank and file of COFO fieldworkers. Lawrence Guyot explained the friction: "[A] large number of people on the staff at the time had not excelled in intellectual rigors. Some of 'em couldn't read and write, but my God, they could do anything else . . . and did." The fieldworkers had shed blood, sweat, and tears for more than a year now, and their work among local people was beginning to pay off. Now, "here they were faced with competing in this newly found constituency that had developed respect for them . . . with these white, competent people."[66]

Charles Cobb, who did not have to bow to anyone's intellectual abilities, objected to including white volunteers in another major project for a different reason: "[I]t was a concession," he later said. "You're conceding that you're not able to deal with the situation."[67] Cobb's protest was reasonable and accurate, but in objective retrospect, this concession was no defeat: no one should have been able to cope with the violence in the state.

Still, there were sound criticisms of the plan to be overcome: several of the Freedom Vote volunteers had struck the COFO organizers as arrogant dictators, and Lowenstein's role in their recruitment had confused the chain of command. On one occasion, a volunteer had refused to obey directives from Moses, the Freedom Vote coordinator, because he understood that he was to answer only to Lowenstein. Willie Peacock, a Mississippi native whom Moses had recruited into SNCC, described another problem: "[I]f you bring white people to Mississippi and say, 'Negro, go and vote,' [many blacks will say,] 'Yassah, we'll go and try to register and vote.'" By itself, this approach could prove counterproductive in the long run.[68]

Guyot and Hamer alone among the COFO foot soldiers supported Moses' vision for a summer project. Guyot, the classic political realist, remembered the federal protection that had shielded white volunteers during the Freedom Vote. Hamer argued simply (and persuasively), "If we're trying to break down this barrier of segregation, we can't segregate ourselves." Everyone agreed that voter registration should remain a major initiative, and most agreed that black Mississippians needed political candidates for whom the new registrants could vote with pride. The creation of an alternative to the state's "regular" Democratic Party would therefore have to be a goal of the summer program. Dave Dennis, CORE's field director for Mississippi and Moses' first lieutenant in COFO, pushed his vision for community centers that would provide a broad range of educational and recreational services for poor blacks, eventually forming a nucleus for community organizing. Charles Cobb sketched his plan for an alternative school system. The broad outlines for the ambitious project that would be known as "Freedom Summer" came into focus. Somewhere along the way, the conferees went along with Moses and dropped their opposition to including white volunteers.[69]

COFO recruited college students from every corner of the country for the project that became known as Freedom Summer.[70] They planned to gather in June at Western College for Women in Oxford, Ohio, where veteran Mississippi activists would teach the volunteers organizing skills and the racial etiquette of the Magnolia State.

On June 8, McLaurin, James Charles Black (an eighteen-year-old day laborer from Ruleville), and three others left the Delta for Atlanta, where they were to attend a final SNCC planning meeting before the Freedom Summer training sessions began in Ohio. Late that night, a state highway patrolman pulled them over in Lowndes County, Mississippi, near the Alabama border. He spotted summer project brochures and campaign literature for Fannie Lou Hamer in the back seat and hissed, "You goddamned niggers are trying to ruin our way of life." The Lowndes County sheriff then arrived on the scene in an equally foul mood. According to affidavits from the civil rights workers, he punched Black, the driver, about twenty times, then used his blackjack to force him to the ground. "While he was beating me he asked if any white folks had ever treated me bad; I told him yes and he hit me again," Black said.[71]

The law officers transported the group to the county jail. In the sheriff's office, they asked Black if he was "a Negro or a nigger." "A Negro," he answered. The highway patrolman resumed beating him with the black-jack and repeated the question. Black could tell where this was headed, so this time he answered, "A nigger," and was released. The sheriff and pa-trolman repeated the process with each occupant of the car. At one point, Sam Block, one of the civil rights workers, heard the jailer say, "The river's just right [for dumping a body]; let's carry them out and rifle them right now." The civil rights workers were never allowed to make a phone call or consult a lawyer. On the following morning, the five were tried before a county magistrate without a lawyer present, and Black was found guilty of reckless driving—a charge he vehemently denied—and fined $7. The other four were charged $4 apiece for a night's room and board in their cramped cell. After paying the fines—plus an additional $2.08 to get their car out of storage—the crew was back on its way to Atlanta, each of them bruised and bloodied. A week later, they arrived in Ohio for the training session. The white college volunteers wondered why McLaurin wore dark sun-glasses all the time.[72]

I inquired further as to the COFO activity in and around Indianola since I observed several Negroes in the courthouse halls being talked to by a beatnik white youth. I was told by Sheriff Holloway that the white youth was Charles Scattergood, age twenty-four, whose home address is 2514 N. 24th Street, Arlington, Virginia. ... He was coaching some Negro women as to how to pass the voter registration tests. ... He has every earmark and has the background and activity of being a young communist. He is being assisted by a Negro youth from Birmingham, Alabama, by the name of John Harris. Sunflower County, it appears, is in for a thorough working over by this type of agent.

State Sovereignty Commission Investigation Report, 1964

CHAPTER FIVE

Sunflower County Is in for a Thorough Working Over

Freedom Summer and After

While COFO trained volunteers for the Freedom Summer project in Ohio, officials in Mississippi prepared for their arrival. Shortly before the volunteers appeared, the state legislature passed a "criminal syndicalism" statute prohibiting anyone in the state from teaching or advocating "a change in agriculture or industrial ownership or control or in affecting any political or social change." The State Sovereignty Commission also investigated rumors that white hate groups were preparing to import huge weapons shipments into the state to preempt the coming "invasion," even as the commission's investigators canvassed the state for incriminating information on civil rights activists.[1] Before Freedom Summer even began, the state of Mississippi was well on its way to proving exactly the point that the project was designed to publicize: that the U.S. Constitution was not the law of the land in the Magnolia State.

At the Ohio training center, COFO veterans ran workshops on Mississippi's political and economic history and taught the volunteers how to protect themselves from police batons and dog bites. After a well-publicized incident in which Mississippi veterans took the volunteers to task for underestimating the resolve of powerful white racists, the volunteers came to expect the absolute worst from Mississippi. By the end of training, the volunteers took an almost perverse pleasure in the reception that they anticipated, especially after John Doar of the U.S. Justice Department warned them not to expect federal protection. "There is no federal police force," he said in Oxford.[2]

When the volunteers who had been assigned to Sunflower County arrived in Ruleville, however, the atmosphere was anticlimactic. "We were really expecting worse," one wrote home. "Most of us would not have been too surprised if everybody had been arrested as we crossed the Miss. border and/or beaten."[3] Upon arrival, they learned that Ruleville's Mayor Dorrough had prepared for their visit by telling local blacks that the volunteers were coming to kill them. The sense of high adventure many volunteers had brought to Ruleville gave way to absurdity. Days later, however, the volunteers learned the sobering news that three COFO workers—whom some of the Ruleville volunteers had befriended at the training session in Oxford—had been "held for questioning" following a traffic stop in Philadelphia, a small town in Neshoba County in the central part of Mississippi, and had disappeared. They were assumed dead. McLaurin had been "held for questioning" in a similar situation less than a month before. His mind began racing, but he remained outwardly calm. Tracy Sugarman, a participant-observer of the summer project in Ruleville who both canvassed voters and covered the project for CBS News, marveled at McLaurin's cool composure as the civil rights veteran set up a communications system in Sanctified Quarter. He hoped it would prevent a similar tragedy from occurring in his own project.

The disappearance of the workers gave a terrible legitimacy to the argument that national attention would focus on Mississippi only after whites had spilled some blood. Taped White House telephone conversations show that President Johnson was quick to act on the disappearance. He immediately lit a fire under FBI director J. Edgar Hoover, who in turn sent additional agents to Mississippi; the state capital of Jackson would eventually house the largest FBI field office in the country. On June 23, two days after the three had disappeared, Johnson phoned Senator Eastland for advice on the matter. Eastland deemed the disappearance "a publicity stunt." The civil rights workers had not really disappeared, he informed the president, because "there's not a Ku Klux Klan in that area, there's not a Citizens' Council in that area, there's no organized men in that area, so that's why I think it's a publicity stunt."[4]

A subsequent investigation revealed that Neshoba County's deputy sheriff Cecil Price, a member of the Klan, had stopped the trio—James Chaney, Andrew Goodman, and Michael Schwerner—on the afternoon of June 21, then held them for questioning until after ten o'clock that night. When the three left the Philadelphia jail, Price again stopped their car and handed the civil rights workers over to fellow Klansmen. Chaney, Goodman, and Schwerner were murdered and buried within an earthen dam, where their bodies remained hidden until early August.[5]

Mississippi governor Paul Johnson Jr. explained to President Johnson that cofo's "professional agitators" had simply gotten the college volunteers in over their heads and that these agitators bore the responsibility for the three civil rights workers' disappearance. "This sort of a thing could not have been prevented, no matter what anyone had done," he told the president. "It's an isolated incident." Lyndon Johnson disagreed. "I think we're gonna have a *looong* summer." Governor Johnson had reason to stonewall the investigation. His State Sovereignty Commission had provided a description of the core veteran Schwerner, his car, and its license tag to county sheriffs across the state, including Neshoba County sheriff Lawrence Rainey.[6]

The Freedom Summer project got off to a horrible start. In Ruleville, the project workers accepted the news and pressed on in their tasks, considerably more sober than they had been when they arrived. The volunteers began to have nightmares. Ruleville volunteer Heather Tobis wrote to her brother Jon, "Last night I was a long time before sleeping, although I was extremely tired. Every shadow, every noise—the bark of a dog, the sound of a car—in my fear and exhaustion was turned into a terrorist's approach." Tobis sang freedom songs to herself to relax. "The songs help to dissipate the fear," she wrote. "Some of the words in the songs do not hold real meaning of their own, others become rather monotonous—but when they are sung in unison, or sung silently by oneself, they take on new meaning beyond words or rhythm."[7]

For obvious reasons, life among the poor blacks of Ruleville took some getting used to for the white college students. One awestruck volunteer wrote home soon after arrival, "There are people here without food and clothing. Kids that eat a bit of bread for breakfast, chicken necks for dinner. Kids that don't have clothes to go to school in." The problem of social niceties loomed large in the initial relationships between volunteers and grateful locals. One volunteer despaired, "I felt that at any moment they would be willing to say 'Ma'am' to me if I should raise my voice. How can I help create an honest relationship after years of lies, of words that came from the lips and not the heart?"[8]

The volunteers acclimated themselves to life in the Delta, a transformation made somewhat easier by the heavy amount of work to be done in the early weeks of the campaign. Sympathizers across the country had responded to SNCC's urgent appeals for bail money and supplies at the outset of the summer, and when the volunteers arrived in Ruleville, their first task was to sort through more than 7,000 books that had been donated to the Delta's Freedom Schools. COFO staff continued to organize mass meetings, and volunteers scattered throughout the community asking people to attend and participate. At the first mass meeting of the summer, they heard Charles McLaurin tell stories about how he had been beaten for his civil rights activities in Columbus (he had by this point accumulated twenty-one arrests since his jailing at the state fair demonstration) and why he believed it was important to continue the struggle. He beseeched his listeners to try to register to vote. The mass meetings allowed wary sharecroppers to begin to realize their strength in numbers, their mass aspirations.[9]

"What Is Relevant to Our Lives Is Constantly Defined for Us"

Soon the volunteers had the Ruleville Freedom School up and running. The Freedom School was open to anyone who wanted to attend, and in Ruleville it seems to have appealed equally to teenagers and to illiterate adults who wanted to learn at least enough to pass the county's complicated voter registration tests. The institution of the Freedom School was essential to the creation of an alternative movement culture. For Freedom Summer to have a lasting impact, it would have to create new institutions in the African American community that could sustain themselves. It would have to begin the process of teaching black Mississippians a new system of values, completely different from that of the white-supremacist system under which they had been educated to that point.

To that end, the creation of Freedom Schools comprised the main impetus of the summer project. In 1963, Charles Cobb had reported from the Delta his realization "that oppression and restriction is not limited to the bullets of local racists['] shotgun blasts, or assaults at county courthouses, or the expulsion of sharecroppers from plantations." Rather, the larger culture of Mississippi—"radio, T.V., newspapers, etc."—was the real oppressor, the force that most restricted the minds of black Deltans and kept them inferior. Aurelia Norris Young, a leader of the Jackson movement, later remembered, "Back in the thirties and forties there were few positive black images in Mississippi, because we had no newspapers, we had no TV, no radio." "What is relevant to our lives," Cobb despaired, "is constantly defined for us." At the core of SNCC's philosophy was a movement to help black Mississippians make these decisions for themselves. Creating an alternative educational system was the starting point.[10]

Mississippi schools trained blacks to be subservient farm laborers and nothing else. Fannie Lou Hamer noted pointedly, "We Negroes know Mississippi education hasn't prepared us to live in any other state." Racist white individuals and institutions defined what was acceptable for black Mississippians—what constituted a "qualified voter," just as they had once decided who was a "good nigger"—and the larger culture allowed it. Black Mississippians were just beginning to question the assumptions behind this system, Cobb claimed in 1963, and that was an important first step that COFO could not afford to waste. "If we are concerned about breaking the power structure," Cobb argued, "then we have to be concerned about building our own institutions to replace the old, unjust, decadent ones which make up the existing power structure."[11]

For Cobb, the key to the alternative educational system would have to be instigating students to question everything around them. "To encourage questions is to encourage challenge, which is to encourage overthrow," Cobb reasoned. Every question had a ripple effect: "To talk about why a policeman hits a Negro across the head is to talk about why that policeman does not feel responsible to Negroes, and who he is responsible to, and why they don't feel responsible to Negroes, and what can be done to make them feel responsible, or who can be placed in those positions that will feel responsible, and how they can be placed in those positions, and whether or not those positions are necessary."[12]

Cobb's questions illustrated the assumptions behind SNCC's organizing strategy. Rather than organize the social classes and individuals that the larger society defined as natural "leaders"—black teachers, clergymen, and business owners—SNCC's mantra was "Let the people decide." (Indeed, when they moved into Ruleville, Cobb and McLaurin found that teachers and preachers were "the most hated people in the community.") Organizers like Cobb and McLaurin were to raise questions and educate—by offering help, not by lecturing. "The people" were perfectly capable of choosing their own leaders. The strategy would bear fruit over the next several months and years. If enough people questioned the "authority" that Cobb discussed, then the concept of authority would have to be re-defined so that people could make the decisions on issues that affected them purely by themselves. To reach that lofty goal, however, he and his fellow SNCC workers had to define political problems in the simplest and most local terms possible, then work up the scale to analyzing and resisting systems of oppression.

To become first-class citizens in the larger culture, Cobb theorized, African Americans would have to define for themselves how they related to the larger culture. In Sunflower County, that meant creating an entirely new educational system. Cobb knew that the segregated school system in Mississippi intentionally kept African Americans separate, ignorant, and afraid. Local people had come to resent the black teachers and principals who ran the inferior schools, in some cases for very legitimate reasons. Poor parents were constantly asked to come up with money for vaguely defined school fund-raisers—candy sales, cosmetic sales, doughnut sales, raffles—that they had reason to expect lined the pockets of black school officials. The school schedule also allowed practices under which schools forced students to pick cotton and assured that non-air-conditioned black schools were in session during the hottest part of the year, while white students were on vacation.

Irene Johnson could not help noticing that shortly after her own children and their schoolmates raised money for a new school bus, the principal of Ruleville Central High School bought a broken-down bus for the school and a new car for himself. There were reports that students who did not raise enough money either received failing grades in their courses or were suspended from school until they could come up with the ransom.

The worst indignity was the forced picking of cotton to raise money for the schools. For as long as anyone could remember, black students had gone to school on schedules that made them available for cotton chopping in the early summer and for picking in the late fall. By the 1960s, the practice of black principals renting out the labor of their students during picking season was common throughout the county. Students were told that their labor was raising money for the schools, but they suspected otherwise. One angry student affirmed that he and his classmates had spent several days working in the fields without lunch. "We did not get paid for our work in the fields picking cotton," he complained to SNCC workers. "When we returned from the field the teacher would go to the principal's office. I think the teacher gave the money for picking cotton to the principal. As far as I know the curtains in the gymnasium were the only things purchased [for the school] with the money." Black students in Ruleville lodged complaints with Cobb about everything from the state of their schoolbooks to the practice of forcing students who did not produce money they were to have raised into begging for it in the street.[13]

Cobb tapped into a ready-made topic of concern. By 1963, the rank and file of African Americans in Ruleville were thoroughly disgusted with the town's educational system. Parents were tired of the system's second-class and underfunded facilities but were even more offended by what local people perceived as a failure of black teachers and school administrators to speak up for the community and demand better, if not equal, schools from the state of Mississippi. Fairly or not, local people increasingly perceived black teachers and administrators as parasites sucking from African Americans' scant resources, not as leaders in the community. It was easy and natural for the civil rights workers to exploit this common complaint, but it remained for them to provide an alternative.

Cobb looked to the schools as a means of consciousness-raising. He stripped the concept of public education to its roots and saw that school systems teach values. An alternative school system could teach alternative values, which would be crucial to the creation of a movement culture. In the words of Liz Fusco, a Freedom Summer volunteer in Ruleville who would later become state coordinator of the Freedom Schools, Cobb's vision encompassed a revolution in black Mississippi "more revolutionary than voter registration alone: more personal, and in a sense more transforming, than a political program."[14]

To break the bonds of the hegemonic power Sunflower County whites held over the majority of their neighbors, the movement would have to begin by attacking on the most local level possible, at the most basic building block of education. The people who had begun to ask the kinds of questions that Cobb described had no alternative to the Mississippi schools. Because the existing education system was not "geared to the relevancies [local people] discover while building this new life," the civil rights workers would have to create an institution to fill that void. Cobb asked COFO to take that responsibility, to create an educational system whose goals were not the "development of intellectual skills, but a preparation for participation in living" as free and equal citizens of a democratic republic.[15] The idea for the Freedom Schools was born.

In the early months of 1964, SNCC staffers argued about what should be taught in the schools, how, and by whom. Staughton Lynd, a white radical historian from Yale University, oversaw the development of the curriculum and eventually "imposed a kind of beautiful order on the torment" that characterized the SNCC bull sessions on curriculum. The program that emerged was heavy on African American history, civics, and the arts. Above all, it encouraged students—most of them schoolchildren, but many of them adults who wanted to learn to read along the way to becoming full citizens—to ask questions that did not have easy answers.[16]

After one class studied documents regarding the history of slavery and abolition, the teacher asked, "[W]hat do you think about Frederick Douglass's talking so straight to the President of the United States?" Taking the question a step further, the teacher asked, "[H]ow does the picture of [SNCC's] Jim Forman in the Emancipation Proclamation issue of *Ebony* suggest that same kind of straight talking?" In another instance, the questions for discussion were even more loaded: "[W]ho do you think the movement is proving right—Booker T. Washington or W. E. B. Du Bois? And what comment on your own upbringing is made by the fact that you all knew about Booker T. Washington but most of you had never heard of W. E. B. Du Bois?"[17]

Even approaching these questions required an intellectual curiosity and a political sophistication that Sunflower County's black schools, which were dependent upon the generosity of powerful whites, had never attempted to teach. (In fairness, few American schools have ever tried to teach the way the Freedom Schools did, either.) According to radical historian Howard Zinn, a part-time Freedom School teacher himself, the schools were an experiment "that cannot be assessed in the usual terms of 'success' and 'failure,'" a unique "combination of disorder and inspiration." They violated every tenet of classic American educational orthodoxy.[18] And by every single account, Sunflower County's Freedom School students responded beautifully to the program.

The Ruleville Freedom School materials housed in the archives of the Martin Luther King, Jr., Center for Nonviolent Social Change are revelatory. Classroom compositions illustrate the enthusiasm with which students responded to the radical curriculum, and they demonstrate that increasing self-esteem among students was a valuable by-product of the schools' program. Asked to describe how it felt to be a Negro in Mississippi, thirteen-year-old Jerry Shields responded, "I feel that it is very bad in Mississippi because most of the people are afraid to vote. . . . The white[s] don't want to communicate with us because they say we haven't gotten any sense and we are ignorant." Willie Shields, a fifteen-year-old, equivocated: "I feel good about being a Negro in Mississippi, but I want all of my freedom and rights." Fourteen-year-old Flozell Shields wrote, "I feel very good to be a Negro." Nor was he ashamed of being poor. "[B]eing poor is not a sin. Because when God's son came into this world, he was born a poor baby. His mother and father were poor." The Freedom Schools allowed their students to hope. Shields used lessons he had learned from his Sunday school and African American history classes and applied them to the reality he experienced as a self-aware Afro-Mississippian and a member of the Freedom Struggle. "Before now the Negroes were something like slaves and are [still] slaves in a way," he wrote. "But in a little time the Negroes will be able to do what they would like to do. They will have better jobs and better homes and many other things that I think Negroes should have."[19]

Freedom School compositions show how clearly lessons on the history of the antislavery struggle resonated with Mississippi blacks more than a century after emancipation. Bettye Butler wrote, "To have freedom means a lot to me. To have freedom is a rejoice for life. . . . Maybe some day I'll have the freedom I've been waiting for so long." Charles Evans promised, "We will like freedom in Mississippi if we can get it." Lessons on the struggle for freedom echoed contemporaneous discussions on the public accommodations bill being debated in Congress. (Eastland called the bill, which would become the Civil Rights Act in 1964, a "complete blueprint for the totalitarian state.") Willie Shields noted, "I don't have all of my freedom of speech, freedom of going in any place I want, I don't have the freedom to go with white boy[s] and girl[s]." Willie Hatchett complained, "Negroes do not have their freedom to go in any place they wish to go, because some of the white people think we [are not] good enough for them."[20]

Taken as a whole, the Freedom Schools' students deemed the experiment a resounding success. Ruleville's Bessie Mae Herring explained, "I have learned a very much more this summer than I learned in many many years. This have been a great summer and I hope what we did will not be in vain. . . . Freedom School ment more to me than I can explain." Gertrude Beverly determined simply, "I don't thank nothing could have come to Ruleville eny better than the Summer Project." At the end of the summer, Rennie Williams concluded, "I am sorry that our school is closing. I pray God we will meet again soon."[21]

Kirsty Powell, the class's teacher, was no less enthusiastic and encouraged by the experience. "I have enjoyed Freedom School because I am a teacher, and I love to teach people who want to learn," she wrote in her own assessment. "And because I love to read, I have been happy when I felt you were enjoying reading too." Powell, in fact, thought she had gained more from the experience than any of her students. "I have learned a great deal from Freedom School," she wrote, "because it is the first time in my life I have ever been part of a movement where together people were standing up to work for freedom and for a better world. It is good to have even a tiny part in a great work like this."[22] Freedom School teachers throughout the county had similar reactions to the project. One wrote of a Freedom School's students, "I can see the change. The 16 year-old's discovery of poetry, of Whitman and Cummings above all, the struggle to express thoughts in words, to translate ideas into concrete written words." The students' changes were evident far beyond the classroom, too: "After two weeks a child finally looks me in the eye, unafraid, acknowledging a bond of trust which 300 years of Mississippians said should never, could never exist. I can feel the growth of self-confidence [in my students]."[23] A true movement culture finally began to take hold in Ruleville.

Extending the Movement Culture

The Ruleville Freedom School was firmly established by the end of June, but the Freedom Summer staff and volunteers had not yet set up a beachhead outside of Fannie Lou Hamer's town. Charles McLaurin first tried to spread the summer project into Drew, the cotton mill town north of Ruleville. Ruleville teenagers who had joined the movement began canvassing in Drew, but McLaurin warned them, "We don't want to be in Drew after dark." If Mayor Charles Dorrough treated Ruleville as his personal fiefdom, Mayor W. O. "Snake" Williford ran Drew as his own police state. Drew whites were considered the most recalcitrant of Sunflower County, and perhaps of the state.

The town's proximity to Parchman Penitentiary had throughout its history made Drew a dangerous place to be black. In the 1930s and 1940s, overzealous (or sadistic) lawmen in Drew had used the cover of escaped prisoners to shoot unarmed blacks with regularity. If anyone questioned the murders, they deadpanned, "We thought he looked like he'd escaped from Parchman." Black life at Parchman was worth next to nothing. There was also talk among Sunflower County blacks about a sharecropper named Joe Pullum who had been lynched near Drew sometime in the 1920s, but only after he had killed thirteen and injured twenty-six members of the lynch mob.[24] Mae Bertha Carter, whose family sharecropped on plantations near Drew for decades before they moved into town, remembered at least two other lynchings. Her uncle was one of the victims.[25]

When local people from Drew finally agreed to attend a Ruleville mass meeting, they were introduced to "tremendous applause," according to

David Halberstam, who reported on the meeting for the *New York Times*. "You don't know what a victory it is even to get the Drew people over here," a Freedom Summer volunteer told Halberstam. "We've got to go to Drew and help those people to loosen up," said Irene Johnson, an enthusiastic student in the Ruleville Freedom School and a local leader. "We've got to make them realize what's going on in this country because they've been living in such fear over there."[26]

McLaurin led the first organized canvassing effort into Drew on June 24, but a stream of cars and pickups full of angry and armed whites forced the civil rights workers back to Ruleville. McLaurin and the others were lucky to get out alive, but as they left, McLaurin promised the blacks in Drew who peeked out from their porches, "We'll be back!" On July 14, they returned to distribute leaflets announcing Drew's first mass civil rights meeting. Williford had eight of them arrested for leafleting without a permit and set bail at a minimum of $100. Williford told one of the white volunteers he arrested that "livin' with niggers [was] un-American and un-Christian" and that the volunteers were "Communist and a disgrace to the white race."[27]

The meeting in Drew went on as planned the following evening, but because no church was willing to let the movement use its building— Williams Chapel in Ruleville having recently been firebombed after opening its doors to the Freedom Riders—McLaurin planned to hold the rally in a church's front yard. Student volunteers and movement people from Ruleville and interested teenagers from Drew filled the yard and began to sing freedom songs. A group of black Drew men gathered across the street, separated from the meeting by twenty police officers and deputized white citizens. (Drew residents told the civil rights workers that the Citizens' Council had met that morning, perhaps to plan this police presence.) Immediately, two student volunteers were arrested for passing out sheets of paper with freedom song lyrics, and five others were then arrested for blocking a sidewalk. McLaurin abandoned the freedom songs and went to the edge of the street, yelling above the heads of the policemen to the African American men of Drew who had gathered to watch: "We want all the responsibilities of citizenship. Not tomorra! Now! . . . You're payin' first class taxes, but you're lettin' Mister Charlie keep you second-class citizens!" He crossed the street and began circulating among the men, trying and failing to get even one of the silent men to sign the freedom registration form. Disgusted by their timidity, he yelled, "[I]f you don't sign up to go down to register to vote in Indianola—you say to the white man, 'Don't treat me like a man. Treat me like a boy! We've got to stand up!" But the men knew that under the watchful eyes of the nearby "police force," no one could afford to be the first to sign up. Consequently, none of them did. The atmosphere of terror and suppression hung over the town like the sword of Damocles, waiting to drop. McLaurin and the remaining volunteers retreated to Ruleville again. In the end, McLaurin was forced to decide that "Drew was a pocket of resistance that cost too much to take."[28]

In Indianola, cofo continued to butt against the caution of the town's African American clergymen well into July. To begin creating a movement in Indianola, cofo needed a base of operations along the lines of Ruleville's Williams Chapel. No Indianola church was willing to provide that base.[29] Without a local leader or a base of operations, volunteers from Ruleville began traveling to Indianola a handful at a time as inconspicuously as possible, nagging black pastors and trying to create a groundswell among their congregants. According to another volunteer, they were "delighted with the quick response they . . . found," especially among the town's high school students. By late June, they had drummed up enough interest among Indianola teenagers to hold an outdoor mass meeting. When the cofo workers rolled into Indianola it was raining heavily, but a young man standing in the middle of the downpour demanded, "Where have you people been? We've been waitin' and waitin'!"[30]

McLaurin scouted out the town a little more methodically and found a structure that several of the black Baptist churches owned jointly and had been using half-heartedly as a school building. The structure was perfect for Freedom Summer's purposes: it had one spacious meeting room and indoor plumbing. "It's great!" McLaurin exulted. "It's not only great, it's brick!" It would be hard to burn down. Because several congregations owned the building jointly—and had title over it, making it impervious to Citizens' Council pressure—the churches' decision also served the purpose of getting the pushy, nagging civil rights workers off of several backs at once. Now the pastors could stop worrying about putting their own churches in harm's way.[31]

By mid-August, cofo had assigned several civil rights workers to the new center at the Indianola Baptist school building. The workers canvassed the county seat and felt confident enough to call a mass meeting within two weeks. McLaurin predicted that about ten people would show up. Instead, hundreds packed the hall, and for the first time many of them were middle-aged. The meeting commenced with a freedom song, but as sncc staffer John Harris was introducing McLaurin, who was to lead the event, an uninvited guest, Nathaniel Jack, burst in. "Slim," as everyone in Indianola knew him, had been a charter member of the Indianola branch of the NAACP in the 1950s, a close friend of Clint Battle's father. He was now the first and only African American police officer in the state of Mississippi. Black Indianolans considered him a mean sonofabitch. Indianola's chief of police had promised COFO that there would be no harassment, but Jack entered the mass meeting and pulled his service revolver on McLaurin and Rabbi Al Levine, a volunteer, when they asked him to leave. This quelled the meeting's enthusiasm.

McLaurin took advantage of the situation, however, telling the crowd that he knew all about Slim and why he was there. McLaurin informed the audience that he had learned something from an arrest in neighboring Leflore County. A white police official there told him, "If a white policeman shoots a Negro, you have a racial crisis. But if a Negro policeman shoots a Negro, you don't have a racial crisis." After a long dramatic pause, McLaurin shouted, "And that's why they hired Slim!"[32] Flashing the flexibility and the political didactics that successful political organizers have to demonstrate in trying circumstances, McLaurin turned what could have been an embarrassing setback into a dramatic political lesson. Fortunately for McLaurin, Jack backed down.

To the civil rights workers' delight, the preliminary energy they had devoted to Indianola paid off with great momentum after this climactic breakthrough. Students at Indianola's Gentry High School organized a formal chapter of the Mississippi Student Union, which was in essence a youth wing of the youthful SNCC, and participated as canvassers for the Freedom Summer project. As fruitless as the aborted attempts at organizing Indianola had seemed in 1962 and 1963, the town was by the end of Freedom Summer a bubbling movement center. High school students and older Indianola blacks kept the Freedom School packed. Before long, younger adults like Oscar Giles and his wife Alice, who owned a small grocery store in town, and Bernice White, who taught school in neighboring Leflore County and was therefore slightly less vulnerable to white economic pressures, began to attend mass meetings. According to McLaurin, between 1962 and 1964, "Our aim was to get the grass roots, because we knew that there would be more of them. Once we got the masses together, we could *push* the elites, those professionals and others, because they would have to either come along or get run over. That's just the way we felt about it."[33] The civil rights workers did organize the grass roots first, in Ruleville and later in Indianola. Once groups like the National Council of Churches and the National Council of Negro Women got behind Freedom Summer, the black middle class of Indianola also began to lend its support to the movement.[34]

"Ain't gonna let nobody turn me 'round." Charles Cobb and Charles McLaurin
(second and third from left) lead a freedom song at a Ruleville mass meeting.
(Danny Lyon/Magnum Photos)

Prior to Freedom Summer, McLaurin's missives to the VEP included at least a dozen reports detailing unsuccessful trips to Indianola. In one, from April 20, 1963, he wrote, "I went into the Negro community [of Indianola] to talk with the people who might be able to help me. I was trying to get names of some of the ministers who might have church[es] in the city. . . . I got the addresses of some of the ministers with large churches, who I am planning to contact about using their churches [for] mass meetings, and Voter Registration workshops." Again on April 24 he wrote, "On Monday, April 29, I will go to Indianola, Mississippi to see if I can really get started to registering Negroes to vote." But on June 16 he referred to the "so[-]called Negro leaders of Indianola," who were more interested in trying "to get the city to build them a swimming pool" than in leading a social movement.[35] The struggle to create a people's movement in the county seat was a long one.

When the movement did finally make it to Indianola, McLaurin applied lessons he had already learned in Ruleville and in a shorter campaign in Greenville. By the end of 1963, before Freedom Summer even began, the

Ruleville movement was essentially a self-sustaining one. McLaurin stepped to the side and Joe McDonald led mass meetings. McDonald also took responsibility for the periodic trips to the registrar's office in Indianola. Fannie Lou Hamer developed into a full-scale movement leader in her own right and began to expand her influence far beyond the county. The Ruleville movement's core consisted of teenagers, older men and women, and a small number of independent businessmen. When this base had been consolidated and it became possible to expand the movement to Indianola, McLaurin concentrated on an identical constituency. McLaurin had cultivated a cadre of devoted teenagers who did the bulk of the canvassing in Ruleville by mid-1963. When he tried to branch out into Greenville and Indianola in June, McLaurin realized that the strategy of organizing students provided the most immediate results. It also had the benefit of providing the possibility of greater long-term change. McLaurin first spent two weeks in Greenville trying to drum up support among young adults and middle-aged citizens. The tactic failed, and McLaurin decided to concentrate on organizing students, whom he then trained as canvassers. It may have been wishful thinking, but McLaurin claimed that the number of adults at the mass meetings increased exponentially after he had organized and trained the youngsters and sent them back into the community.[36]

In any case, McLaurin employed the tactics he and other SNCC workers had learned through a painstaking process of trial-and-error to great effect in Ruleville and, by the end of 1964, in Indianola. The SNCC workers' incessant canvassing had produced by the end of the year a movement culture that provided a legitimate alternative to the culture of the planters. All over Sunflower County, even in Drew, African Americans openly questioned the right of planters to run their lives. Mike Yarrow, a Ruleville Freedom Summer volunteer, witnessed the change in black attitudes toward white Sunflower Countians and the dismay that the change elicited in whites. "Time and again [the whites] talk about how we are just spoiling a beautiful relationship," Yarrow wrote home from Ruleville. "They take great pride in their solicitude for Negroes. When I ask Negroes about whether whites are just lying or really think they are good to the colored, Negroes always answer that they are lying."[37]

Yarrow said that blacks could cite without difficulty instances in which whites who claimed to be great friends of the black people had beaten up blacks, or worse. "What's more," Yarrow wrote, "the lopsided power relationship in this system makes the Negro lie to whites in order to stay alive. This lying reinforces the whites' illusion and destroys the Negro's self-respect."[38] By the end of Freedom Summer, however, the shuffling, deferential attitude that Yarrow described among Sunflower County blacks competed with a new, assertive attitude, particularly among teenagers. It seemed obvious that at least a vocal minority of black Sunflower Countians would no longer defer to whites as they had in the past. It remained, however, for McLaurin, Hamer, and others to translate this new attitude into real political power.

"We Must All Work to Make the Preamble to the Constitution a Reality"

To that end, COFO laid the groundwork for an alternative to the omnipotent Mississippi Democratic Party. In the one-party state of Mississippi, the Democratic Party was arguably the most repressive of all the institutions that maintained white hegemony. The Mississippi Freedom Democratic Party (MFDP), as the alternative party was named, was a logical outgrowth of the Freedom Votes that were first held in 1963. Every aspect of Freedom Summer described what the civil rights movement was *against* in Mississippi. The MFDP did as much as anything else to describe what the movement was *for*: democracy, defined as broadly as it ever has been in the American experience. When William Scott of Indianola was asked to give a short speech at the Sunflower County chapter meeting of the MFDP in August 1964, he said, "We must all work to make the preamble to the Constitution a reality so we can all celebrate the Fourth of July." There is not a more succinct statement of the MFDP's political vision. The Freedom Democrats took the democratic rhetoric of Lyndon Johnson, the national Democratic Party's leader, seriously and forced a showdown with Johnson that dared him to put his money where his mouth was at the 1964 national party convention in Atlantic City.[39]

Fannie Lou Hamer emerged in Atlantic City as the MFDP's unofficial public spokesperson, fresh from her experience as a candidate in the Democratic primary to be the representative for Mississippi's Second District in the U.S. House. That Hamer cast her first vote for herself in the spring of 1964 attests to the speed with which voter registration had changed the Delta's political landscape. Hamer received word that she had successfully registered to vote in January 1963, and she tried to vote in the Democratic primaries held that August. She was denied because she had not paid her poll tax for two consecutive years. In 1964, having paid her poll taxes, she ran for the U.S. House of Representatives against the powerful Jamie Whitten and voted for herself. As Hamer's biographer Kay Mills notes,

"The candidacy was doomed from the start, if the objective was winning the congressional seat." But this was not Hamer's sole objective. Hamer knew she would probably lose—even with a black majority—but ran to get blacks used to voting.[40] According to Charles McLaurin, Hamer hoped to help African Americans see that there was no mystery to the electoral process.

Hamer's campaign platform combined her lifelong commitment to interracial equality with the beginnings of an economic critique. "Mrs. Hamer said that all Mississippians suffered in their present circumstances and that their elected officials really didn't represent the people. She pledged that if elected, she would work hard to develop all parts of the state and help all people, regardless of race or personal circumstances."[41] Hamer's unofficial campaign slogan—which would be identified with her for the rest of her life and which now appears on her tombstone—was "I'm sick and tired of being sick and tired."

Charles McLaurin became Hamer's campaign manager by default. In early January, the MFDP's political scientist Lawrence Guyot called McLaurin and told him that Hamer would be running for Congress and that McLaurin had to drive her to the Mississippi secretary of state's office in Jackson by 5:00 that afternoon for her to qualify for the election. McLaurin told Hamer what they had to do. "Man, what do we know about runnin' for Congress?" she demanded, but Hamer prepared herself and made it to the state capitol in time to qualify for the election. They filled out the necessary forms and learned that they would have to pay a $500 fee. While Guyot tracked down the money, the secretary of state forced Hamer to name a campaign manager. Hamer took the demand in stride and said under her breath, "Shit, McLaurin, you're my campaign manager. You know as much about being a campaign manager as I know about being a Congressman."[42]

The campaign itself continued in a similar vein: on what could only charitably be described as a shoestring budget, Hamer traveled the Second District—which included the Delta and a few hill counties to the east—throughout the spring. Along the way, she spoke to as many African American church groups as her managers could assemble. At Hamer's first campaign appearance, in Ruleville, an armed, uniformed policeman and an armed white citizen arrested two campaign workers. "We don't have no nigger politics in Ruleville," the policeman told the pair. Hamer "feels that as an American citizen she has the right to conduct a campaign for Congress the way candidates all over the country do," her campaign literature announced. "People should have a right to choose their representatives, and you can't do that without the vote." These sentiments branded Hamer a dangerous threat in Sunflower County. Still, no one expected her to challenge Whitten seriously. Guyot, who realized that Hamer had no chance of winning an election, used the campaign to publicize the obstacles that Mississippi blacks faced as voters. Whitten crushed Hamer in the Democratic primaries, but she campaigned throughout Freedom Summer as the MFDP's candidate for office in the fall's general election.[43]

The MFDP occupied a middle ground from 1964 to 1968. It strained to include both the black Mississippians who still believed that mainstream electoral politics had rewards to offer them and the black citizens of the state who distrusted politics but wanted to create autonomous black institutions. The tensions inherent in such an effort eventually proved powerful enough that the party disintegrated without ever achieving practical successes. But at the end of Freedom Summer, the MFDP seemed full of promise. As a conclusion to Freedom Summer, COFO prepared a challenge to the "regular" Mississippi Democratic Party at the Democratic National Convention, and the challenge appeared—on paper, at least—to have a real chance of succeeding.

In July, COFO's Bob Moses advised the Freedom Summer project staffers who were not working in the Freedom Schools to shift their focus from registering voters to organizing for the MFDP. Warning that "[t]he various political programs which comprise the Freedom Democratic Party's Convention Challenge are in very bad shape," Moses ordered every available hand to work on "the massive job which remains to be done in order to be prepared for the challenge."[44] If the MFDP could prove that its members had been consistently excluded from the regular party, the MFDP might stand a good chance of winning Mississippi's seats in Atlantic City. Joe Rauh, an attorney for the United Auto Workers and a major player in the District of Columbia Democratic Party, went to work on the MFDP's legal brief.

The "regular" Democrats made no attempt to open the party's doors to African American voters. The party's statewide convention in July began with a band playing "Dixie" and an invocation from the Reverend W. M. Cascade that affirmed, "The segregated way is the Christian way." Several delegates drove cars that had been festooned with Barry Goldwater bumper stickers to the convention.[45] Party literature boasted, "The Mississippi Democratic party, completely free of both national parties and solely an instrument of the citizens of this State, now is safely in the hands of a conservative, responsible majority of Mississippi voters."[46] Certainly the regular Democrats had no intention of supporting a ticket headed by

Lyndon Johnson after he had led the Civil Rights Act past Eastland and through Congress early that summer.

White Democrats in Mississippi had had a complicated relationship with the national party since at least 1948, when U.S. senators James Eastland and John Stennis and Governor Fielding Wright had led a Mississippi delegation to the convention of the States Rights Democratic (or "Dixiecrat") Party. The Dixiecrats had been put out by the national Democratic Party's sudden willingness to court black voters and support civil rights legislation. They had picked up their toys at the party's convention in Philadelphia and had gone home to Birmingham, where they nominated South Carolina governor J. Strom Thurmond to oppose Thomas Dewey and Harry Truman, the Republican and Democratic candidates for president. Mississippi's electoral votes, along with those of Louisiana, Alabama, and South Carolina, had gone to the States Rights Party in 1948, but the Dixiecrats' success was short-lived. Mississippi returned to the Democratic column with safe majorities in 1952 and 1956, though the state's electoral votes went to a slate of "unpledged electors" in 1960.[47]

The regulars knew that Lyndon Johnson feared a repeat of the 1948 southern walkout at Philadelphia and concluded that they could select their delegates as they wished in 1964 without fear of retribution from the national party. They had a strong friend in Senator Eastland, even if he shied away from the media attention that began to focus on the brewing delegate fight. He and Governor Paul B. Johnson Jr. filled the state's delegation with ultraconservative segregationists. By refusing to allow African Americans to participate in the party, they made the MFDP necessary in the first place.

The Freedom Democrats argued this very point. The brief they submitted to the credentials committee of the national party affirmed the MFDP's loyalty to the candidates and the ideals of the national party and questioned the regulars' motives. The major question before the national party, according to the Freedom Democrats, was "whether the National Democratic Party takes its place with the oppressed Negroes of Mississippi or their white oppressors, with those loyal to the National Democratic Party or those who have spewed hatred upon President Kennedy and President Johnson and the principles to which they dedicated their lives."[48]

The Freedom Democrats carefully documented their exclusion from precinct and state Democratic Party meetings. When both parties reached Atlantic City in August, the MFDP presented a carefully worded brief in support of its party's claim, buttressed by affidavits from would-be African American voters. The regulars backed their claim with a legal brief supported by materials that had been collected by the State Sovereignty Commission.[49] The Democratic Party's credentials committee would have to decide which delegation deserved to be seated.

Hamer's appearance before the convention's Credentials Committee seemed to make the national party's decision a simple one. On live national television, Hamer explained how she had been evicted from the Marlow plantation because she had tried to register to vote and how night riders had shot into the homes of other African Americans in Ruleville to dissuade them from registering. Hamer described her experience in a Winona, Mississippi, jail cell, where she had been beaten savagely on her way home to Ruleville from a citizenship training school. "All of this is on account of we want to register, to become first-class citizens, and if the Freedom Democratic Party is not seated now, I question America," Hamer boomed. "[I]s this America, the land of the free and the home of the brave where we have to sleep with our phones off the hooks because our lives be threatened daily because we want to live as decent human beings, in America?"[50] Hamer's address was followed immediately by an appearance from Rita Schwerner, the widow of one of the three martyred civil rights activists in Neshoba County. Surely, it seemed, the party would recognize the loyal Freedom Democrats and not the openly antagonistic, lily-white regulars, as the legitimate Democratic representatives of Mississippi.

However, in the new era of televised political conventions, Lyndon Johnson found it difficult to jettison the Mississippi regulars. He worried that a public embrace of the Freedom Democrats would initiate a massive walkout from southern white delegates on the floor of the convention. Indeed, as Hamer addressed the Credentials Committee, the president preempted national coverage of her speech by calling an impromptu press conference. (The tactic backfired; the networks merely waited until prime time to show Hamer's testimony in full.) Johnson did not want to be remembered as the Democratic president who wrecked his party over the issue of civil rights—"We will lose fifteen states without even campaigning [if we seat the MFDP]," Johnson told Hubert Humphrey—so he crafted what has been called a "compromise" meant to solve the seating controversy. Johnson passed the responsibility of selling the compromise on to Humphrey, who understood implicitly that he had to succeed if he wanted to become Johnson's vice president.[51]

Johnson manipulated the MFDP and civil rights leaders who attended the convention. The FBI bugged Martin Luther King's motel rooms and telephones and relayed the results of strategy sessions to the White House. (John Dittmer calls the Atlantic City campaign "a Watergate that worked,"

"All of this is on account of we want to register, to become first-class citizens, and if the Freedom Democratic Party is not seated now, I question America." Fannie Lou Hamer testifies at the 1964 Democratic National Convention. (Warren K. Leffler, U.S. News and World Report Collection, Library of Congress Prints & Photographs Division [LC-U9-12470-B-frame #17])

and Taylor Branch makes extensive use of FBI reports and White House telephone conversations in his treatment of the convention's proceedings.)[52] In essence, the MFDP had the compromise, which gave the party two at-large seats in the convention, accepted for it. Aaron Henry, the MFDP's chairman and one of two delegates who would be seated under the arrangement (Ed King, Henry's former running mate in the 1963 Freedom Vote, was the other), advised the group to accept the compromise.

McLaurin, an MFDP delegate from Sunflower County, had originally deferred to Aaron Henry and the national civil rights leaders who urged acceptance. He began to have second thoughts, however, when Bob Moses spoke up against the settlement. Finally, Hamer announced at a meeting that "[w]e didn't come all this way for no two seats!," and McLaurin made up his mind to reject the agreement. Hamer especially bristled at the treatment the MFDP received from Roy Wilkins, the executive secretary of the NAACP. According to Hamer, Wilkins tried to sell Johnson's compromise by telling her, "You don't know anything, you're ignorant, you don't know anything about politics. I been in the business twenty years. You people have put your point across, now why don't you pack up and go home?" For Hamer, this was among the first indications that the black middle class did not necessarily share her political goals.[53] The rift between MFDP chairman Henry and the party's rank-and-file would widen over the next several years.

In 1997, McLaurin described his 1964 self as a country boy who learned about big-time politics by the minute as he sat in on meetings with Joe Rauh and Walter Reuther and famous national politicians. He had originally favored accepting the compromise because he thought that it would immediately open doors for the MFDP's leaders and that these openings might eventually translate into increased opportunities for blacks throughout the state. "In other words, Mrs. Hamer, and Aaron Henry, and Ed King, could have been a big deal," he thought. Lyndon Johnson might have offered them appointed positions if the compromise went through without a hitch. "That could have opened up some opportunities, that's all I could see. Maybe something could have come out of that for me, that's all I could see. I didn't see the big picture."[54]

Hamer's refusal illuminated the big picture for McLaurin, who "got a lesson in what the movement was about. If they had taken that [compromise], the movement would have come to a standstill. They would have co-opted the people who were organizing, who were building this movement. That would have shut the rest of us up." The lesson for McLaurin was, "The movement was bigger than just getting some recognition. . . . I couldn't have gotten this lesson in school." McLaurin returned to Sunflower County and ran for a seat in the state senate. He knew that he could not win but hoped he could "raise the consciousness of the black people to the fact that they could run." He would have been satisfied, he said, to hear someone say, "There's ol' McLaurin, just a little country hick-town fella from Jackson, runnin' all around the Delta. If he run, and he don't get killed, [I can do it, too]."[55] By 1966, hundreds of African American candidates were running for political office all over Mississippi.

The End of Freedom Summer: A New Beginning

The Summer Project as a whole provided a decisive turning point in the history of race relations in Sunflower County. Ruleville was the site of the oldest and most entrenched freedom movement in the county, but even Indianola now had the framework of a justice movement that was broadly supported by the members of several black social classes. By the end of the summer, the national civil rights movement had won qualified support from the federal government. Lyndon Johnson pushed a strong civil rights bill outlawing the segregation of public facilities through Congress and signed it into law in June. The president prodded the FBI to investigate the disappearance of the three civil rights workers in Neshoba County, and his Justice Department prosecuted the victims' murderers vigorously (on the charge of violating the trio's civil rights, because the state had not proceeded with murder charges). To be sure, Johnson had pulled the rug out from under the MFDP, but his championing of civil rights legislation and aggressive prosecution of white violators of civil rights apparently scored points even with the Freedom Democrats. Sunflower County's MFDP delegates, Hamer among them, returned from Atlantic City to Sunflower County and campaigned hard for Lyndon Johnson.[56]

The 1964 Civil Rights Act had the potential to eliminate segregation in Sunflower County, but the law was unlikely to enforce itself. It remained for the Freedom Summer volunteers who stayed in the Delta to test the legislation's implementation. When volunteers asked Ruleville mayor Charles Dorrough how he planned to enforce the new law, he answered that he was under no obligation to do so because both of Mississippi's senators had voted against it. COFO staffers informed Indianola police chief Bryce Alexander in August that they were about to begin testing public accommodations, and he told them that if they broke the law, he would have to jail them. "City law or federal law?" they asked; "he replied that he was hired by the city so he would enforce municipal law, which mandated segregation of the races." Clearly, the stroke of Johnson's pen in Washington meant nothing by itself in Sunflower County.[57]

On October 4, eleven local people from Indianola, Moorhead, and the town of Sunflower, along with two COFO staff members, attempted to enter Dan's Restaurant, an all-white establishment, in Indianola. In a scene that repeated itself throughout the South in the early 1960s, the owner of the restaurant blocked its entrance and told the protesters that the establishment was closed. The event catalyzed a chain of events that showed what depths Sunflower County police were willing to plumb in order to maintain segregation—federal law or no federal law. The restaurant owner demanded that the integrationists wait in the parking lot while he called the police. They obliged, then observed several customers filing in and out of the "closed" restaurant. In a matter of minutes, Indianola policeman Ernest Sharp drove into the lot and screeched to a halt behind one of the COFO staffer's cars, in order to prevent "the culprits from escaping." The "culprits," who were willing to go to jail, were standing in the lot waiting to be arrested. As COFO staffer James Dann radioed in a report on the group's situation to the Indianola Freedom School, Sharp dragged him from the car and struck him several times with his billy club. Dann said that he would go peacefully; there was no need for violence. This so incensed Sharp that he cracked the civil rights worker over the head.[58]

The thirteen integrationists were escorted to the Indianola police station and lined against a wall. When a member of the group dared to ask what they were being charged with, Officer Sharp "let out a storm of abuse, waved his clubs and threatened to beat the next person who opened his mouth." Then the prisoners noticed known leaders of the Indianola Citizens' Council trailing in and out of a conference in Police Chief Alexander's office. The cabal decided that the thirteen integrationists would be charged with trespassing and that Dann would also be charged with resisting arrest. A highway patrolman then began interrogating an Indianola high school student who had been arrested as a member of the group. With the members of the Citizens' Council standing by, the patrolman coerced the young man into stating the names of his parents and the names of their employers. While the COFO staffers gestured wildly, trying to convince the young man to hold his peace until his lawyer arrived, the patrolman got the youngster to "admit" that he was a Communist.[59]

Before COFO's lawyers arrived, James Clay, an African American Indianola resident who had loaned his car to COFO for the demonstration, arrived to try and claim his automobile. Clay suffered from epilepsy and had an artificial leg. An Indianola police officer ordered Clay from the station, but the man was slow in complying. Officer Sharp turned his attention to Clay, striking him several times with the billy club and banging his head against a jailhouse wall. Clay was thrown in jail with the rest of the demonstrators. "Thus," concluded the COFO report on the incident, "the Indianola Police Department subdued and imprisoned a one legged . . . epileptic, whose only crime was to loan his car to civil rights workers." Bail for the fourteen totaled $3,750. One minor was ordered to a reformatory, Clay was released, and the other twelve spent two nights at the county penal farm. Based on the uncovering of "new evidence," a municipal judge dropped the charges against them on October 6, but even this was little victory for the thirteen who had been insulted, kicked, and beaten for attempting to enter a restaurant.[60]

The members of the Citizens' Council who had conferred with the police chief did so under the auspices of the "Police Auxiliary." The auxiliary had been organized in 1956 by Representative John Hough, who was then Sunflower County's voice in the state legislature. (Hough was also identified in oral history interviews as the plantation owner who had put the financial squeeze on Clint Battle at approximately the same time.) A glorified posse, the auxiliary force was made up almost entirely of Citizens' Council members who were willing to assist the police with armed force in the event of emergencies such as the attempted integration of Dan's Restaurant. In 1960, the force had received training in firearms and arrest techniques from an FBI agent at Hough's plantation south of Indianola. Throughout 1964 and afterward, the auxiliary cooperated with Sunflower County's suppression of civil rights activities, to the extent that COFO could complain with some justification, "[A]t a moment's notice any white man in the county can be deputized."[61]

The incident at Dan's Restaurant was an exception that proved a general rule. Desegregating public facilities was never a primary concern for COFO in the Delta, due at least in part to this characteristic series of events: desegregating facilities took too many man-hours and too much bail money, and a poorly organized effort could put local people in real physical danger. More typical was the work of Freedom Summer—registering voters, running the Freedom Schools, and distributing food and clothing—which continued after the majority of the volunteers returned to their colleges and took national media attention along with them at the end of the summer. COFO even increased its voter registration activity in Sunflower County, though actual registration continued to progress in only a trickle.[62]

SNCC staff members remained in the county after the Summer Project ended, along with at least four summer project volunteers who stayed in Indianola and two who remained in Ruleville.[63] The movement held its momentum. However, outright white resistance, which publicity-conscious political leaders had kept under wraps while the national news media focused on Mississippi during the summer, emerged into the open again. Pent-up frustrations manifested themselves in sometimes familiar, sometimes creative ways. The Indianola Freedom School's local insurance carrier dropped the center's fire policy on October 21 after an MFDP meeting took place there. On October 25, a low-flying crop duster disrupted a meeting of 250 people at the Freedom School when it buzzed the building and threw homemade bombs that exploded in midair. On October 27, an unknown party firebombed the Freedom School. Indianola firemen reportedly stood by and watched the blaze as it consumed a mimeograph machine, shortwave radio, office supplies, and 2,000 books. When SNCC workers led an outdoor rally at the site days later, Indianola police broke it up with billy clubs.[64]

In November, Lela Mae Burks, who had been attending the Indianola Freedom School, lost her job as a housemaid (and her $3 per day paycheck) after Sunflower County sheriff John Sidney Parker informed the woman's employer that Burks had gotten involved with the civil rights agitators. When an African American teenager applied for a membership at the all-white county library, he lost his job as a truck driver. Two children, ten and twelve years old, were arrested for handing out leaflets to announce an Indianola mass meeting and were held for questioning at the Indianola police station. After the same meeting, unidentified whites drove by the church where it had been held and dropped off Klan literature. The car drove by again later and fired bullets into the church. This time Robert McCraney, an MFDP leader, returned fire. He was arrested for firing a gun within the Indianola city limits, but police did not pursue the whites who had fired first. The mayor of Indianola warned McCraney that SNCC was "leading him into hell." On the day of McCraney's arrest, the Indianola police arrested two more children, these aged eight and nine, for leafleting.[65]

SNCC's Freedom Schools and community centers continued to operate despite the various forms of intimidation, having lost little momentum from the summer project. SNCC consolidated its gains in voter registration from the summer by organizing local "citizenship clubs" and voters' leagues in Ruleville, Indianola, and the town of Sunflower. Local people led the groups entirely by themselves and held regular mass meetings. Much of this activity coincided with MFDP party political maneuvers, but much of it concentrated on local issues that had nothing to do with party politics—as when the Sunflower County Civic League organized a "Freedom Week" to protest the lawlessness of local police. As thousands of African Americans attempted to register in Sunflower County, thousands more (an estimated 2,000 in the winter of 1964–65) were "Freedom registered" for the shadow elections that the MFDP continued to hold. Local people organized a county-wide Civic League and raised money for a relief fund to aid the victims of Citizens' Council reprisals.[66]

Field reports from SNCC staff revealed that the Citizens' Council was alive and well in the wake of Freedom Summer; its actions in Sunflower County were by now indistinguishable from actions taken by local officials and law officers. John Harris, a staff member of SNCC, reported, "Police, W[hite] C[itizens'] C[ouncil] and plain harassment from whites has greatly increased since the summer, to both COFO workers and local Negro citizens." When COFO attempted to rent a building in Moorhead, the mayor informed civil rights workers that the building would be bombed if the organization moved in; he then saw to it that the Citizens' Council rented the structure before COFO could finalize its lease. Harris chronicled numerous examples of Freedom School students who had been fired from their jobs, in many cases after local police had taken it upon themselves to inform the pupils' employers of their activities. Police intimidation of civil rights workers was endemic throughout the fall and winter. Nonetheless, activists in Sunflower County took as their motto "Freedom by Christmas" and announced that they were "plunging ahead into a more intensified program designed to bring about fundamental social, political and economic change in Sunflower County."[67] Through the winter, SNCC staffers and volunteers assisted Indianola youth in their effort to desegregrate the town's library. They succeeded in 1965, but the library removed all of its tables and chairs—lest white schoolgirls sit next to black schoolboys.

Civil rights work was hard work, and frustrations began to manifest themselves during the winter. COFO staff in Sunflower County began to criticize the statewide operation in increasingly harsh terms. John Harris concluded a report to COFO headquarters in Jackson by announcing that "[i]nsufficient funds, lack of cooperation, and incompetence [on the part of the state coordinating office] have led the Sunflower County Project to the point of almost complete disregard and loss of respect for the Jackson office."[68] The movement's momentum began to wane in Ruleville early in 1965. The town's African American community had been the first in the county to embrace civil rights activity, in 1962, but spirits there faded noticeably after Freedom Summer. Many sharecroppers in the area had

"We are soldiers in the army of the Lord." Voter registration meeting at Ebenezer Baptist Church in the town of Sunflower. (Charles Moore/Black Star Photos)

been to Indianola to attempt to register more than a dozen times, and by 1965 canvassers had surely reached everyone who was interested in voting. Indeed, Ruleville and its environs had become something of a burned-over district for voter registration workers by 1965; the civil rights activists had worked long, continuous hours for nearly three years but had little in terms of concrete gains to show for their labor. A SNCC staff member described what ailed the movement in Ruleville, which he considered "a pretty well organized town." He reported, "Local people are taking responsibility for just about everything. The problem here is the despair and subsequent apathy of some people who have been working hard for over two years and who don't see any change. Some people have been down to register fifteen, eighteen, even twenty-three times" without success.[69] The voter registration workers and the local people whom they convinced to put their livelihoods on the line met with continued resistance at the county courthouse in Indianola.

The federal Voting Rights Act that Congress passed and President Johnson signed in August should have solved these problems conclusively. After the bill was signed into law, the Sunflower County board of supervisors did direct the county circuit clerk, Sam Ely, to register all applicants regardless of race, and Ely complied. Ely maintained separate registration rolls, however, for illiterate African American voters so that he could strike their names at a moment's notice in the event that a suit that the U.S. Justice Department had already filed against his office went his way. Even the State Sovereignty Commission investigator who was assigned to report on voting in the Delta, hardly an advocate of equal voting rights, remarked that the practice was "contrary [even] to Mississippi's lenient voter registration law." When the Voting Rights Act became law, there were fewer than 600 registered African American voters—less than 5 percent of the total voting age population, which was estimated at more than 13,000 in the 1960 census—in Sunflower County. Clearly, the civil rights groups that hoped to bring about change in Sunflower County via the ballot box still had a long row to hoe. And many of them began to believe that for true change to come to Sunflower County, they would have to explore alternatives to electoral politics.[70]

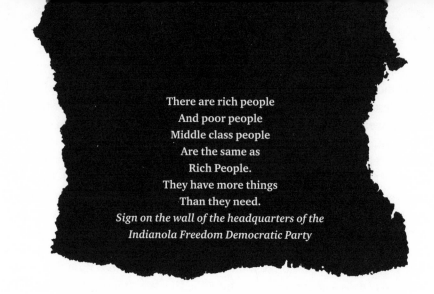

There are rich people
And poor people
Middle class people
Are the same as
Rich People.
They have more things
Than they need.
Sign on the wall of the headquarters of the
Indianola Freedom Democratic Party

CHAPTER SIX

Questions That Liberalism Is Incapable of Answering

Organizing Alternatives, 1964–1977

Fannie Lou Hamer's civil rights movement began to lose faith in the electoral process after the disappointment at Atlantic City in 1964. A Freedom Summer volunteer who remained in Sunflower County wrote home that when Hamer returned to Ruleville, she "launched into a high-powered, oft-times bellowing account of the Convention in Atlantic City." Hamer and the members of the MFDP had gone to Atlantic City with the expectation that they would expose injustice at work in Mississippi and that Democrats from the rest of the country would then do everything in the party's power to correct it. This is not what transpired. According to the same Freedom Summer volunteer, Hamer "said how disillusioned she was to find hypocrisy all over America. She felt [Lyndon] Johnson had really showed his hand against the MFDP by preventing a floor fight." Worse,

Hamer said, "[Martin Luther] King, Roy Wilkins, Bayard Rustin, James Farmer, and Aaron Henry had been willing to sell out the FDP by their willingness to accept the compromise."[1]

Things had not gone as the MFDP had planned, but party members in Sunflower County believed that the delegates were right to have refused the compromise. The Freedom Summer volunteer reported on an MFDP meeting that was held after the delegates returned from Atlantic City in late August. "I realized that for southern Negroes, Mississippi Negroes especially, to see that crowd sitting down meant something that would have been completely lost if a compromise had been accepted that simply hushed everything up. . . . One woman at the mass meeting said, 'I looked at that convention [on television] from the time it started. All the time til now I never seen no nigger in a convention, but they was there! Lots of them! Big ones and little ones, they was there!'"[2] In that sense, the MFDP did what it had set out to do. The MFDP's "Freedom Primer" explained:

President Johnson and Hubert Humphrey could not understand why the Freedom Democratic Party would not give in. And many of our Negro and white friends could not understand either. Very few people in the country understand what it means to say "No!" to what is wrong and to say "Yes!" to what you believe in.

Most people think you have to give in at some point so that other people will not be mad. They think that you are supposed to accept what you are offered by powerful people because that is the way things are done in this country.[3]

In rejecting the compromise, the MFDP succeeded, at the very least, in speaking truth to power and exposing the injustices that constrained them. They did so more effectively than they could have by being seated in the first place. In September, the executive committee of the MFDP agreed: taking the long view, their challenge had been successful, and they had made the right decision.[4]

The MFDP's disaffection with the national Democratic Party was real, but it has been exaggerated. Journalist Milton Viorst wrote in 1979, "At Atlantic City, the civil rights coalition shattered into fragments. . . . Militant blacks . . . declared that you could never trust a 'dirty white liberal.'" MFDP delegate Cleveland Sellers later remembered, "We left Atlantic City with the knowledge that our struggle . . . was not for civil rights, but for liberation."[5] Hamer herself was terribly disappointed with the results of the Atlantic City convention, as her words demonstrate, but she and the other members of the MFDP in Sunflower County were not so dejected that they refused to vote Democratic or even to campaign for national Democrats in Sunflower County. Hamer continued to press her challenge against the "regular" Democrats' U.S. congressman for the Second District, Jamie Whitten, and took her challenge as far as the House floor before it was dismissed.

The MFDP supporters who campaigned for national Democrats in Mississippi did not do so blithely. Party chairman Lawrence Guyot cabled the Democratic National Convention's John Bailey in late October to chronicle at least nine separate incidents in Sunflower County alone in which MFDP campaigners met with violence over a span of nine days. On October 20, an unidentified white man punched an MFDP worker in the face, and a crowd of whites beat up a SNCC photographer in Indianola. On October 22, a crop duster passed over an outdoor Indianola MFDP rally, dropping flares and explosives. On October 24, someone threw rocks through the window of the one black-owned store in Ruleville that dared to post Johnson-Humphrey campaign posters. Five days later, someone fired shots into the same storefront, this time riddling the pictures of Johnson, Humphrey, and a local candidate, most likely Hamer, with bullet holes.[6] The candidates of the national Democratic Party and the electoral process still mattered to the MFDP's supporters if they were willing to endure this kind of harassment to campaign in the Delta. The MFDP did not surrender its goal of replacing the regular state Democratic Party after Atlantic City, and MFDP members in Sunflower County did not immediately give up on political organizing.

After Atlantic City, Hamer and the members of her camp did, however, begin to look for alternatives to liberal politics. It was only natural that they should do so. Bob Moses told a reporter in 1965, "We are raising fundamental questions about how the poor sharecropper can achieve the Good Life, questions that liberalism is incapable of answering."[7] The MFDP continued to operate, registering voters, sniping at the "regular" party through the national press, and preparing for the next seating controversy at the 1968 Democratic convention in Chicago. After 1964, however, the MFDP was a different political animal from the party that had challenged the regulars in Atlantic City, and party members began exploring alternatives to traditional electoral politics.

Tellingly, by 1967 at least one county chapter of the MFDP openly advocated violence. The Hinds County *Freedom Democratic Party News* editorialized, "We must learn what the White Man learned in 1776. There can be no peace or freedom for any oppressed people until that people is ready to pick up guns."[8] The MFDP's 1968 state party platform called for a guaranteed minimum income and guaranteed health care for all Mississippi citizens, and its foreign policy section made those demands seem timid. The MFDP proposed an end to the draft, the complete removal of American troops from Vietnam, cessation of arms shipments to the Middle East, resumption of normal relations with Cuba and China, and an arms embargo against South Africa. In 1969, the party also became the first entity in Mississippi to call for an end to the Sovereignty Commission.[9] These views placed the MFDP far outside the mainstream of black voters, to say nothing of whites. But the MFDP continued the exciting work of introducing new voters to the mechanics of political participation. The minutes of a May 18, 1969, MFDP executive committee meeting recount the "crackle of excitement of people involved in the basics of [the] political process for the first time." The party did not abandon its commitment to introducing local people to the political process—the dispensation and use of power.[10]

The Mississippi Freedom Labor Union

COFO workers who remained in the Delta helped organize a truly quixotic effort to unionize farm laborers in the spring of 1965. About fifty cotton choppers (who worked for wages weeding the cotton rows between planting and harvest, and whose livelihoods were most threatened by mechanized farming) and tractor drivers went on strike in April in the environs of Shaw, just to the northwest of Indianola in Bolivar County. The Mississippi Freedom Labor Union (MFLU) soon spread to ten Delta counties, including Sunflower, and had as many as 1,000 members (according to one conservative estimate) at its peak. In 1965, Delta cotton choppers made $3 per ten-hour day, and tractor drivers earned about twice that amount; they went on strike when plantation owners threatened to cut those wages almost in half. The MFLU called for a minimum wage of $1.25 an hour. The strike came at a time when mechanization had replaced every task but cotton chopping; tractors and other machines by now planted the seed and harvested the cotton, and the use of chemical pesticides was increasing. On a given day during the cotton-chopping season, 3,000 equipment operators and 25,000 men, women, and children worked the cotton fields of the Delta, but their days, too, were numbered.[11]

The spring strike was a resounding failure. Plantation owners whose laborers struck simply borrowed excess labor—of which there was no shortage—from neighboring plantation owners or nearby towns. The MFLU had no realistic chance to effect change in a world where machines were rapidly replacing farm laborers. Not surprisingly, in the 1965 growing season—the first after Freedom Summer—cotton planters embraced liquid herbicides and insecticides that did the work of choppers to go along with their mechanical sowers and pickers. In this atmosphere, human workers were fast becoming superfluous to the cotton economy. If every single farm laborer in the Delta did not support the MFLU, the strike had no chance of success.[12]

According to one estimate, 32,300 day laborers worked the Delta's cotton fields during one peak week in June, but only 11 of the thousands of day laborers from Indianola joined the MFLU strike. This only had the practical effect of ensuring that 11 Indianolans gave up their incomes for the hoeing season. A strike fund of over $14,000 did not begin to cover the living expenses of the choppers throughout the Delta who did strike, and planters controlled the local committees responsible for distributing federal welfare dollars.

The lack of organized, overwhelming support doomed the strikes. McKenna Mack, an African American native of Sunflower County and a member of the MFLU, explained how the union started off on the wrong foot. "Only just one town in Sunflower County [perhaps Shaw, which straddles the Bolivar/Sunflower County line] was on strike and that didn't help any," he said. "If the county was goin' to go on strike, the whole delta shoulda went on strike and not just one town in Sunflower County and that's why I think it's messed up." He concluded, "[I]t will be a mess until the whole delta goes on strike." The whole Delta never did go on strike, but there were small victories to celebrate nonetheless. On June 3, a busload of day laborers refused to work on the Eastland plantation in Doddsville after they learned that "Big Jim" refused to pay African American employees who had registered to vote.[13]

Other plantation owners were simply unwilling to listen to their workers' demands or to allow union organizers on their property. On the day when MFLU-organized tractor drivers went on strike against the Andrews plantation in Tribbett, just west of Sunflower County, for a small raise in pay, owner A. L. Andrews evicted all of his employees, forbade them from trespassing, and borrowed laborers from neighboring plantations—all before sundown. An unidentified MFLU organizer explained how dangerous it could be to canvass Delta plantations. "[T]he longest we ever stayed on any plantation was at night, for an hour and a half, talking to people," he said. "As a usual thing, conversations last from five to ten minutes before the plantation owner comes driving along to chase you away." To talk any longer could be dangerous: "[T]hey'd shoot you. There's no joke about that, because they made boasts in 2 or 3 towns around here that if they ever caught any one of us on their plantation, we wouldn't go on anybody else's."[14]

While civil rights workers with little experience in union organizing canvassed for the MFLU, pressures mounted on traditional labor unions to recognize and support the farmworkers' union. E. T. Kehrer, the director of the new Civil Rights Department of the American Federation of Labor and Congress of Industrial Organizations (AFL-CIO), had no illusions that the MFLU's strikes could succeed in winning a living wage for the farm laborers, or that the MFLU might overthrow the plantation system. But he did believe that the national union movement owed something to the farmworkers who had been left behind by modernization. "I shudder to think what would happen to us if we turned our backs and just let all these things go on," Kehrer told *Business Week*.[15]

However, Claude Ramsay, the longtime president of the Mississippi AFL-CIO and a political foe of the MFDP, opposed the MFLU on all grounds. He made certain that the upstart union would not receive anything more than bare-bones financial support from the national union movement. During Freedom Summer, Ramsay had reviewed the plight of Delta farm laborers "from stem to stern" with clergymen affiliated with the Delta Ministry, a civil rights project of the National Council of Churches. He tried to convince the clergymen that "the situation was impossible to deal with from a trade union point of view," in part because he considered farmworkers "among the most difficult groups to organize." Ramsay did not dispute that the Delta farmworkers' wages and working conditions were "among the worst existing anywhere in the nation." He simply denied that union organizing could help to alleviate these problems. "How do you organize and produce benefits for some twenty-five thousand seasonal workers who are employed only two and a half months each year and who are largely unemployable elsewhere?" Ramsay asked with justification. He argued that it was simply impossible to organize people who were so poor and so unskilled. However, Bob Williams, an organizer for the MFLU, disputed that belief. "It seems like it could be a lot harder organizing these people and getting them to strike than it is," Williams said. "[But] these people are ready . . . they're just sitting back and waiting for somebody to come tell 'em what to do, and how to do it."[16]

Ramsay did offer to the MFLU the use of experienced organizers and assistance in lobbying the federal government to extend the minimum wage to farmworkers. These suggestions, he said, "went over like a ton of bricks" with the MFLU's advisers. The reaction was characteristic of Ramsay's complicated relationship with the MFDP and its collaborators. By

1965, Ramsay had had a long and honorable history of opposition to segregation and the Eastland wing of the Mississippi Democratic Party; it had come at great personal cost. The leader of the union movement in the nation's most antiunion state, he had been far in front of his membership on civil rights issues since at least 1954 and had been the victim of Klan violence as a result. Yet he received no respect from the radicals of the MFDP and MFLU. MFLU members told him that "they did not want any one coming in to tell them what to do" but that they did want the AFL-CIO's monetary support. Ramsay disdained black radicals and white college-students-cum-labor-organizers; he thought that the MFDP, for example, excelled at creating problems "and then left them for others to resolve." After Atlantic City, he began organizing a liberal-labor Democratic coalition in Mississippi to oppose both the regulars and the Freedom Democrats. He refused to throw his full support behind the MFLU.[17]

Having strained its relations with the liberal establishment and the MFDP, without funds to support striking members, without overwhelming support on the part of Delta farm laborers, and in the face of widespread white opposition, the MFLU disintegrated during the summer of 1965. A planned strike during the 1965 harvest season fizzled. By the time farm-workers were finally included in federal minimum wage statutes in 1967, the plantations had shifted almost completely to the use of pesticides and tractors. By Hodding Carter III's estimate, this was twelve times cheaper than employing cotton-choppers at the newly mandated minimum wage of a dollar an hour.[18]

There was simply no place for these unskilled workers to go in the Delta's mechanizing economy. Many of them followed relatives north. Others scraped by on what they could grow for food in vegetable patches and what little they received in the form of government welfare. It became ever clearer that traditional approaches could not address their increasingly complex problems.

"The Country's Number One Freedom-Fighting Woman"

Fannie Lou Hamer did not retire from public life after her appearance at the 1964 Atlantic City convention. She challenged the legitimacy of the 1964 statewide elections that sent another all-white congressional delegation to Mississippi, which kept her in the national spotlight through 1965. After that point, Hamer continued to cultivate relationships with a wide range of groups on the political left. By 1967, Hamer was corresponding with antiwar groups, feminist groups, and civil liberties groups from around the nation, all of whom sought her advice concerning organizing strategies.[19] Hamer was especially popular among women's groups; she told a 1971 meeting of the National Women's Political Caucus that she had suffered more discrimination as a woman than she had as an African American. (In 1961, at the age of forty-three, Hamer had been sterilized without her permission by a white Ruleville doctor and had been prevented from suing him.) Hamer certainly kept feminists on their toes, though: she opposed abortion and birth control in all cases and was proud not to be "hung up on this about liberating myself from the black man. . . . I got a black husband, six feet three, 240 pounds, with a [size] 14 shoe, that I don't *want* to be liberated from," she told one group. Significantly, while sncc abandoned its commitment to integration and its willingness to work with any whites who were willing to work with them, Hamer refused to surrender the ideal of an interracial democracy. For Hamer, the ideal was grounded firmly in Christ's message to the world. As Malcolm X garnered increasing publicity and sncc chairman Stokeley Carmichael formulated a "black power" ideology that jettisoned integration—both of which the national press interpreted as antiwhite—Hamer maintained, "Ain't no such thing as 'I can hate anybody and hope to see God's face.' "[20]

Hamer nevertheless became a heroine of young black radicals. Malcolm X introduced her to an audience at Harlem's Audubon Ballroom in December 1964 as "the country's number one freedom-fighting woman." In 1974, the Black Panthers' minister of information, Emory Douglas, informed Hamer that the radical group wanted to use her image for a poster series of great black leaders. Hamer joined the pantheon of W. E. B. Du Bois, Harriet Tubman, Marcus Garvey, and Sojourner Truth. Through such experiences, Hamer and her ideas received increasing recognition in the rest of the country, if not in the Delta.[21]

As Hamer drifted away from electoral politics, she began to concentrate on economic development. With so many problems to solve for the black people of the Delta, she had a hard time deciding on the best path to take. She debated whether she should work to increase federal welfare giveaways, attempt to begin an affordable housing program, try to bring a jobs-training center to Sunflower County, or move in an entirely new direction. Characteristically, she decided on all of the above. Hamer embarked on a speaking tour along the East Coast in 1966, earned honoraria from the unions and women's groups to whom she spoke, and solicited individual contributions along the way. These funds served as the nest egg for Hamer's new idea: the Freedom Farm Co-operative. The sclc, entertainer Harry Belafonte, the Southern Cooperative Development Corporation,

Frank Porter Graham's National Sharecropper Fund, the American Freedom from Hunger Foundation, and Measure for Measure of Madison, Wisconsin, also made major donations.[22]

The core of Freedom Farm as Hamer conceived it was a vegetable patch that local people could help farm and then harvest for free. But true to its creator, Freedom Farm evolved into much more than a communal garden, eventually metamorphosing into a farming cooperative, craft-making cooperative, Head Start center, housing development, meat-lending operation, adult education center, and headquarters for civil rights agitation all rolled into one. Joe Harris, a SNCC veteran, signed on as manager of Freedom Farm. He soon found himself registering voters, working on school desegregation projects, helping local people fill out welfare paperwork, and running financial management courses for local farmers who tried to escape the trap of sharecropping, often without being paid.

Surely the most ingenious aspect of Freedom Farm, and the best illustration of its pragmatic approach to the complicated problems of the people it served, was its "pig bank." With help from the National Council of Negro Women, Hamer purchased twenty female and four male pigs in 1968, and she created one of the great capitalist enterprises in all of American history. A Freedom Farm employee explained the pig bank's standard operating procedure: "When a gilt [the principal] was found to be pregnant she was loaned to a needy family who had the facilities to maintain her. (The family also made and kept the promise that when they had a pregnant gilt they would pass it on to another needy family.) When the interest was born, usually [in the form of] 9 to 20 baby pigs, the family would return the principal to the pig bank. The family would then raise the remaining interest as meat for their tables."[23] Within three years, the bank produced a fabulous return on its initial investment in the form of as many as 3,000 pigs, which fed more than 300 hungry Sunflower County families.

In 1969, Hamer bought Freedom Farm's first forty acres, planted food crops, and began selling memberships in the farming cooperative for a dollar apiece. Thirty families signed up and paid their dues, and Hamer allowed another 1,500 families who could not afford the nominal fee to share the vegetables without paying for them.[24] Freedom Farm was flexible to the extreme. Not until 1972 did the cooperative's officers decide that managing Freedom Farm as "an independent operation capable of sustaining its own existence" was a priority. Both before and after they made this decision, Freedom Farm's goal was to help poor people improve their material conditions in the most pragmatic way possible, not to build an institution. After 1972, however, the cooperative began reinvesting its profits from farming operations back into the farm. The organization curtailed its social programs but continued to help local poor people negotiate the welfare bureaucracy, register to vote, and receive food and clothing. Freedom Farm also awarded partial scholarships to twenty-five area college students. At any given time, there were as many as thirty-two people on the Freedom Farm payroll, which was hardly negligible in a cash-poor region with precious few available jobs.[25] The number of poor blacks in Sunflower County and its environs who received relief in the form of cash and supplies from Freedom Farm would run into the tens of thousands. Freedom Farm also cultivated local leaders. Its board of directors included George Jordan, the Ruleville farmer who had tried to convince other black Christians to register to vote in the 1950s, and Matthew Carter, the sharecropper whose family integrated the Drew city schools. At the same time, a new generation of black leaders trained at the right hand of Fannie Lou Hamer.

Freedom Farm struggled mightily to find creative solutions to the problems brought about by the new order of mechanized agriculture in the Delta. According to Joe Harris's estimate, the demand for unskilled man-hours on Delta farms dropped from 175 million in 1940 to less than 20 million in 1960. After 1960, the demand for unskilled, uneducated black workers had shrunk further. The U.S. Department of Agriculture estimated that mechanization and reductions in cotton acreage would eliminate demand for 30,000 Mississippi farmhands in 1966 and another 100,000 in 1967. The entire state created fewer than 100 new manufacturing jobs in the same period. The median annual income for African Americans in the Delta was $456 in 1960 and shrank during the decade.[26]

Freedom Farm never enjoyed complete independence from white planter control. The organization had to bank with the Eastland-controlled Bank of Ruleville, the only such institution in the area, and surely felt constraints.[27] The co-op did find unlikely friends among the white professional class, however. Perry ("Pap") and Fannie Lou Hamer were able to establish a strong working relationship with Pascol Townsend Jr., a white Drew attorney who was close to Eastland and who had earlier worked with Mayor "Snake" Williford to keep Freedom Summer volunteers out of Drew. Townsend handled all of Freedom Farm's legal affairs. In return, when Eastland nominated Townsend for a federal judgeship, Hamer spoke up for him, lest liberals in the Senate associate him too closely with the reactionary Eastland.[28]

Freedom Farm perennially suffered under poor financial conditions compounded by its employees' lack of formal financial training. In 1973,

Nora Campbell, a secretary for Freedom Farm, informed Joe Harris that creditors had repossessed the organization's typewriter and Xerox machine, and the phone company had disconnected service. Campbell herself had missed several paychecks, and her own car and furniture had been repossessed.[29] When poor people who had been ill-educated by a state that regarded them as racially inferior in the first place and who had been denied jobs that would have taught them the skills of money management participated in the leadership of a program like Freedom Farm, mistakes were inevitable. To expect otherwise, the Delta Ministry pointed out, was "not only to ask here a level of performance absent from even highly experienced bureaucracies" but to fail to recognize that the purpose of Freedom Farm and similar projects was to provide "training in leadership and administration."[30] Allowing uneducated sharecroppers to operate Freedom Farm did perform this function. Hamer and the other officers of the cooperative could have balanced this aspect of Freedom Farm's operations with experienced managers who might have saved the institution from financial headaches in the long run, but they did not.

In 1974, Hamer tapped into her network of liberal allies in order to buy more land for Freedom Farm's programs. A series of young peoples' "Walks against Hunger" across the United States netted $120,000; Hamer used the money to purchase 640 acres of Sunflower County farmland for the cooperative. The Measure for Measure organization of Madison, Wisconsin, chipped in with cash and new tractors. Freedom Farm then used the revenue from its crops grown on the new land and the farm's preexisting tracts to underwrite loans from local banks and the federal Farmers' Home Administration to purchase thirty-five new homes for Ruleville families. After Joe Harris, who had done the work of at least three mortals for Freedom Farm, passed away unexpectedly in 1974, however, the cooperative slipped into financial chaos. Freedom Farm had to sell the 640 acres to keep the cooperative from losing the remainder of its assets, and the co-op never recovered from the setback.[31] Freedom Farm died a slow and surprisingly unnoticed death.

The Return to Electoral Politics

An April 1966 federal district court order permitted African Americans to register en masse for the first time in Sunflower County. Municipal elections were to be held in the town of Sunflower in the following months, but town officials did not take sufficient pains to inform black voters of the election. They also demanded to see receipts for two years' worth of poll taxes from would-be voters and refused to let anyone who had registered to vote within 120 days of the election into the polls.[32] The MFDP challenged the validity of this election and eventually amended its suit to challenge municipal elections in Ruleville, Doddsville, and Moorhead. Federal district court judge Claude F. Clayton ordered new elections in the towns of Sunflower and Moorhead to take place in May 1967.[33]

Hamer and her allies had tried electoral politics and been burned, but they again allowed themselves to place their hopes in the 1967 county elections. "If we could win the election in Sunflower County," Hamer said, "it would give hope to all the peoples who have been struggling so long and ain't saw nobody win nothing."[34] The MFDP cobbled together a full slate of candidates and enlisted the help of liberal African American and white allies outside of Mississippi. Martin Luther King Jr., Harry Belafonte, and John de J. Pemberton, executive director of the American Civil Liberties Union, created a National Committee for Free Elections in Sunflower County, Mississippi, to publicize the elections and rally financial support for the MFDP's candidates. The committee also included civil rights veterans Bayard Rustin, A. Philip Randolph, and Stokeley Carmichael and the white liberal stalwarts John Kenneth Galbraith, Eugene McCarthy, and Franklin D. Roosevelt Jr. at a time when black and white liberals and black radicals had little else on which they could agree.[35]

The MFDP's candidates were not household names, for the most part, even to those who had paid attention to the Freedom Movement. Hamer, embroiled in an internecine war over the administration of Head Start funds in the county, ran for a seat on Sunflower County Progress, Inc., the county board that oversaw federal antipoverty spending, but lost to a black Ruleville man supported by whites. (This particular loss had much to do with Hamer's growing belief that members of the black middle class in Sunflower County were "selling out" their poorer sisters and brothers.)[36] She did not run for political office in the election, though she did run for a seat in the state senate again in the fall.

The candidates who ran for office in Sunflower and Moorhead were not in most cases familiar names from the civil rights struggle, but they were all leaders in their communities who had distinguished themselves in other ways. Thelma L. Barry, a sixty-six-year-old candidate for justice of the peace in Moorhead, was typical in this regard. Her campaign literature mentioned her church affiliation and the leadership roles she had performed in that capacity. "Have served as Sunday school teacher, Prayer and Bible Band teacher and President of the Home and Foreign Mission," it read. "[A]lso presently serving as President of the Mother's Board.

Elect

INFORMED

CHARLES McLAURIN

STATE SENATOR
District 11 – Post No. 1
BOLIVAR AND SUNFLOWER COUNTIES

NOVEMBER 2, 1971

HE WILL DO THE JOB FOR YOU BECAUSE HE CARES

"If we could win the election in Sunflower County, it would give hope to all the peoples who have been struggling so long and ain't saw nobody win nothing." MFDP *members like Charles McLaurin and Fannie Lou Hamer ran campaigns they had little hope of winning in order to demystify elections for newly enfranchised blacks. These photographs were taken in 1971; note how much Hamer had aged just since 1964. (Mississippi Department of Archives and History)*

Elect
INFORMED

SINCERE

CAPABLE

MRS.

Fannie Lou HAMER

STATE SENATOR
District 11 – Post No. 2
BOLIVAR AND SUNFLOWER COUNTIES
NOVEMBER 2, 1971

Reared and educated five children in this community. Became a midwife in this county in December, 1932. Became a registered voter in 1965."[37]

MFDP campaign literature succinctly defined the most important issues for new voters. James Wesley Davis ran for a seat on the Moorhead city council. A forty-eight-year-old father of seven, Davis was a World War II veteran and a successful farmer, a deacon of Sunrise AME Church, and a Mason. Davis had first registered to vote in 1966 and immediately joined the MFDP. Davis's campaign promises covered a wide range: he pledged to improve municipal services, to work toward establishing a health clinic, to pressure the Moorhead schools to integrate, and to bring federal spending programs to Moorhead.[38] Clover Green, a forty-three-year-old Navy veteran, ran for constable in Sunflower County. In listing his qualifications, Green also mentioned his church affiliation and membership in the NAACP and MFDP. He urged African American voters, "[I]f you want to go to jail because someone wants you to, if you want to pay extra fees in order to pay the Justice of the Peace and the Constable, if you want to be carried to jail while the White man goes free, then vote for my opponent! Now, my dear friends, if you want justice done toward you . . . if you want whites as well as negroes carried to jail if the need arises, then vote for me, Clover Green, I am your man."[39] James Lewis, a Moorhead city council candidate, had also served in the U.S. Army and joined the MFDP in 1964. He taught Sunday School at Swan Lake Missionary Baptist Church in Moorhead. He, too, promised better city services.[40]

Otis Brown, a product of the Freedom Schools in Indianola, ran for mayor of Sunflower. He had an interesting (and, no doubt, effective) way of reminding voters of who he was: "I sold peanuts and Hot Tamales [in Indianola] on Saturdays and Sundays, and sometimes at ballgames for my father."[41] Following Freedom Summer, Brown had served as COFO's Sunflower County project director (after McLaurin left the county to attend college) and as the county chairman of the MFDP. Brown promised that if elected, he would "reach out to industry[,] which is one of the most important things we need if [the town] is to continue its existence," and pointed out, "This is something the past administration has never done." Brown, too, pledged to bring a doctor to the town and had already hired a lawyer to research what could be done to bring War on Poverty dollars into Sunflower. Like the other MFDP candidates, Brown promised to improve municipal services. He added to these promises a vow to enact a curfew to keep children off the streets at night and in school during the day and to create a recreation center for the town's children, a jobs training program, and programs to help constituents with welfare and social security paperwork.[42]

These campaign promises separated the MFDP candidates from the regular Democratic candidates, who were interested primarily in keeping property taxes on the area's large farms as low as possible. It goes without saying that they did not favor increasing costly city services, subsidizing health services, or attracting federal welfare dollars. To defeat the MFDP candidates, the white Democrats would have to convince African American voters, now a majority of the electorate, that the MFDP candidates were not prepared to govern. They produced political fliers like the following, reproduced in full:

Citizens of Sunflower:

You have a chance to vote for a good town or a bad town in the election. The choice is yours. If you are smart you will not be mis-lead [sic] by paid racial agitators who would promise you everything and give you nothing but misery if they succeed in fooling you into following their leadership. Look at them! Are these people the kind you want as leaders of the Negro community? Think about it—these agitators should not be trying to run your business. Your homes and property are at stake and we had better think seriously about this when we vote. They give you lots of promises but can give you nothing but disappointment and sorrow. The sensible leaders of both races can make this community a good place to live, but this group would not like to see this happen as they make their living on stirring up division and mis-trust. Don't be a fool, or a tool for this bunch who will bring you misery if they have their way.

Think for yourself when you vote! All your property, and everything you own is at stake. Vote for a sensible, sane government.[43]

The incumbent mayor and aldermen of the town of Sunflower mailed letters to black voters thanking them for "the fine support you have given this administration in the past." "We have had complaints from some of our local [African American] citizens," the white politicians claimed, "that they have been threatened and harassed by people working for the Freedom Democratic Party. As your city officials, we want to take this opportunity to assure our citizens that we will take any and all means to protect the citizens of this community." For the first time, white politicians had to pander for black votes and even referred to African American residents of the town as "citizens." The mayor and aldermen assured black voters that the State Highway Patrol would be there on Election Day to protect them from "outside lawbreakers or radicals who use threats or violence to accomplish their goal"—referring, presumably, to MFDP members rather than violent whites.[44] The whites in power also showed a gift for more subtle forms of intimidation. A month before the election, the Sunflower County Selective Service Board called Jimmy Lee Douglas, an African American candidate for mayor of Moorhead, in for a reexamination. He had already been examined once and rejected for service.[45]

The editors of the *New Republic* pinned their hopes on an MFDP victory in the 1967 elections, optimistically opining that "[a] victory in Eastland's backyard would send shock waves throughout the state." But Hamer was more realistic. "Nothing has changed in Mississippi," she admitted in a rare moment of public pessimism before the elections; she knew that victory at the polls was only a means to an end. Winning the elections was important, but by itself not even political victory would not change the realities faced by black Deltans in their daily lives.[46]

When Hamer filed suit against county registrar Cecil Campbell in April 1965, before the passage of the Voting Rights Act, only 13 percent of the eligible African American population of Sunflower County was registered to vote. Two years later, after the passage of the landmark legislation and an intensive voter registration drive, only 24 percent of the eligible African Americans in the county had registered. Federal registrars had moved into the surrounding counties of Bolivar, Coahoma, Leflore, and Humphreys to uphold the Voting Rights Act, but they were held out of Sunflower to avoid upsetting Senator Eastland. Only those brave and stubborn enough to withstand a gauntlet of white intimidation won the franchise in Sunflower County. "The only people registered to vote now are the ones who have gone through a living hell to get registered," Hamer claimed in 1967. Given the reality of low black registration, even if every registered black voter made it to the polls and every one voted for MFDP candidates, the challengers still faced an uphill battle.[47]

Black voters actually formed a majority in the town of Sunflower precinct, where the MFDP fielded six candidates. According to the Delta Ministry, 95 percent of the black voters of the precinct tried to vote on Election Day. The Sunflower chief of police greeted each voter at the door, and a white man photographed each black voter. Precinct officials had previously agreed to allow Joe Harris to help illiterate African American voters who requested help in filling out their ballots. However, the election officials provided only local whites to assist in the delicate task on Election Day. The black voters of Sunflower knew all too well that if they voted for MFDP candidates and powerful whites learned of it, they would be susceptible to white pressure. The Delta Ministry reported that "after years of fear and intimidation," the mere presence of whites in the polls "was enough to frighten some [African American] voters into voting 'white.'" The MFDP candidate who received the most votes of the six (Otis Brown, with 121) still received 45 fewer votes than the white candidate with the fewest votes. The MFDP's candidates were no more successful in the Moorhead precinct; the election itself went more smoothly there, in part because white voters composed a strong majority of the electorate.[48]

Curiously, the triumphant white candidates insisted that their opponents from the MFDP—the leaders of local black churches and local farm-owners, all of whom had lived in Sunflower County for all or most of their lives—were "foreigners" or "radical agitators." J. R. Romine Jr., an incumbent alderman from Sunflower, attributed his reelection to the fact that "we have enough sensible Negroes in this community to realize these foreigners are not the ones to lead them in their politics." Sunflower mayor W. L. Patterson was more blunt in his assessment: he defeated Otis Patterson 190 votes to 121, even though twenty more African Americans voted than whites, he claimed, because he had ignored the "radical" voters of his town but *had* sought the votes of the "good niggers." In all, the MFDP fielded sixty candidates across the state in the 1967 election season, six of whom won. In the June Democratic primaries for statewide races, a Ku Klux Klan candidate for governor won 727 votes in Sunflower County, and Byron De La Beckwith (having been acquitted by an all-white jury of murdering Medgar Evers) outpolled every other candidate for lieutenant governor. If anything, white supremacy was making headway in Sunflower County politics.[49]

The MFDP finally participated in a successful political crusade in 1968, when the remaining members of the organization helped drive the Dixiecrats out of the Democratic Party. The Mississippi "regulars" again tried to exclude African Americans from their delegation to the Democratic National Convention in Chicago as they had in Atlantic City. This time, what remained of the MFDP joined forces with the state chapters of the AFL-CIO and NAACP, the Prince Hall Masons, the Negro Mississippi Teachers Association, the State Baptist Association, and a coalition of white liberals to send an integrated delegation to the convention.

It initially appeared that President Johnson would side with the loyalists and end the controversy once and for all. But Johnson decided he could not risk offending Eastland as chair of the Senate Judiciary Committee or Stennis as chair of the Senate Defense Subcommittee. The latter's support was especially crucial to the administration's Vietnam policy.[50]

The loyalists succeeded anyway. For the first time, an integrated delegation represented Mississippi at a national Democratic convention. But within the state, the loyalists could do no better than an only-in-Mississippi balancing act with the regulars for nearly a decade. The regulars continued to elect candidates in Mississippi who ran as nominal Democrats but could not participate in national party politics. The loyalists had little power within the state but represented it at national conventions. They healed the breach in 1976, just as conservative white Democrats in Mississippi and throughout the South were beginning to pledge their allegiance to a strengthening Republican party.[51]

Stirrings in Indianola

In 1967, Carver Randle, a young black schoolteacher from Indianola, rejuvenated the county's NAACP chapter with a nontraditional power base: the Saint Benedict the Moor Catholic Center. Father Walter Smiegel, a white priest, opened the doors of the Catholic Center on Church Street to the movement, and he helped Randle organize a December campaign for Indianola mayor. Randle promised to revise the city's tax system to place a heavier burden on the wealthiest (white) tax brackets; he would have used these increased revenues to provide municipal services to the poorest (black) parts of town. Parts of southern Indianola suffered from deplorable sanitation and absentee landlords who still rented properties without plumbing facilities. Randle also promised to increase police protection for black sections of town while forcing the department to treat all of the citizens it served fairly. Randle made it into a runoff election with Ed Cole, the white candidate, but when 800 black voters tabbed Cole in the January election, Randle conceded defeat.[52]

In 1968, Randle and Smiegel led a boycott of white Indianola merchants who either refused to hire African American employees or paid them unequal wages and who failed to use courtesy titles toward African American customers. After unknown parties bombed the Indianola Freedom School, the home of Inez Magruder (which she had used to house SNCC workers), and Oscar Giles's store (Giles was a leader in the MFDP, and his financial independence surely galled some whites) in 1965, the situation had begun to simmer down in Indianola. From Randle's perspective, this was not an entirely positive development.

Randle had graduated from Indianola's Gentry High School in 1961 and won a football scholarship to Mississippi Valley State University. He chose not to risk his football career by joining the COFO workers, but the 1965 bombings shocked him into action. "I'm sure I was naive, but I just didn't think that we had white people here who could be that mean, to burn up someone's business or home. It was hard to understand," he recalled in a 1997 oral history interview. When he returned home after his 1965 graduation, Randle joined a coalition of African Americans who were working to improve the public schools, create jobs, and improve the public facilities that were available to black Indianolans. The coalition disintegrated when moderate members of the black middle class could not agree with younger radicals on tactics, and the boycott effort was Randle's attempt to jumpstart the movement again in Indianola. He "felt like we had to shake things up in the black community to get that going again."[53]

The boycotts did shake things up. In April, 400 black Indianolans marched with Randle to the Sunflower County courthouse to publicize the boycott. Their presence must have been expected, because a low-flying crop duster buzzed the courthouse several times and drowned out the voices of Randle and other speakers. When the boycotts began, they had enough of an effect to elicit a response from the white business community. The *Indianola Enterprise-Tocsin* made appeals to the "responsible Negroes" of Indianola not to honor the boycott, and editor Wallace Dabbs printed a series of attacks on Father Walter Smiegel. Dabbs accused Smiegel of inciting blacks to violence (the *Enterprise-Tocsin* reported on several acts of vandalism to local businesses, but it is far from certain that boycotters did the damage), and Smiegel deflected the criticism gracefully. "[E]ven a white fool knows that if black youths were responsible for this felony, they would have been apprehended within seconds," he countered. Jack Harper, president of the Indianola chamber of commerce, mailed letters to local African American citizens urging them to defy Randle and Smiegel.[54]

The boycott movement fizzled within a matter of months without concrete concessions from white businesses. But Randle still considered it a qualified success. "The purpose of a boycott is not only an all-or-nothing thing where you make these demands and if you don't get all of them the boycott fails," Randle said. "The purpose is also to heighten awareness. . . . After that boycott in 1968, we had people thinking about courtesy titles and all that, you see. So sometimes you just have to shake things up a little bit, shake the status quo." The boycotts did shake the status quo, but they did not upset it. African American political candidates in Indianola and throughout the county failed throughout the late 1960s and the entire decade of the 1970s to capitalize on blacks' majority in the county's total population. Appeals for racial solidarity simply could not overcome African Americans' economic dependence on whites or their fears of economic reprisal. Without a flashpoint of an issue to rally wide-scale support for a mass protest movement, civil rights organizing would founder in the county for a generation.[55]

Civil rights activists faced horribly daunting obstacles in the late 1960s and 1970s—worse, in many ways, than what they had faced during Freedom Summer. The members of the Subcommittee on Employment, Manpower, and Poverty, of the U.S. Senate's Committee on Labor and Public Welfare, toured the Delta and held hearings in Jackson during the spring of 1967. They observed for themselves "conditions of malnutrition and wide-

spread hunger . . . that can only be described as shocking" and asked
President Johnson to declare the Delta a disaster area so that its poor
residents could be eligible for a massive influx of federal dollars.[56] Bob
Williams, an organizer for the MFLU, described the housing of farm workers in Sunflower County as "shacks, where you could probably throw a cat
through [the holes in] the floor or the wall, if you tried anywhere real
hard." They were "just little shacks, three or four rooms, built out of two by
fours and tarpaper," Williams said. "That's all the room they got, and . . .
some of these families are pretty large families . . . [with] ten to fourteen
kids."[57]

As of April 1967, more than a quarter of a million black Deltans received
food from a government surplus program. The Delta Ministry distributed
food and clothing to more than 2,200 families in Sunflower County during
1968 and gave away cash to thousands more for the purchase of food
stamps.[58] One particular measurement of Sunflower County's poverty rate
gauged the depths of this poverty. In 1968, the federal Office of Economic
Opportunity calculated the minimum "level of income necessary for sur-
viving on a minimum diet with none of the amenities of prosperity" for
each county in Mississippi and determined that in Sunflower County, the
figure was a modest $2,953. Of 8,681 total families in Sunflower, 3,916, or
45.1 percent, earned less than this absolute minimum. If anything, economic conditions for African Americans in Sunflower County deteriorated
drastically during the decade that followed Freedom Summer. Attorney
Marian Wright testified at Senate hearings on poverty in the Delta in 1967,
"Starvation is a major, major problem now."[59]

The federal government did not retreat from all spending in Sunflower
County, however. The Eastland plantation received a $168,524.52 subsidy
for cotton price supports and acreage reduction in 1967. Federal welfare
policy—which Eastland himself helped to create—eased the burden on
planters like Eastland by "keeping his workers alive during the winter,
then [permitting] counties to withdraw their meager support during the
planting season—forcing the workers to accept near-starvation wages in
order to survive." Jamie Whitten, the Delta's voice in the U.S. House of
Representatives, chaired the House Appropriations Subcommittee on Agriculture for so long that Washington wags knew him as "the permanent
secretary of agriculture." His maneuverings in the 1960s killed a federal
program to teach unemployed black farmworkers how to drive tractors
and a Johnson administration plan just to study the problems of poverty
and hunger in Mississippi.[60] The election and reelection of Eastland and
Whitten came at great cost to the people of Sunflower County. Eastland

and Whitten actively—and successfully—opposed the interests of the majority of Sunflower County's people while they supported policies that enriched themselves and their staunchest supporters.

The black population of Sunflower County dropped by 7,758 between 1960 and 1970, and another 1,670 left the county between 1970 and 1980.[61] As mechanization eliminated farm employment and as Delta whites remained entrenched in positions of power, more and more blacks left the state. Surely, however, an even greater number would have left had the civil rights movement not given them hope that Mississippi was on the road to democracy.

Those who remained in Sunflower County, black and white alike, relied increasingly on the assistance of the federal government. Tony Dunbar, who traveled through the Delta in the late 1960s and again in the 1980s, found that "[t]he Delta is sort of a substation of Washington." The feds now dictated "[w]hat to plant, when to plant it, where to plant, whom to hire, how to house farmworkers, how to finance the farm, not to mention public welfare," and the list went on. Historian James Cobb found that the Delta's socioeconomic system as it existed in the early 1980s was a product not of its isolation from mainstream America but of "pervasive global and national economic influences and consistent interaction with a federal government whose policies often confirmed the Delta's inequities and reinforced its anachronistic social and political order as well."[62]

Change would obviously be slow to develop in Sunflower County; the struggle to bring it about gradually destroyed the county's most tireless agent for transformation. By 1977, Fannie Lou Hamer had been jailed and beaten for trying to vote. She had been sterilized without her permission. She had seen housemaids fired for joining the NAACP, and she had seen children, including her adopted daughter, die from complications of malnutrition. She had been hospitalized twice for nervous exhaustion. Suffering from breast cancer, hypertension, and diabetes and desperately disappointed by her African American sisters and brothers—to say nothing of whites, whom she also believed capable of redemption—Hamer died at the age of sixty-nine.[63]

At the time of her death, Mississippi had 210 African American elected officials, 204 more than there had been at the onset of Freedom Summer. By 1980, Mississippi would have 387 black elected officials, more than any other state in the Union. This reflection of increased black voting power was directly attributable to the efforts of Hamer and other dedicated freedom fighters. But Hamer knew that a movement for civil and human rights was as necessary in 1977 as it had been in 1957, if for no other reason than to keep the newly elected black officials from behaving like the old white ones.

Poverty and racial discrimination still bedeviled Sunflower County. Hamer died with bitterness toward her black neighbors in the county, whom she thought were not doing enough to help themselves, and she directed the bulk of her displeasure toward black middle-class "sell-outs." This was not a new opinion for Hamer. In a 1966 interview she had said, "The NAACP don't work with the people. . . . There ain't nothing I respect about the NAACP. It's awful." In Hamer's opinion, the NAACP represented only the black middle class, and the middle class, like the government, had failed to address, much less solve, the problems of black Deltans. She knew that for African Americans to win respect as equal members of a civil community and for truly democratic practices to take hold in the heart of the Delta, much work remained to be done.[64]

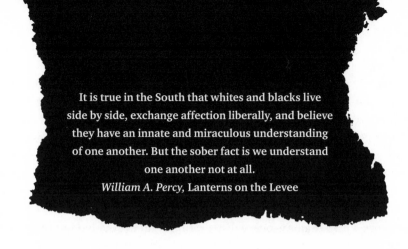

It is true in the South that whites and blacks live
side by side, exchange affection liberally, and believe
they have an innate and miraculous understanding
of one another. But the sober fact is we understand
one another not at all.
William A. Percy, Lanterns on the Levee

CHAPTER SEVEN

Concerned Citizens

*Civil Rights Organizing in the
Wake of the Civil Rights Movement*

For Indianola and Sunflower County, 1986 promised to be a proud year. As
the year began, Indianolans made plans for the town's centennial celebration, which would take place in May along the banks of picturesque Indian
Bayou. Would-be planters hoping to cash in on the expanding plantation
cotton and timber economies had organized the town during the aftermath of America's first Reconstruction. In the century that followed, Indianola persevered through booms and busts in cotton prices, floods of
biblical proportions, disease epidemics, the rise and fall of the sharecropper socioeconomic system, technological changes with enormous social
consequences, a Great Migration, and a second Reconstruction. Somehow, while scores of other small towns throughout the Delta had slipped
into economic irrelevance and simply faded away, Indianola had endured.

Economic development and diversification provided grounds for cautious optimism for Indianola's future. The town truly had something to celebrate.

In 1986, Sunflower County was still the state's largest producer of agricultural products, but it had begun to escape the trap of a one-crop economy.[1] U.S. highways intersected the county, making their juncture in Indianola the hub of a minor regional transportation network. In the county seat, a light industry employed nearly 1,000 semiskilled and unskilled workers, and a major grocery distribution center provided hundreds more nonagricultural jobs. The world's largest catfish processing plant hummed on the outskirts of town. Locals bragged about the new Wal-Mart and McDonald's franchises, sure signs that Indianola had finally arrived. But as Indianolans prepared for their centennial celebration and congratulated one another on the persistence that had carried them through so many trials in the past, the most trying episode in the town's social history was about to unfold. As they did in so many communities throughout the United States in the years following the "classical period" of the civil rights movement, debates surrounding the town's public education system divided Indianola.[2]

The mass movement that Indianola's middle-class blacks organized around a public education crisis in 1986 cut across classes within the black community and drew powerful whites into coalition. The alliance they crafted and the resolution they helped negotiate highlighted the promise of a movement led by the middle class but also illustrated such a movement's limitations. The movement's leaders worked with the Indianola business community to win a seat at the table where decisions affecting the lives of black citizens were made. They did not address the more dramatic and fundamental issues of social and economic reorganization.

The Schools

The U.S. Supreme Court's 1955 edict to end segregated public schooling "with all deliberate speed" had no effect whatsoever in Sunflower County for more than a decade. The process of desegregating the county's public schools did not even begin until lawyers associated with the MFDP started to challenge the dual school system with piecemeal legal assaults beginning in 1965. With help from the U.S. Department of Health, Education, and Welfare, these civil rights lawyers hammered out a "freedom of choice" compromise with Sunflower County education officials. Under the euphemistically named plan, which was soon approved by the federal courts, parents of school children received "freedom of choice" forms that allowed them to choose which schools their children would attend. On paper, African Americans could choose to send their children to previously all-white schools, and whites, too, could send their children to whichever school they chose. In reality, however, black families found their choices severely limited. One scholar observed, "In theory, the child's choice was free. In practice, it depended on black initiative, stamina, and fortitude to circumvent the numerous bureaucratic obstacles set in their path."[3]

Truth be told, bureaucracy was the least of black families' problems. Civil rights activists had a difficult time convincing black parents throughout the county, particularly in the town of Drew, that they truly were free to register their children in previously all-white public schools without reprisal. MFDP canvassers from Ruleville who tried to organize black families in Drew to respond to "freedom of choice" reported that they could not even step foot into the town without being arrested.[4]

Only a small handful of Sunflower County families took the authors of the freedom of choice papers at their word. One of these families, the Carters—Matthew and Mae Bertha Carter, along with their seven school-age children—sharecropped on the Pemble plantation in the Drew school district. The family lived on the food they grew in a vegetable patch and the $85 that their landlord advanced to them each month and subtracted from the cash value of their crops after every harvest.

The Carters were not new to the struggle for civil rights. Several members of the family had participated in protest marches throughout the state. Two daughters had been arrested at a demonstration in favor of the 1965 Voting Rights Act, which led to their being jailed along with hundreds of others in the livestock pens at the state fairgrounds in Jackson. Matthew and Mae Bertha Carter had been members of the NAACP since 1954, and everyone in the family had attended civil rights meetings in nearby Cleveland. Amzie Moore, the legendary Cleveland civil rights leader, was a family friend and adviser.[5]

The Carters had long-standing grievances against the Drew school district. Mae Bertha Carter rued the split sessions that kept black children out of school during the cotton planting and picking seasons, thereby interrupting their studies. She seethed when her children had to walk past an all-white school to get to what she considered an inferior institution. Like many before her, Carter also complained about fund-raising activities at the black schools. Her particular concerns reached the boiling point in 1964 when the Drew Negro High School principal ruled that students who had not paid club dues and book fines, bought the school newspaper and the yearbook, and sold candy for the school could not take their final examinations. Such fund-raisers created a prodigious hardship for large sharecropping families such as the Carters. When faced with a similar choice, one Carter child, twelve-year-old Gloria, had used her lunch money to pay club dues and gone without food for days on end. When Larry Carter, fourteen, faced steep book fines, a teacher suggested that he stay out of school for a few days and chop cotton to earn the necessary money. Mae Bertha Carter complained to the faculty of the high school that the fund-raisers were interfering with her children's education. When Amzie Moore counseled that further complaints would likely get them thrown off the Pemble place, the Carters held their tongues.[6]

The Carters received their "freedom of choice" papers in May 1965. On August 11, they returned the forms, indicating that they intended to enroll their children in previously all-white schools. Drew school officials had agreed to "freedom of choice" in the first place only because they assumed that no blacks would be brave—or foolhardy—enough to attempt to send their children to superior schools. From the white officials' perspective, the "compromise" rested on the premise that an all-white school board knew what was best for blacks and that blacks would in any case be too terrified to act against whites' wishes. Mae Bertha Carter still wondered at the arrogance in a 1997 oral history interview: "They think they know black folks," she said of the school board members. "They think they know 'em. See, this was an all-white school board, all male . . . and I can imagine 'em sitting there now, working out this proposal: 'Well, if we send out this freedom of choice [form], these people from the plantation won't be coming.'"[7]

The Johnson administration demanded that local schools desegregate only the first through fourth grades under the first phase of "freedom of choice" in 1965. According to Carter, the whites in Drew "knew us so well, they went on and said, 'Let's just put down there the first through the twelfth grade, 'cause ain't nobody comin' noway.'"[8] Constance Curry, an early adviser to SNCC and in 1966 a staff member of the American Friends Service Committee (AFSC), visited the Carters to see what her organization could do to help the family. What in the world, she asked the Carters, had ever possessed them to sign the "freedom of choice" papers in the first place? "We thought they meant it," Matthew Carter told her matter-of-factly. His answer may have been disingenuous, but it was a powerful one, and it exposed a determination that would be crucial if the Carters were to succeed.[9]

Within twenty-four hours after filing their intention, the Carters were threatened with eviction from the plantation. The white owner of Bob's

Grocery Store, the commissary where for years the Carters had bought their provisions on credit without incident, told Matthew Carter that he would have to renounce his intent to desegregate the schools or pay his bills in full before nightfall. Carter somehow scraped together the money and paid. Two nights later, gunshots ripped through the Carters' home.[10]

A neighbor of the Carters had also applied to transfer her two nieces into previously all-white public schools. A field representative for the AFSC found that the woman, Lizzie Lee, was "just very, very afraid" in the wake of the shooting incident. The Drew school board had ruled that Lee could not apply for the transfer for one of her nieces because she was not the girl's legal guardian. When Lee learned of the shooting at the Carters' home, she withdrew the other petition.[11]

James Hollman, a sharecropper in Ruleville and an MFDP member, had been active in trying to persuade Drew parents to transfer their children. He found that several African American families were willing to transfer their children to previously all-white schools but would not do so by themselves. Hollman reported, "People expressed fear that their landlords would throw them off the land." He took Prathia Hall Wynn, the AFSC's field representative, to meet the Miller family outside of Drew. Hollman had almost convinced Mr. Miller to transfer his two high-school-age daughters, but when Mrs. Miller learned about the shootings at the Carter home, she refused to consider the matter further. Wynn noted, "The situation seemed to place her in a [d]ilemma since she was very obviously concerned about obtaining the best possible education for her children."[12]

Wynn learned that the "freedom of choice" plan had been a major subject of discussion among the families she visited throughout the Delta. A Mr. Jones who sharecropped on a plantation near the Carters told Wynn that local families had discussed the matter when the forms arrived. Several had expressed interest in sending their children to better schools, but "[t]hey were afraid of reprisals. Then the shooting incident ruled the question out completely." Wynn also reported, "We had heard about the Carter family from several people before we met them. People who did not know them or where they lived had heard their story." The shooting thus discouraged blacks in a wide radius from transferring their children under "freedom of choice." In fact, it discouraged everyone but the Carters; their children were the only blacks in the previously all-white public schools of the Drew school district for two full years.

The effort to keep the Delta's black children in segregated and inferior schools was vigorous and concerted, and it involved a U.S. senator. In March 1967, James Eastland's office requested that the Mississippi State

Sovereignty Commission investigate one of the senator's pet suspicions: whether officials of the U.S. Department of Health, Education, and Welfare (HEW) (one of the more activist pro–civil rights agencies in the Johnson administration) had made unspecified promises to black families in Drew in order to entice them to desegregate the public schools.[13]

Chief investigator Tom Scarborough interviewed several white officials in Drew and learned of a rumor in the white community "that HEW officials did make promises to the Negroes of perhaps getting a scholarship to Howard [University] if they attended the white school." The Drew officials "said they were unable thus far to obtain a statement from any Negro who was present at this meeting that a promise of this kind was made."[14] Drew mayor W. O. "Snake" Williford told the investigator that Matthew Carter "did not have regular employment and the rumors are that he is being paid by the NAACP to send his children to the white school."[15] (How else could a black man in the Delta have gotten it into his head to send his children to the best available school?) The rumors did have one grain of truth: the AFSC had bought a house for the Carters with the assistance of lawyers from the NAACP Legal Defense Fund, but the family repaid the cost of the home. Of course, Matthew Carter did not have regular employment because his family had been thrown off the Pemble plantation, and other Sunflower County plantation owners refused to enter into a sharecropping arrangement with a known "agitator." In any case, the rumors reflect white Mississippians' inability to believe that Delta blacks might be willing to fight for a decent education for their children unless outside forces were prompting them.

The town of Indianola maintained an almost entirely segregated school system, holding out against the nominal law of the land until 1970. Desegregation had little momentum throughout the South after the Supreme Court's two historic *Brown* decisions in 1954 and 1955. In 1964, however, the Court ruled in *Griffen v. County School Board of Prince Edward County, Virginia* that it was unconstitutional to shut down public schools as a means to sidestep integration and proclaimed, "The time for 'mere deliberate speed' has run out."[16] Three black children tried and failed to integrate the previously all-white Lockard Elementary School just north of the railroad tracks in Indianola in 1965; five succeeded in 1966; and nine African American students attended the previously segregated Indianola High School and Indianola Junior High School in 1967. But until 1970, the trickle never amounted to anything more than just that.[17] White students attended Lockard Elementary School, Indianola Junior High, and Indianola High School north of the railroad tracks. Black students attended Carver Elementary School, Carver Middle School, and Gentry High School on the other side of town.

By the late 1960s, however, there was an active civil rights movement in Indianola, and black parents began to push for the desegregation of public schools. The Indianola school district had other ideas. Led by Superintendent O. B. Reno, a former member of the board of directors of the Indianola Citizens' Council, the school district wrestled with HEW lawyers and federal courts over plans to integrate the public schools for half a decade.[18] In 1968, the U.S. Supreme Court ruled in *Green v. County School Board of New Kent County, Virginia* that school boards were "clearly charged with the affirmative duty to take whatever steps necessary to convert to a unitary system in which racial discrimination would be eliminated root and branch." A year later, in its *Alexander v. Holmes County, Mississippi, Board of Education* decision, the Court finally asserted in strong language that it was the "obligation of every school district . . . to terminate dual school systems *at once* and to operate now and henceforth only unitary schools."[19]

At last, on January 16, 1970, nearly sixteen full years after segregated schools had been deemed unconstitutional, U.S. district court judge W. C. Keady ruled that Indianola could no longer operate a dual school system. He ordered the school board to prepare for a completely integrated public school system by February 1, two weeks hence.[20] Keady assigned all students in grades one through four who lived north of the C&G Railroad tracks to Lockard Elementary and all others to Carver Elementary, which in practical terms changed nothing. Students across the district in grades five through seven, however, were assigned to Carver Middle School; grades eight and nine across the district were assigned to the previously all-white Indianola High School (now Indianola Junior High School); and all students in grades ten through twelve were assigned to Gentry High. The decision met with predictable outrage from Indianola's white citizens.

The decision must not have surprised anyone in the white community, however, because whites immediately launched a program to make public school desegregation irrelevant to them. The program had been in planning stages for some time. Plans for Indianola Academy, a segregated private school, had been hatched at a Citizens' Council meeting in August 1964, a time when it first appeared that the federal government might be prepared to enforce desegregation edicts in Mississippi's public schools. The *Indianola Enterprise-Tocsin* reported on the plan and solicited community input.[21] When the Indianola public schools agreed nominally in 1965 to desegregate the first and second grades at Lockard with one grade to follow each consecutive year, First Baptist Church of Indianola set up the town's first private school, the precursor to Indianola Academy.[22] By November 1967, the academy had everything but a central building; 241 students from grades one to nine, all of them white, attended schools at the town's white Baptist and Methodist churches. Academy trustees thought that a new school building to house the nine grades would be completed soon on privately donated land and that one grade could be added each year thereafter.[23]

Similar arrangements were falling into place throughout Mississippi and much of the South. The national leadership of the Citizens' Councils applied the same energy and enthusiasm to organizing all-white private academies that it had once devoted to keeping the public schools segregated. A historian of the segregation academies concludes that their creation may have been the Citizens' Councils' "most significant and lasting endeavor. . . . Without the preexisting organizational work of the Citizens' Councils, the rapid creation of segregation academies in many small southern communities simply would not have been possible."[24]

At the height of the Citizens' Council movement, Senator Eastland and others had proposed segregated academies as a way to keep schools "pure"; following *Brown*, council members even encouraged the state to shut down the public schools rather than integrate. (Instead, the Mississippi legislature repealed the state's compulsory attendance law. As a result, by one estimate only 50 percent of the white students and 20 percent of the black students who began first grade in 1954 graduated from high school twelve years later.)[25] By 1970, whites in the Delta had given up on the public schools completely. By that point, Eastland and Thomas P. Brady (the author of *Black Monday* and since 1963 an associate justice on the state supreme court) were soliciting funds for the "Council Schools," a compendium of three Jackson-area segregation academies that were operated by the state Citizens' Council apparatus and were intended as a pilot program for the movement.[26]

Indianola Academy opened for classes in 1969, and when Keady's ruling came down in January 1970, academy officials received more than 900 applications in less than a week. With the help of the local American Legion post, which offered its building for classroom space, and (tax-deductible) furniture and supplies donated by local businesses, Indianola made the transition from all-white public schools to an all-white private academy without a hitch. Scholarship grants from local individuals and businesses allowed even poor whites to attend the academy. With these grants and powerful amounts of peer pressure, whites maintained racial solidarity across class lines.[27]

Though plans for Indianola Academy had long been in the making, blacks remember that the academy "cropped up over night" in the wake of the ruling in *U.S. v. Indianola Municipal School District*. According to Isabel Lee, who was then the sole African American on the school board, "The decision came down on a Friday, and by Monday all the whites were over at the academy. Not one of them showed up at [Gentry] High School."[28] Contemporary newspaper accounts reported that while the academy had been in the works for quite some time, the white shift from public schools to the academy did take place over a single weekend. Indianola Academy's relatively quick organization and construction could only have been the result of massive organization on the part of white segregationists. While the academy was not officially connected to Citizens' Councils, Inc., its link to council ideology was direct. That ideology had changed since 1954. Where Robert Patterson and others had organized to keep their children's public schools lily-white after *Brown* to save them, their successors now worked to create all-white institutions at the expense of the public school system. Once again, the Delta's planter class led the way.

The Crisis

By the fall of 1985, when Indianola's superintendent of education D. B. ("Mud") Floyd announced his retirement, more than 90 percent of the children and a majority of the teachers in the town's school system were African American. Ten educators expressed an interest in replacing Floyd; nine were white, and all of them were male. Indianola's school board asked for input on the hiring decision from citizens, and black Indianolans rallied behind Robert Merritt, the principal of all-black Carver Elementary School and the one African American who had applied for the job. Four of the five school board members who decided the issue were white, at a time when blacks made up more than 60 percent of Indianola's total population. The school board hired the Mississippi Association of School Boards to assess the candidates, and the consultants recommended Merritt.[29]

The school board then passed a resolution stating that applicants for the position needed a doctoral degree and five years' administrative experience in the city schools' central office to qualify for the position. The latter qualification was a transparent attempt to restrict the candidacy of Merritt, who had not yet retreated from the schools to the comparative comfort of the bureaucracy's central office. Merritt held a Ph.D. in education administration, an educational specialist's degree in educational administration and supervision, and a bachelor's degree in elementary education and had garnered ten years' experience as a teacher in Indianola's schools and sixteen as a principal. He could not have been better qualified for the post. But the school board's tradition of promoting employees— nearly all of whom had been white until the late 1970s—from within the central office raised suspicions that the majority-white board was only interested in hiring someone it was comfortable with and could control. Local blacks suspected that the five-year rule would only apply to Merritt.

Morris Kinsey, chairman of the state chapter of the NAACP's Education Committee, publicly insinuated that the school board had created the five-year rule explicitly to prevent Merritt's candidacy and charged the board with racial discrimination. "It is time to forget race and to look at the person with the qualifications and commitment to educate all students," Kinsey advised. "If the board fails to do what is good and right, we call for their immediate resignation."[30] Kinsey may have been the first person outside of Indianola to take note of the growing controversy, but he would not be the last.

Merritt enjoyed the unqualified support of a majority of Indianolans. He was rejected nevertheless, along with eight other applicants, after the school board secretly interviewed and offered the position to another candidate at the plantation home of board president Odell Godwin. Walter Gregory, the school board's lone black member, confided to the Indianola newspaper that the board had met with the white candidate at Godwin's home but had refused to meet with Merritt.[31] When the revelation surfaced, the embarrassed school board was forced to begin the search for a superintendent anew.

The board consisted of one member elected by the voting population of the Indianola school district and four members appointed by the town's all-white board of aldermen. Indianola did not have a black school board member until 1967, when Isabel Lee became the first African American appointed to the panel. After one term ("They were glad to get rid of me and I was glad to get rid of them," she later said), Lee was replaced by Walter Gregory in 1971.[32] Until 1986, Gregory was the only African American on the five-member board. However, in March 1986—several months into the controversy over the hiring—the school district held an election for the one elected seat on the council. This was unusual enough in itself; normally incumbents faced no challengers, because board members traditionally did not announce publicly when their terms were to expire. For obvious reasons, this cut down on school board elections. This particular election was especially important to the community, though, because the contest involved Odell Godwin.

Godwin, an eighteen-year veteran of the school board and its president, was the member of the board who had been most dismissive of Merritt's candidacy in public. Moreover, his elected position had traditionally been controlled by the large number of voters who lived within Indianola's school district but outside of the town limits. His constituency was dominated by wealthy white farmers who were interested only in keeping their taxes as low as possible. Like other whites in the area, they had abandoned the public schools.

The election attracted the attention of Concerned Citizens, a group that had originally organized in 1985 around the issue of pay raises for public school teachers, most of whom were by now African American. Concerned Citizens first complained that the school board was willing to spend tens of thousands of dollars on the search for a new superintendent when it had a perfectly qualified applicant in Merritt. The group was convinced that Godwin was primarily responsible for turning the hiring into a farce, and it was determined to take action in the upcoming election. Concerned Citizens backed David Jackson, a deputy director of the Delta Housing Development Corporation. If he could defeat Godwin, the group thought, it would surely signal a changing of the guard. (Jackson's children attended Indianola public schools, while Godwin's two sons had been educated at Indianola Academy.) Concerned Citizens waged a stealth campaign, fearing that a public play for Godwin's seat would scare whites into voting in droves. The plan worked. Only 348 Indianolans bothered to vote in the election, and Jackson won the seat with a comfortable majority. When the school board members met for the first time to seat Jackson, they also elected Walter Gregory their new president.[33]

The victory, in the context of the hiring decision, was a major one. It was also highly symbolic. Concerned Citizens understandably considered Jackson's win a victory for the cause of fair representation. Willie Spurlock, a paralegal who had emerged as the group's spokesman, said, "Through [Jackson], we will know more about what is going on."[34]

Concerned Citizens believed that Jackson's election would result in Merritt's hiring. Another black face in school board meetings might not guarantee satisfaction in the Merritt matter, the group reasoned, but surely the board would interpret the effort that went into getting Jackson elected to a traditionally white seat as widespread public support for Merritt. By February, the superintendent decision had become a litmus test for Indianola race relations. A member of Concerned Citizens told the *Enterprise-Tocsin* that naming Merritt would "trample or at least cool the flames of a steadily brewing and potentially explosive crisis which would affect not only the school system, but also the business community, and all races, religions, creeds, and colors in Indianola."[35] The search for a superintendent had become a major controversy.

Concurrently, in the second search for a superintendent of schools, the board narrowed its list from a pool of nineteen applicants to two finalists, Merritt and W. A. Grissom, who was white. Grissom, the assistant superintendent of neighboring Bolivar County's District II schools, had nearly twenty years' experience in Bolivar County's central office and had lived in Indianola for eleven years. Grissom had also worked for four years as the principal of Lockard Elementary, Indianola's lone integrated school. Merritt had served four times longer as the principal of Indianola's all-black elementary school, and his academic credentials were superior to Grissom's.[36]

The Boycott

Concerned Citizens began to hear rumors in late March that Merritt would be passed over again for the position. The group promised a massive economic boycott should the rumors prove true. At an Indianola chamber of commerce meeting on March 23, sympathetic whites and merchants anxious to avoid a boycott demanded that the school board choose Merritt.[37] Nonetheless, on March 25 the board hired Grissom as its superintendent after a 3–2 vote that split along racial lines. The thirty blacks who attended the morning meeting at which the hiring was announced booed the decision. That evening, Concerned Citizens held a meeting that drew 700 Indianolans to Saint Benedict the Moor, the Catholic church that had emerged as a movement center in the late 1960s.

The reaction was remarkably well organized from the outset. Protesters locked arms in a show of solidarity and organized a boycott of downtown Indianola businesses and public schools, to be accompanied by picketing of businesses and the school district's central office. Spurlock, Concerned Citizens' spokesman, told the crowd, "We have tried to maintain peace. The superintendent issue has led us to war . . . a full-scale war," and he warned those who did not want to get involved in the boycott not to get in their way. Concerned Citizens elected picket captains and formed groups to march in front of Indianola businesses beginning the following day. The group vowed to continue the protest until Merritt was named superintendent, "not because he is black but because of his qualifications and his understanding of the community." Because many local blacks, particularly the elderly, lacked the means to drive outside of Indianola for essential

"It is time we get a slice of the pie. We are not asking for the whole pie."
Marchers protest the schools superintendent decision in downtown Indianola, 1986.
*(Jim Abbott/*Indianola Enterprise-Tocsin*)*

items, Concerned Citizens exempted drug stores, banks, and the Piggly Wiggly grocery store on downtown Front Street from the boycott.[38]

The following day, only 317 of the 3,029 students enrolled in the city's five public schools arrived for classes. The 90 percent absentee rate suggested that the boycott movement was founded on a staggeringly high level of unity from the outset. Fearing the loss of attendance-based appropriations from the state, the school board declared a holiday for the city's schools but hoped to reopen them within a week. Students joined adults on the picket lines that were concentrated in front of white-owned businesses such as the town's new Wal-Mart and McDonald's outlets on Highway 82 and the locally owned Ben Fried's Department Store in downtown Indianola and the Double Quick convenience stores that were scattered throughout the area.[39]

Concerned Citizens chose the sites carefully, though for different reasons. The Double Quick convenience stores were the most logical targets. They were owned by the Gresham family, whose patriarch had been active in the original chapter of the Citizens' Council and the rejuvenated state Republican Party. The Greshams had come to wield considerable economic, and therefore political, power in Indianola.[40] Concerned Citizens demonstrated political savvy and perhaps a measure of retribution in its decision to pinpoint the family's financial interests.

The group heaped unwanted attention upon the chain stores in hopes that executives at national corporate headquarters would pressure local management to work toward a resolution of the crisis. It targeted Ben Fried's Department Store because Steve Rosenthal, owner and operator of the establishment that had been in business in the same spot on the banks of Indian Bayou since 1913 (Rosenthal was Ben Fried's grandson), was then the chairman of the Indianola chamber of commerce's Merchants Committee. The chamber of commerce was already on record as favoring Merritt, but Concerned Citizens deduced that Rosenthal, if hit in his own pocketbook, would work doubly hard toward a quick resolution. Indianola's business geography was such that locally owned stores were generally concentrated "downtown" and national chain stores—Wal-Mart, fast-food restaurants, gas stations, and the like—were located along the east-west highway north of downtown. Because the businesses on Highway 82 were spread farther apart, the pickets were necessarily spread thin and protests there were less potent. But fewer picketers could cover more storefronts and concentrate attention on the downtown business district. The downtown protests were devastating for merchants like Rosenthal. Blacks from the county and the surrounding area, upon whom the merchants depended heavily, respected the boycotts and shopped elsewhere. Delta whites stayed away from Indianola in droves, afraid of what the protesters would do to them if they ventured downtown. The chamber of commerce estimated that the boycott cost Indianola merchants in excess of $3 million.[41]

Concerned Citizens issued numerous warnings beforehand, announcing that the group would call for a boycott if the school board failed to hire Merritt. Still, somehow, powerful whites managed to maintain that they had been blindsided by the black community's reaction to the school board decision. Clarke Johnson, a town alderman and small businessman (and a self-described progressive on racial issues), said, "Maybe I was sitting up there fat and happy, but I didn't realize there were any serious problems." "This surprised me, this really surprised me," said Morris Lewis, the founder of Lewis Grocery, one of Indianola's largest businesses and the largest grocery wholesaler in Mississippi, which happened also to employ hundreds of African Americans. "I thought we were living well together."[42]

Other white businesspeople found themselves in a difficult if not impossible situation. Some, perhaps many, agreed with Steve Rosenthal, who had supported Merritt in the abstract but vastly underestimated both the public support Merritt enjoyed and the larger cause he represented. "Unfortunately, and probably by our own mistake, we weren't in tune with it," Rosenthal said. "We had heard there was some unrest going on, but we didn't realize the extent of it. With every political situation there's going to be a happy side and a sad side, but we didn't realize there was a *major* problem going on and major unrest brewing." Ted Moll, the president of Indianola's Modern Line, a light industry that employed hundreds of black workers, said in the wake of the decision, "Personally, I feel that the school board's decision was wrong. I believe that Indianola is ready for a black superintendent. I apologize that I didn't express this opinion vocally enough. . . . This is a progressive community and we have been shackled with civil rights talk that we don't deserve and I think we need to put that fire out quickly." City alderman Bill Coleman, who also managed a downtown store, claimed, "[A]s a city official and a merchant I am appalled at the decision the school board made in their selection. I don't think they were fair to the man they chose and I don't think they were fair to the community which they served. I don't think they took into consideration the signals they were getting from both the black and white community at all."[43]

White merchants who did not agree with Rosenthal and Moll about Merritt's qualifications did agree that the boycott was all too effective and that they had been placed in an awkward situation. Emily Smith, the owner of a downtown clothing store, complained, "I think we are the victims. I don't think this boycott is fair to us. We don't have the power."[44] Mayor Philip Fratesi, who would prove to be unequal to the difficult task of restoring racial peace in Indianola, complained, "They're picking on the merchants, which I think is wrong because . . . the decision was made by the school board and not the merchants. I would like to have seen [Concerned Citizens] take a different course of action. If they didn't like the decision they could resolve the issue through legal means."[45]

But the boycotts did continue. Children manned the picket lines by day, and their parents relieved them to march at night. When the children went back to school, elderly blacks took their places. On several occasions, white youths in pickup trucks yelled obscenities and insults at the protesters, and a few times they threw rocks and water at participants.

The boycott devastated small downtown businesses. Delta merchants counted on the Easter season as one of the year's busiest and most profitable, and the boycott wiped those sales out almost completely. Rosenthal remembered, "For the first week or ten days we did almost zero business.

. . . Every business in town was affected [negatively] in some form or fashion, from the big boys on down." Rosenthal's department store had to write off a warehouse full of Easter clothing that it never sold. Four businesses actually closed as a result of the boycotts. One, a convenience store, had employed as many as twenty blacks and nine whites. Even a month into the boycott, when Concerned Citizens' momentum was waning, local businesses reported that sales were off 33 to 66 percent. Small retail stores could ill afford a one-third slip in sales at any time, much less during a busy sales period. Local businessmen relied on local black customers, but the loss of out-of-town trade was doubly damaging.[46]

On the first weekend of the boycott, 500 protesters marched through downtown Indianola singing "We Shall Overcome" and reciting passages from Martin Luther King Jr.'s "I Have a Dream" speech. For the first and last time, Concerned Citizens allowed outside political actors to participate in events, and this was the first mass protest generated for the benefit of the press. Concerned Citizens' rhetoric remained purposefully mild. Spurlock had told the original boycott mass meeting, "This is not a plaything, people. We did not get to this juncture because we wanted to be here. We were forced here," and he continued to act as a moderating force. His words to the marchers were anything but extreme:

> We are here this afternoon to say to Indianola, Sunflower County, the state of Mississippi and the nation that we're not here to protest against our white sisters and brothers. This is not a matter of dislike. It is a matter of where a decision was made with which we do not agree. . . . We know that this is hard, that this is very taxing on various members of the community. It is a lot of stress. It has caused races to become polarized. But we must conduct ourselves just as we have up to this point, with decency and integrity. . . . The only thing we are asking today is that we are given a chance. We are not asking to take over. . . . It is time we get a slice of the pie. We are not asking for the whole pie.[47]

Spurlock told the crowd that the boycott revolved around the issues of meritocracy and fairness, not race: "Dr. Robert Merritt can serve our community well, not just for blacks but for whites alike," he said. Most tellingly, Spurlock claimed, Merritt "would lead our system to the point where if any citizen chooses to send his child to the public school, he can." Members of Concerned Citizens made it difficult for their opponents to portray them as dangerous radicals or outsiders.[48]

Spurlock and Concerned Citizens maintained that the crisis was about Merritt's qualifications, first, last, and always. By keeping the focus on a single, cut-and-dried issue, Concerned Citizens did not allow its base of protesters to fragment into several factions over disputes stemming from secondary concerns. Members acknowledged, however, that they considered the Merritt controversy an emblem of a much larger problem. "It's bigger than the issue itself," Spurlock maintained. "[I]t's about taking [part of the] power."[49] For Concerned Citizens, the school board's choice was only the most blatant example of Sunflower County's white minority expecting to make all of the important decisions for a biracial, black-majority community.

Members of Concerned Citizens also insisted that they be allowed to settle the problem themselves, without outside help. The decision ultimately made resolution of the crisis easier to manage. After Morris Kinsey, chairman of the state NAACP chapter's Education Committee, accused the Indianola school board of flat-out racism, Concerned Citizens asked him not to comment on the matter again. Later, Concerned Citizens spoke to labor unions in the state about extending the boycott throughout Mississippi, but nothing came of the conversations. Spurlock and others also publicly threatened to enlist the help of Reverend Jesse Jackson on several occasions. Privately, they agreed that this was Indianola's problem and Indianolans needed to settle it themselves. Spurlock told the *Indianola Enterprise-Tocsin*, "This is a local matter and it should be resolved on a local basis. I feel there is enough decent people, both black and white, to get this resolved locally."[50]

The refusal to import non-Indianolans rested on one of the many valuable lessons Concerned Citizens had learned from earlier movements in the county, when moderate and conservative whites warned rural blacks from getting involved with "outside agitators" and successfully kept blacks from winning their rights as equal citizens. In 1986, Concerned Citizens could have brought in experienced outside organizers to help with the boycott, but such a calculation involved considerable risk. In her 1939 study of Indianola society, Hortense Powdermaker described the phenomenon of "the intruder . . . [whose] outside efforts are felt as a threat not only to the existing order, but also to the serenity of those who identify their interests with it."[51] Concerned Citizens knew that its white neighbors in rural Sunflower County were as unwilling in 1986 to accept the social critiques of "outsiders" as they had been when Powdermaker studied Indianola in the 1930s and when northern college students "invaded" the county in 1964. Concerned Citizens thought that any "outsider" it brought in to help solve the problem could not have arrived with a complete understanding of local politics, local personalities, or the local lifestyle.[52] This time, members bargained that an "outsider" without the savvy that came from growing up in the Mississippi Delta could not help their cause in the long run.

Inviting Jesse Jackson or someone of his stature to Indianola undoubtedly would have thrust Concerned Citizens into the national limelight. It would have transformed the town into a national symbol of southern blacks' struggle to win permanently the rights that the civil rights movement of the 1960s had not been able to guarantee them. Concerned Citizens knew that. But the group decided that only local people could and should solve this local problem. As a result, members of Concerned Citizens declared that they expected to be treated as equal political actors by whites in Sunflower County. They affirmed that African Americans in Sunflower County had confidence in their own abilities as political actors and had no real need to call in "outsiders" to help them solve what they defined as their own problem. Finally, they let it be known that they liked it in Indianola and were not going anywhere else—so whites had better get used to living with them as equals.

Concerned Citizens, unlike its white neighbors, demonstrated a devotion to Indianola's public schools, which translated to a devotion to Indianola's civic life and the future of the town. By 1986, the Great Migration had ended and had even begun to reverse itself. Economic alternatives to sharecropping had become available to African Americans in the Delta. At least a significant number of the blacks who stayed in Sunflower County lived there because they wanted to, not because they were without options. Among other things, the actions of Concerned Citizens emphasized this point and demonstrated the members' deep commitment to the civic life of Sunflower County.

Merritt steered clear of the demonstrations on his behalf and publicly disavowed the use of boycotts. He told the *Jackson Clarion-Ledger* that he was happy to have the unified support of Indianola's black community but that he did not support Concerned Citizens' tactics. He remained out of sight during mass rallies, but his daughter and wife walked at the head of at least one march.[53] Merritt himself had to walk a fine line. Proud enough to believe that he was the best man for the superintendent's position, he fought hard to attain it. As a career educator, however, he had to have swallowed hard when his ambition resulted in thousands of black children staying home from school. That in itself made his plight with the school board difficult enough, because he had to continue to position himself not only as the best qualified candidate but also as the one who knew most

about and cared most for Indianola's school children. Had Merritt participated in mass marches or pickets in downtown Indianola, the white community and the majority-white school board would have interpreted his
actions as self-aggrandizing, and in all likelihood the struggle over his
hiring would have become irredeemably bitter. The code of acceptable
behavior for the "good nigger" had certainly changed since Luther Holbert's day, but Merritt's actions were nevertheless severely constrained by
whites' expectations of how he should behave. Nor could Merritt come off
as ungrateful or aloof in the collective eyes of the black community, lest
support for him wane and his goal become unreachable. If Merritt had to
fret over appearing too selfish and uppity before the white community, he
also had to worry about appearing thankless, remote, and "too white" to
his core of supporters. By successfully negotiating this Scylla and Chary-
bdis, Merritt kept an already tense situation from deteriorating.

Concerned Citizens continued to view the school boycott as an extremely serious tactic that should be employed only in an emergency. After
the first week of picketing, parents sent their children back to school. As
soon as the students returned to the classroom, however, the school
board's three white members reaffirmed their commitment to hiring Grissom, and Grissom announced that he had every intention of taking office
when his contract took effect in July. One week after the children went
back to school—fifteen days into the boycott—Concerned Citizens announced another school walkout. Absentee rates the next day rose again
to nearly 90 percent.

Walter Gregory and David Jackson, the two black school board members, now broke ranks from the white members of the board for the first
time. For the first three weeks of the crisis, Gregory and Jackson had
acknowledged voting against Grissom but had agreed to support him publicly as members of a unified school board. On April 13, they bowed to
pressure from the black community and withdrew their support for the
board's decision. Grissom somehow maintained that he had the community's full support, but the ground was crumbling beneath him. On April 3,
the *Enterprise-Tocsin* published an open letter to Grissom that had been
signed by 506 parents of public school children. It read, in part, "For many
years the black community has sat idly by while the leaders of the white
community have made important decisions that dictated our lives and our
children's lives. That day no longer exists when our community will allow
others to direct our children's future." On April 14, the all-white Indianola
board of aldermen called unanimously for Grissom's resignation.[54]

On the same day, the school board closed the five Indianola public

"Truly the man of the hour in the city of Indianola." Robert Merritt.
*(Jim Abbott/*Indianola Enterprise-Tocsin)

schools indefinitely, pending resolution of the boycott. All 166 teachers and 30 teachers' aides, 5 principals and 3 assistant principals, 17 bus drivers, and 122 support personnel—over 350 employees, the majority of them African American (and many of whom were participating in the mass meetings and pickets)—were relieved without pay. The board also canceled all extracurricular activities, including sports, which in the small-town South meant serious business. Tensions in Indianola ratcheted up another level.[55]

When the boycotts carried on into the third week of April, they began to interfere with plans for the town's centennial celebration. Concerned Citizens announced that if the celebration's planners did not make major changes, the boycott would be extended to include the festivity. An exhausted Spurlock pointed to the lack of black faces on the centennial planning board—one more example of a "plantation mentality," in his words—as reason enough to forego a celebration. "I just don't know what there is to celebrate," he said. "We still have racial problems. There have been no great racial strides [since 1886]. Whites are still predominant. They hold the power positions, and they don't want to share." Reverend Michael Freeman, the pastor of a black Methodist congregation, pointed out, "We live in two separate communities—black and white."[56]

Concerned Citizens mainly objected to the site of the celebration's opening ceremony, Legion Field, which had been the site of a prisoner of war camp for German soldiers during World War II and later served as the home field for generations of football teams at all-white Indianola High School. While white students romped on its well-manicured playing field, Gentry High School football players played on a gridiron that bordered a cotton field. ("If you scored a touchdown and kept running too far," one former player remembered, "you were in the cotton. It was embarrassing.") After Indianola High School had been ordered to desegregate and Indianola Academy cropped up, Legion Field became the home of the IA Colonels—yet more proof that the segregation academy had replaced Indianola High School as the civic rallying point for whites in Indianola. Members of Concerned Citizens interpreted the decision to locate the centennial celebration's most important ceremony at the field as an undisguised message that they were welcome there only on whites' terms. Henry Paris, the chairman of the Centennial Committee, responded that blacks should be grateful that an entire day had been reserved for a B. B. King concert on their side of town.[57]

As the boycotts ground on, the two communities that had existed in such close proximity for a century became increasingly wary of one another. Concerned Citizens saw whites trying to tell blacks how to act in every situation. Whites were certain that what they perceived as their own progressive attitudes and behavior had generated a stockpile of racial goodwill over the years in Indianola. They now identified their black neighbors as ungrateful, irrational, and destructive. Support for the school board's decision eroded, but the board's three white members entrenched themselves and refused to budge.

The Solution

Almost immediately after the boycotts began, the Indianola chamber of commerce decided to resurrect the town's Bi-racial Committee, a project that had begun as an effort to make sure cooler heads prevailed during a similar, though less serious, controversy in 1968. In the years since, it had died a quiet death. When the boycotts began, there was literally no place where representatives of Indianola's black and white communities could discuss grievances on an equal footing and in a formal, or even informal, manner. The chamber's decision to revive the committee was major news during the crisis; it signaled that Indianola's business community took black complaints seriously. Members of the chamber of commerce realized, to their credit, that the committee needed African Americans who could speak freely for their community: if rank-and-file blacks thought that powerful whites had "hand-picked" the black members of the group, the chamber reasoned, it would have no legitimacy. "It has got to be people who represent the black community, whether we agree [with them] or not," Henry Paris acknowledged, "and we need people from the white community who can communicate and speak out."[58]

To ensure that the Bi-racial Committee's black members were not hand-picked and "co-opted," the chamber asked Concerned Citizens for the names of black leaders who would be willing to serve. Concerned Citizens provided the committee with four names: Willie Spurlock; attorney Carver Randle, a longtime Indianolan and former president of the county NAACP branch; Reverend Michael Freeman, the pastor of Raspberry United Methodist, whom local whites considered a hothead; and Reverend David Matthews of Bell Grove African Methodist Church, whom local whites (if not always local blacks) appreciated as a moderate. Representing whites were Ted Moll, the president of Modern Line; merchant Steve Rosenthal; chamber of commerce president and merchant Maurine Lipnick; Planters Bank's Henry Paris; and Reverend Stan Runnells of St. Stephen's Episcopal Church, who was considered something of a racial liberal.

The Bi-racial Committee began meeting at least twice a week at the headquarters of Lewis Grocery for hours at a time. After black members of the committee had successfully explained their grievances, the committee began to discuss possible solutions to the crisis. It quickly became clear that Concerned Citizens, as it had iterated on numerous occasions, would not accept a solution that did not include hiring Merritt. Grissom, however, refused to resign. According to David Matthews, the idea of buying out Grissom's contract first came to light during one of these early discussions, but the suggestion was apparently tabled because of its exorbitant price tag.⁵⁹

The Bi-racial Committee was critical to the maintenance of racial peace in Indianola. The committee also served as something of a distillery: African American citizens knew that they could speak freely, often times in an impolitic manner, about their predicament at Concerned Citizens meetings. The Concerned Citizens leaders who sat on the Bi-racial Committee then toned down those remarks for white ears but got the essential point across. White members further distilled those remarks and reported them to their community; they also toned down rhetoric from the white community for black ears at Bi-racial Committee meetings. What was important and revolutionary about the meetings was that powerful black and white Indianolans sat at a negotiating table and spoke as equals. Jack Harper, the county's chancery clerk who was instrumental in organizing the original Bi-racial Committee, said, "That committee has been worth its weight in gold to the community."⁶⁰ The committee's work was indeed precious, not necessarily because it was instrumental in maintaining racial peace and averting violence, but because it provided a rare arena in which powerful whites treated blacks as their equals. Eventually, Bi-racial Committee deliberations generated concrete proposals to break the schools' impasse.

Three weeks into the boycott, Tommy McWilliams, an attorney for Delta Pride whose family had lived in Sunflower County for four generations, announced a dramatic plan. McWilliams, a partner in the Drew law firm that had previously represented the interests of both Jim Eastland and Fannie Lou Hamer, declared that he represented sixteen "influential business leaders" who wanted to bring the superintendent controversy to a quick and final resolution. He began negotiations with Grissom's attorney in hopes of convincing the school board's choice to step down from the office he had not yet technically assumed, but Grissom refused a reported $90,000 buyout package. When negotiations stretched out to a third week, McWilliams warned the readers of the *Enterprise-Tocsin*, "The quality of life which we have enjoyed will not continue unless we learn to live together and work together for the common good."⁶¹

It is difficult to imagine a local white attorney with the respect that Tommy McWilliams carried making a similar statement during, say, Freedom Summer. McWilliams had grown up near Indianola and attended Ole Miss Law School in the late 1960s; his credentials as a recognized leader in the white community were impeccable. (Even as hidebound and traditional as white Delta society is, residence of four generations is almost unheard of. Tommy McWilliams was no newcomer.) His willingness to listen to Concerned Citizens' demands with a sympathetic ear represented a major shift in whites' expectations of how men like McWilliams should wield power in the community, and the example McWilliams set in risking his own reputation to broker a compromise was invaluable.[62]

In late April, McWilliams also publicized for the first time the names of the businesspeople he represented. The list read like a Who's Who of Indianola moneymakers. Officials from Lewis Grocery, Modern Line, Delta Pride, and local banks, along with several respected small businessmen, had all felt the impact of the boycott, and sixteen of them believed so strongly that the situation had to be resolved that they came together, pooled their resources, and organized a buyout.[63]

The group of sixteen was composed of the same type of men who had organized the original Citizens' Council. Morris Lewis, who had helped to organize the council in the 1950s as a wholesale grocer, now lent his weight to the resolution of the superintendent crisis as the closest thing Indianola had to a captain of industry. Henry Paris's predecessors at Planters Bank had also been vocal supporters of the Citizens' Council, but now Paris became a major player in the crisis's resolution. The Gresham family that had been integral to council machinations and to hiring Grissom in the first place now put its money behind moderation and compromise.

The white businessmen who pushed the solution as a way to keep their black employees and customers happy in 1986 had much in common with the farm owners who had pushed the council movement as a way of keeping the children of black workers out of "white" public schools in the 1950s. One could scarcely have imagined plantation owners brokering a solution with blacks during the "classical period" of the civil rights movement, much less supporting it financially. The dynamic of white capitalists responding to the demands of black workers and black consumers spoke volumes about how much and in what ways Sunflower County had changed since Robert Patterson organized the first meeting of the Citizens' Council.

In comparison to the rest of the United States, by 1986 Sunflower County had dabbled with modernization, industrial development, and economic diversification only lightly. For decades, Mississippi's official economic development policy had been to "balance agriculture with industry," but in the Delta the theory had been put into practice only in fits and starts.[64] The Delta remained the least industrialized area of the South's least industrialized state. The legislators who passed Governor Hugh White's Balance Agriculture with Industry (BAWI) proposals during a 1936 special session had hoped that economic diversification and modernization would create wealth by attracting industries to process the state's raw materials over the next few years. "Subsequently," according to one student of BAWI, "the effort to attract new industry became an article of faith in state government and apparently among the people of the state."[65] Later, BAWI adherents hoped that industrial development would liberalize Mississippi society. They could not have looked for a less likely place to test their hypotheses, it seemed, than in Sunflower County.[66]

The resolution of the superintendent crisis would, however, seem to validate the arguments of those who sought to diversify the Delta's economy and liberalize its social relations. A member of the group of sixteen businessmen, a merchant, claimed that Indianola's three industrial powers provided most of the money and nearly all of the muscle behind the settlement. According to Steve Rosenthal, Modern Line, Lewis Grocery, and Delta Pride all "hire[d] a lot of blacks. They knew that for good workers and for good life in Indianola, the employees have to be happy, and [the industrialists] had to be involved in the situation, so they jumped in, too."[67] The group of sixteen recognized that an injustice had been done to the black community, which was something of a victory in itself for Concerned Citizens.

Faced with an organized response to the injustice, the group of businessmen then decided that Sunflower County's business climate (another new phenomenon in itself) would suffer if the injustice was allowed to remain and fester. Finally, the group decided that the happiness of Sunflower County's blacks—as employees, as consumers, and as citizens—was important enough to warrant a huge cash expenditure. Indianola's politicians and the white community followed the group of sixteen's lead. One day after Grissom finally agreed to the $90,000 buyout, the school board voted unanimously to hire Robert Merritt as the superintendent of Indianola's schools. Concerned Citizens had won a seat at the table where decisions were made.

Concerned Citizens clearly acted on the lessons it had learned from earlier civil rights struggles in Sunflower County and elsewhere. From campaigns like the SCLC's 1963 boycott of Birmingham merchants and NAACP efforts in Port Gibson, Mississippi, members of Concerned Citizens learned how well-organized boycotts could force a local power structure to the bargaining table. They also learned that when a business community leads, the elected officials will follow. A boycott that cripples local sales also denies sales taxes, thereby making elected officials all the more eager to end the boycott. From the campaigns of the "classical period" of the civil rights movement, Concerned Citizens learned the importance of good public relations and management of the news media. From their own community's history, members learned the risk of bringing "outsiders" into local situations. They used mass meetings in local churches to disseminate information, discuss strategy, and energize their troops. It was no coincidence that they sang the same freedom songs civil rights workers had sung twenty years before to steel their purpose in similar struggles.[68]

The Aftermath

The superintendent's crisis and its resolution can be read as the culmination of the struggle for black equality in Sunflower County. The resolution marked the first time that members of Sunflower County's small but growing black middle class had organized around a justice issue and thrown themselves wholeheartedly behind a cause that black workers also supported. What had taken them so long? Why did they organize a civil rights movement during the second term of the Reagan administration, long after the civil rights movement was supposed to have ended?

During the "classical period" of the American civil rights movement, between the Supreme Court's *Brown* decision in 1954 and the death of Martin Luther King Jr. in 1968, Sunflower County's black middle class was small, weak, and vulnerable.[69] In the 1950s, black teachers and clergymen who absorbed the bourgeois ideals of an almost equally small white middle class in the Delta could not have hoped to be accepted as social equals in Delta society. They could not exercise their most basic rights as American citizens, and if they thought of speaking out against the injustices they faced, they had the negative examples of Luther Holbert, Clinton Battle, and others to consider.

In the 1960s, the black middle class's timidity attracted the wrath of a newly politicized black working class.[70] Fannie Lou Hamer and her likeminded neighbors, for example, reserved their greatest scorn for other neighbors whom they dismissed as "scared teachers" or "the people peepin' through the bushes."[71] Black activists came to consider the stereotypical frightened teacher or clergyman—the "Uncle Tom" figure, transferred for these purposes to the middle class—as more of an obstacle than the stereotypical fat, tobacco-chewing white farmer who knew what was best for his "nigras." That the members of this class came to lead a civil rights movement in 1986 represented a change in the African American social order.

The black neighborhoods of Indianola welcomed news of Grissom's buyout, but selling the compromise to the white community took hard work.

Hard-liners disparaged the group of sixteen for "giving in" to what they regarded as economic blackmail. Howard J. Davis, a white Indianolan, grumbled to the *Enterprise-Tocsin*, "We are certainly all thankful that the boycott has ended, and I hope that no group will ever try to hold Indianola hostage again." He and other whites criticized Merritt for allowing the boycotts to proceed in his name.[72] The five weeks of black protest did little to clarify the protestors' position for many whites who had had terribly little communication with blacks in the first place. In another letter to the local newspaper, another white sang a tune that would later become all too familiar in the Delta and elsewhere: "In the 1960s black people were being discriminated against and you had white racist[s] all over the South. Those days have long been gone. Today, black people are given a more than equal opportunity and in a lot of cases jobs are only available to black people regardless of qualification or capabilities. . . . In the 1980s white people are being discriminated against and you have black racist[s] all over the country."[73] Indianola's 1986 civil rights movement was complicated by debates over affirmative action taking place simultaneously on the national level. "A lot of the [white] community, I don't think, was really aware of what the situation was, as far as what had transpired to get [Concerned Citizens] upset," says Steve Rosenthal. "They didn't know who Dr. Merritt was or about his involvement with the schools, what his credentials were, and that kind of thing." The group of sixteen's next task was to soothe this faction, and the assignment was no simpler than placating Concerned Citizens had been in the first place.[74]

For the most part, however, Indianolans recognized the resolution of the crisis as a major victory, perhaps the greatest and most meaningful in the county's history. *Enterprise-Tocsin* editor Jim Abbott observed, "There is an increased interest in the black community to participate in the improvement of the public school system here." Just as important was the fact that the "interest [is] shared by many white citizens, many of them younger whites, who see the necessity of a strong public school system as key to the progress of Indianola and who see improved education as the key to Mississippi's future." For Abbott, the generational component was key. In conversations with Indianola whites after the boycott, he noticed that younger white Indianolans—with fewer expectations of how blacks should behave—resented the way the older generation had turned the situation into a crisis. A white man who had been a senior at Indianola Academy during the boycott (and thirty years old at the time of a 1997 interview) said, "The problem with Sunflower County is these aristocratic farmers. They used to be civic-minded when they could run everything, but desegregation changed all that. Now all they care about is holding on to their money." The man hoped and thought that his generation of whites would do better.[75]

Concerned Citizens got what it wanted and encouraged Sunflower County's blacks to let bygones be bygones, even inviting people to shop in Indianola again. Spurlock urged blacks and whites alike to "[s]how that you care about the future growth of our city by supporting our local businesses. . . . In a concerted effort we can cause our community to become unified and bring about the cohesiveness that is needed in a progressive city." Spurlock and Tommy McWilliams both expressed a belief that the lines of communication across racial lines in Indianola had improved to the point that such drastic measures as the boycott would never again be necessary.[76] Carver Randle, the black lawyer who emerged as a leader in Concerned Citizens, concurred. Even Mayor Phillip Fratesi, who refused to place blame on the whites on the school board for creating the crisis, admitted, "The boycott certainly wasn't something we wanted, but I believe it's going to make us a closer-knit community."[77]

The sense of relief among Indianola merchants was palpable, and not just because sales were improving. Johnny Duease, owner of a local small business, told the *Enterprise-Tocsin*, "Business is better, much better, maybe by 100 percent" one week after the boycott had ended. "But as important as that," he said, "is the fact that everybody seems to be in a good mood again." Steve Rosenthal echoed the sentiments: "Most of our customers would prefer to shop in Indianola not only for the merchandise but also because they like to shop with friends. I've had several [African American] shoppers comment to me personally that they're glad it's over."[78]

A vindicated Merritt told the community, "Leadership does not mean controlling people. It means creating opportunities, removing obstacles, providing guidance and promoting growth. And believe me, when we do this we become the recipients of our own efforts. We all profit from it. . . . We must become a human community . . . of forces helping each other."[79]

Energized by the outpouring of support that had gone into his rise to the top of Indianola's schools hierarchy, Merritt embarked on an ambitious and unprecedented campaign to improve the town's schools for all of its children. In June, Jack Harper introduced Merritt to a meeting of the all-white Indianola Lions Club as "truly the man of the hour in the city of Indianola." Merritt outlined a twelve-point program for the improvement of community schools that stressed community involvement. By this juncture—two months into his appointment—Merritt had already proven that he was the right man for the job, not because he was black, but because he was imaginative, energetic, and capable. A group of white parents at Lockard Elementary was so impressed with what they called Merritt's "fresh ideas" that they began pushing for changes from the school board. These changes included a request for more money from the federal government —a clear shift from Delta whites' traditional inclination to reject federal monies for education because they might come with strings attached that would compromise local sovereignty.[80] Merritt's listed goals for the school system would eventually increase from 12 to over 100—and he would accomplish every single one of them before retiring.[81]

One Indianolan went on record with lingering bitterness toward the controversy and its resolution. W. A. Grissom told a Jackson newspaper, "It was nothing but an overthrow of the United States government, and it could have tremendous impact not only on Mississippi but nationwide." Grissom did see what he thought was a silver lining: had he stayed on, Concerned Citizens might have started a voter registration drive that could have resulted eventually in black domination of the school board. He believed that his decision to step aside had averted such a disaster.[82]

The Strike

Grissom's bitterness aside, the superintendent crisis had an ending that the town's citizens found satisfying. Less than two months later, however, another emergency would erupt and bring into doubt the durability of the racial peace that Indianola had won at so high a cost. This episode would show that Concerned Citizens' victory over Delta paternalism may have been less than total, and in any case had ambiguous consequences. It also brought into question the strength of the cross-class cooperation that had been so evident in the African American community during the superintendent crisis.

In early May, the United Food and Commercial Workers labor union accused Delta Pride, Inc., of unfair labor practices. The company employed 1,041 Deltans with an annual payroll of $11 million. Delta Pride's Indianola plant was the largest catfish processing facility in the world, capable of killing, filleting, and packaging as much as 600,000 pounds of catfish in a given day.[83] In 1986, Delta Pride's Indianola facility was the crown jewel of an agri-industry that residents prayed would finally save the area's chronically poor, one-track economy.[84] (The 1985 Sunflower County catfish harvest was valued at $44 million, nearly as much as the $47.9 million cotton crop.)[85] Organized as a cooperative among local catfish farmers in 1981, Delta Pride had enjoyed 30 percent annual growth each year thereafter. Of 1,041 total employees, 903 people worked the facility's cleaning line; 856 of them were black.[86]

The racial composition of the company's workforce lay at the heart of the unionization effort at Delta Pride. The African Americans who worked the monotonous processing lines (the "kill line" and the "cutting line") found the work there no better than it had been on the plantation, and often times worse. The repetitive motion of beheading or filleting fish was no more interesting than hoeing or picking row upon row of cotton, and the working conditions in most cases were no more comfortable. The responsibilities of a "header" required a worker to remove fifteen catfish heads a minute, and a "filleter" was required to cut 800 pounds of fillets per shift. Workers were allowed one five-minute bathroom break in the morning, one fifteen-minute coffee break per shift, and a lunch break. While on the job, workers had to meet strict quotas, "standing on the kill line or at the cutting table, working hard and fast."[87]

Reports in the *New York Times* referred to "management philosophies akin to those of the plantation era" and "the culture of an Old South plantation [that] permeates the industry and is in some ways more offensive than when people picked cotton."[88] Rosa Walker, who worked the Delta Pride cutting tables for eight years, developed carpal tunnel syndrome and was subsequently fired. "They hire you, cripple you, and fire you out at Delta Pride. . . . It's like being back on the plantation," Walker remarked acidly. She was not alone. Walker's coworker Mary Young eloquently described the kill line as "pure-dee hell."[89] The catfish plant in Bebe Moore Campbell's 1992 novel, *Your Blues Ain't Like Mine*, is named, appropriately enough, "New Plantation." Campbell has a white line worker who is pushing for unionization complain, "Them same people that own the New Plantation, they worked the niggers to death picking cotton. Now they're trying to pull the same shit. They work us all like dogs. That goddamn Reagan don't give a good goddamn if you ain't rich. I'da been better off with Jesse Jackson for President."[90]

According to a May 1986 complaint filed by United Food and Commercial Workers with the National Labor Relations Board, several Delta Pride employees who had pushed for unionization had either been fired or threatened with termination or the loss of benefits. United Food and Commercial Workers claimed that the company offered low pay, poor benefits, and dangerous working conditions. Line workers, they complained, had to arrive at work at an appointed hour but were then forced to wait as long as an hour or more for trucks to arrive with fish before they were allowed to "clock in." Once they did, these employees worked at least eight-hour shifts, pushing back the time when they could leave the plant and thereby hopelessly complicating child care arrangements and family schedules.[91]

According to the Indianola chamber of commerce, Delta Pride wages were $3.85 an hour, with the average employee getting 5.5 overtime hours per week at $5.23. (The federal minimum wage in 1986 was $3.10.) Delta Pride had never had a general layoff like other processing plants in the industry and pointed to its generous fringe benefits, including five days' paid vacation after one year's employment, five paid holidays, a Christmas bonus of a week's extra pay for those who had worked a full year, and a package that included 70 percent coverage of health insurance and 100 percent of life insurance.[92] A journalist calculated in 1990 that the average Delta Pride worker made $4.05 per hour, which worked out to $8,424 per year, or $4,251 below the federal poverty level for a single mother of three children. Dick Stevens, president of the Country Skillet Catfish Company just south of the Sunflower County line in Isola, admitted, "People can't live on what we're paying."[93]

Willie Spurlock, still the spokesman for Concerned Citizens, suggested that Delta Pride should address worker concerns to head off a unionization vote. His stance indicated that Concerned Citizens—or at least the organization's leaders—did not perceive an affinity between the union movement and the struggle for civil rights.[94] (Spurlock would later accept a position in management with Delta Pride.) If Delta Pride workers expected support from the Concerned Citizens apparatus, they must have been disappointed to hear from Carver Randle, who encouraged them to look favorably upon the changes management had already made. "Where management does everything it should to keep its employees as happy as possible," Randle reasoned, "you don't need a union."[95]

Editor Jim Abbott and Jack Harper both urged workers to reject the union, afraid that increased wage and benefits costs would drive Sunflower County's largest employer out of business. Isola's WelFed plant, they noted, had closed after a seven-week strike in 1981. To make sure its workers appreciated the cause and effect of that situation, Delta Pride carried busloads of workers to the empty processing facility in the days leading up to the unionization vote for tours of the plant's rusting machinery. When the workers at Pride of the Pond in Tunica voted to unionize in September 1986, the plant shut down immediately. Union organizers claimed that Pride of the Pond was merely trying to scare the workers at Delta Pride, where the stakes were much higher. (Pride of the Pond did reopen following the Delta Pride vote.) Abbott reminded Delta Pride workers that Sunflower County had an 18 percent unemployment rate and that a WelFed Catfish plant in Belzoni and Ludlow Industries of Sunflower County had both recently unionized, only to have the companies close down within weeks. Despite these warnings, Delta Pride's line workers voted 489–349 in favor of unionization in October, and company president Sam Hinote shifted tactics, hastening to quash rumors that the plant would shut down or curtail operations.[96]

Union organizers succeeded in the Delta when they framed labor-management relations in civil rights terms. The 1986 unionization effort was successful, in part, because Drew's Cleve McDowell, state field representative for the NAACP, threw that organization's weight behind unionization on the grounds that nearly all of the nonsupervisory workers were black women and all of the management and ownership positions belonged to white men.[97] United Food and Commercial Workers Local 1529 struck against Delta Pride again in September 1990, protesting working conditions and the high incidence of work-related injuries.[98] The strike caught the attention of Jesse Jackson, who accused Delta Pride of "turning the plant into a plantation," and the Reverend Joseph Lowery, then head of the SCLC. Lowery forecast a new chapter in the civil rights movement, this time "in the arena of the economy," focused on industries like catfish processing. (Fannie Lou Hamer must have rolled over in her grave. For Hamer and her supporters, the civil rights movement had always involved "the arena of the economy.") "Ninety percent of the workers in the catfish industry are black and 90% of the money in the industry goes to whites," Lowery claimed. The SCLC instituted a boycott of Delta Pride products throughout the South.[99]

Delta Pride consistently avowed that labor issues were not civil rights issues, insisting that the economic problems facing the catfish industry had nothing to do with race. The problems catfish processing faced were "rising costs, excess processor capacity and softening sales demand," not modern-day Simon Legrees on the processing line.[100] This was not an abstract issue, for Delta Pride knew that black southerners composed the catfish industry's primary consumer base; allowing the strike to turn into a racial issue could have spelled disaster for the industry as a whole. The 1990 strike stretched into its thirteenth week before Local 1529 voted overwhelmingly to accept a new contract with modest concessions from Delta Pride. Their decision said more about the economic hardships strikers faced and the easy availability of replacement workers than it did about the attractiveness of the new agreement. Even minimum wage jobs were scarce and attractive in the Delta, and Delta Pride actually put more people to work on the lines during the strike than it had before.[101] Significantly, one of the concessions that the catfish workers' union won from Delta Pride was recognition of the federal Martin Luther King Jr. holiday.

In 1991, Reverend Michael Freeman told writer and former civil rights activist Tom Dent, "The strike helped break down class stratifications within the race; people had to unify."[102] It is difficult to agree with this analysis: the middle-class leaders and supporters of Concerned Citizens clearly did not consider the Delta Pride unionization fight their own. Without their support, the striking workers had little chance of constructing major reforms. The proximity of the school boycott, in which middle-class leaders enjoyed support from both the black middle class and black workers, to the Delta Pride strike, which the middle class did not support, highlighted the fragility of cross-class alliances in Sunflower County's black community.

This frailty underscores how difficult it truly is to build and sustain a civil rights movement. But the success of a movement can be measured in ways other than its durability and cut-and-dried results. Freeman also told Dent, "[T]he workers themselves, for probably the first time in their lives, began to understand their own strength; they felt good about themselves."[103] For all of the thousands of men and women who worked for greater civil, political, and human rights in Sunflower County throughout the twentieth century, this may have been the most important consequence of all.

The 1986 movements were successful by these and other measures. White moderates met the old SNCC demand to "let the people decide" halfway. Fannie Lou Hamer's vision of a beloved community of equal citizens did not materialize, but by the end of the superintendent crisis, the African Americans of Indianola, and by extension those of Sunflower County, had become agents of their community's destiny. At the very least, they had won the right to participate in civic life as full citizens. As a result, by any measurement, at the end of 1986 Sunflower County was a much more democratic community than it had been at the end of World War II. It had certainly come a long way since Luther Holbert's day. Whatever else they might or might not bring, at the very least a majority of the county's citizens knew that voting and political organizing would not invite economic and physical terrorism. To be sure, this may seem a small victory for citizens who should have been protected by the U.S. Constitution all the while, but it was a real victory that has had real consequences.

By 1986, blacks in Sunflower County had begun to flex their collective voting muscle. The percentage of African American elected officials continued its slow climb toward the black percentage of total population. At the same time, economic development and diversification worked toward the creation of a black middle class, which in turn created more common ground between black and white residents of the county. Blacks and whites learned a great deal about one another in 1986. By forcing the county's citizens to look for points of agreement, Concerned Citizens gave the community a gift.

Ultimately, the crisis over Indianola's schools superintendency and Concerned Citizens' reaction to it were great for business. The resolution of the schools crisis and the unionization effort at Delta Pride created a racial peace—or (perhaps more important) an image of peace—that other towns in the Delta could not claim. Developments in the years since 1986 have proven that the creation of nonagricultural jobs, along with the creation of an image of biracial cooperation, literally saved the people of Sunflower County. In this case, a successful civil rights movement created a better business climate. For the people of Sunflower County, this may have been the most important lesson to be learned from a forty-year struggle for civil rights.

EPILOGUE

> See, now . . . to understand why we say that . . . you got to go
> back to slavery time. See, our family was owned by a fellow
> named Sutter. That was Sutter's grandfather. Alright. The piano
> was owned by a fellow named Joel Nolander. He was one of the
> Nolander brothers from down in Georgia. It was coming up on
> Sutter's wedding anniversary and he was looking to buy his
> wife . . . Miss Ophelia was her name . . . he was looking to buy her
> an anniversary present. Only thing with him . . . he ain't had no
> money. But he had some niggers. So he asked Mr. Nolander if
> maybe he could trade off some of his niggers for that piano. Told
> him he would give him one and a half niggers for it. That's the
> way he told him. Say he could have one full grown and one half
> grown. . . . So Sutter lined up his niggers and Mr. Nolander
> looked them over and out of the whole bunch he picked my
> grandmother . . . and he picked my daddy when he wasn't but
> a little boy nine years old.
> *August Wilson,* The Piano Lesson

The characters in August Wilson's *The Piano Lesson*, the 1990 Pulitzer Prize winner for drama, migrate from Sunflower County to the urban North, but they cannot escape the ghosts of slavery. Like the members of Wilson's fictional Charles family, Americans are still haunted by the heritage of human bondage. Throughout the South's history in particular, the region's citizens have invariably made decisions within a world whose fundamental structures were created to serve the institution. In many parts of the South, the Mississippi Delta chief among them, the twin legacies of slavery and emancipation are palpable and dramatic even at the dawn of the twenty-first century.

The poor people's movement led by Fannie Lou Hamer from 1962 to 1977 was the first successful challenge to the structures of Sunflower County's slave/sharecropper society. Around Hamer's example, poor blacks created a movement that defied the received culture of the Mississippi Delta and asserted African Americans' rights as American citizens. Hamer's movement forged homegrown solutions to the problems created by the slave/sharecropper regime. As a participant in the civil rights movement, Hamer established herself as a true heroine in the American patriotic tradition. As a social organizer, she proved herself a genius who imagined creative ways to attack a flawed social system. But Hamer enjoyed little if any measurable success in her lifetime; she died with a broken spirit, bitterly disappointed in her black sisters and brothers, to say nothing of the white Americans whom she also hoped to help find redemption.

In comparison, the Indianolans who rallied around the unlikely civil rights figure of Robert Merritt built upon the movement culture that Hamer and her followers had developed, applied the lessons they had learned from that earlier struggle, and succeeded in realizing their narrowly defined goals. They won respect from whites with power, and they won the right to participate in making decisions that affected their community. Their movement succeeded in part because they did not challenge the legitimacy of a rich white power structure so much as demand to be respected by it and to be allowed to participate as equal partners within a civic community. Taking the long view, sNCC's strategy to "let the people decide" has paid off, and it has transformed Sunflower County's social life in a myriad of ways. The beneficiaries of these changes have been middle-class blacks and whites almost exclusively, however. Adherents to the sNCC philosophy who had hoped to reshape the Delta's economic hierarchies can see the glass in Sunflower as no more than half full. Those who emphasized the need for black self-assertion and self-determination can find satisfaction in the changes their work brought about.

Concerned Citizens' success in 1986 was due in part to economic transformations that had changed the Delta over the five previous decades. By 1986, it was comparatively difficult for a white planter class to dominate whichever social class it chose, least of all the county seat's growing black middle class. African Americans moved in to assume the positions that white schoolteachers abandoned when white parents gave up on the public schools, and they staffed many of the new white-collar positions that were created in the Delta's diversifying economy.[1] These economic transformations weakened the once-dominant planter class and shifted power to a business-oriented group of whites who could not afford to alienate their base of African American customers. Concerned Citizens took advantage of this transformation and forged a protest movement that owed as much to the amorphous ideology of Black Power as it did to the integrationist ideals of the classical civil right movement.

Concerned Citizens asserted a collective power as united black consumers who deserved the same rights and positions of responsibility as their white neighbors. Economic transformations had weakened the social power of plantation owners in the years between the *Brown* decision and the Indianola superintendent crisis. Because of these changes, Concerned Citizens found a kindly reception in the white business community in 1986 that Clinton Battle and Fannie Lou Hamer and their followers, so bedeviled by the Citizens' Councils, could not have dreamed of enjoying in 1954 or 1964. Sunflower County's African American professionals and wage earners found it possible in 1986 to assert a collective strength that Battle's and Hamer's sharecroppers could never have wielded. Concerned Citizens was responsible for the creation of an atmosphere that greatly expanded occupational and political opportunities for all of Sunflower's citizens. For that reason, Concerned Citizens was more successful in seeing a justice struggle through to completion than any other civil rights movement in Sunflower County's history.

Concerned Citizens was successful in other ways, as well. Protests such as the superintendent boycott erupted in part because black Indianolans believed that they had a stake in Sunflower County's future. Had its members adhered to Indianola whites' stereotyped expectations of African Americans—had they behaved as "good niggers," to use the phrase that applied in Luther Holbert's day—Concerned Citizens could not have protested the school board's decision overlooking the superior candidate Merritt. In their protest movement, members of Concerned Citizens displayed anything but apathy and laziness, and by demanding seats at the table of power, they showed a devotion to Sunflower County. At base, Concerned Citizens demanded that white Indianolans recognize that the time had come to let African Americans share in making important decisions that affected a biracial community. The group did not demand that the whites who had abandoned the public schools remove themselves from decisions affecting black children's educations. It did not demand that the school board raise property taxes on the outlying plantations whose owners had mismanaged the Indianola school district as reparations for past grievances. In many ways, Concerned Citizens was no more radical than any PTA in America. In the specific context of the Mississippi Delta, however, Concerned Citizens' program of action was revolutionary.

In the years since the resolution of the superintendent crisis, Sunflower County's integrated political leadership has taken advantage of the county's status as a federally defined "empowerment zone" and attracted a number of new businesses to the area. The crowning jewel of this development is Indianola's Dollar General distribution center, which, when it opened in 1998, created more than 400 new jobs and had an annual payroll in excess of $5 million. It is expected to bring more than $10 million into the county annually. Clanton Beamon and Carver Randle, the first African American members of the county board of supervisors and former allies of Fannie Lou Hamer, were credited with bringing the financial windfall to Indianola. The Indianola Vocational-Technical School, one of the pet projects of Robert Merritt, also opened in 1998; it will eventually train thousands of Indianola students to work at the distribution center and elsewhere for wages that far exceed the Delta average.[2]

It is safe to assume that without the visible leadership of citizens like Merritt, Beamon, and Randle, and without the Indianola white business community's newly found civic commitment to interracial democracy, national corporations like Dollar General would not have considered investing in the area. In that sense, the civil rights movement inarguably saved Sunflower County from economic disaster. It should also go without saying that whatever vibrancy exists in Sunflower County's civic life is a direct result of the civil rights movements participants' dedication to democracy. Activist and writer Tom Dent toured the South in 1991 and returned to the hot spots of the civil rights struggle. Dent visited Indianola and left feeling optimistic for the town's future. "Those towns [like Indianola] with an active, issue-oriented and engaged black community, supported by those in the white community who shared the concern with issues, were alive towns," he wrote. "They were the places that were most conscious of their Movement heritage, and saw themselves as continuing a change that began in the sixties or even before then."[3]

I have been fortunate to see this commitment at close range. In researching this study, I lived for a time in Indianola and recorded oral history interviews with Sunflower County residents. I lived in what was becoming the town's only mixed neighborhood, on Forrest Street—which was surrounded by Lee, Jackson, Hood, and Stuart Streets. (I assumed my street was named for Nathan Bedford Forrest, the Confederate cavalry general and founder of the Ku Klux Klan, and not his brother Aaron, who as an early white settler in the county reportedly locked his slaves in cages at night.) My adopted neighborhood had once been the only white neighborhood south of the Columbus and Greenville Railroad, Indianola's proverbial "wrong side of the tracks," but African American families had been buying the neighborhood's small but comfortable homes in increasing numbers since the late 1980s. They were in the majority by the time I got to the neighborhood, and I could tell that it would not be long before they

began flexing their political muscles. In the newest New South—the post–
Voting Rights Act South—which heroes, I had to wonder, would replace
the Confederate generals on the neighborhood's street signs? (I don't
mind suggesting that Merritt Street has a nice ring to it.)

Through blind luck, the first person I met in Sunflower County was Jack E.
Harper Jr., the county government's longtime chancery court clerk. I knew
nothing about Indianola when I first arrived; I was surprised to find what
looked like a swamp running through the middle of the county seat. More
surprising was the sense of excitement that hung in the air over the small,
languid town: a Hollywood film crew was busy constructing what was
supposed to look like a lawyer's office on a vacant lot across from the
Sunflower County courthouse, only to blow it up later that afternoon.
(They were in Indianola to film a crucial scene for a movie adaptation of a
John Grisham novel.) I watched the proceedings for a while, then ducked
into the courthouse and asked a woman what was going on. She explained
why men were running around the courthouse with walkie-talkies, and I
asked her another question: Did she by any chance know anything about
the state of the county's records? "Oh, you'll want to talk to Mr. Harper
about that," she answered. I came to learn that I would want to talk to Mr.
Harper about a lot of things.

Jack Harper could not have been more cordial. After I explained to him
what I was contemplating, he asked what I suppose was the inevitable
question: "Son, do you have a Mississippi heritage?" My answer—No, sir, I
grew up in Georgia and both sides of my family are from North Carolina—
didn't seem to count for much, but Harper was no less generous after
learning that I was an "outsider." In the course of our conversation, he told
me that he had held the same political office since 1956. This was extraordi-
nary for a white politician in the Black Belt South, not only for the improbably long time span it covered but also for the milestones it encompassed. By
the 1990s, Mississippi had more African American elected officials than any
other state, a reflection of the voting power of citizens who were allowed to
register to vote after the Fifteenth Amendment was finally enforced. It
seemed highly curious to me that a man who had been elected by an all-
white constituency to multiple terms before the Voting Rights Act took
effect in 1965 in the majority-black county could have held on to power for
so long afterward. He would have had to serve two almost completely
opposite constituencies on either side of the landmark legislation.

Harper told me with evident pride about his service on the state Democratic Party committees that finally reconciled the "regulars" with the

remnants of the Freedom Democrats in the mid-1970s. Harper had been a political ally of the white liberal governor William Winter in the 1980s, and I have since seen video footage of Winter and Harper stumping for Robert Clark Jr., who in 1982 nearly became the first African American from Mississippi to be elected to the U.S. Congress since Reconstruction. He and Aaron Henry—the World War II veteran who had run for governor on the Freedom Vote shadow ticket—were old friends, Harper told me, but for some reason that did not quite square with the autographed picture of James Eastland I saw displayed prominently on his office wall.[4] Harper assured me that the county's records were extant, if disorganized, and encouraged me to dive into the history of Sunflower County.

I later learned that Jack Harper had sat on the first board of directors of the Indianola Citizens' Council. I also learned that as the chairman of the Indianola chamber of commerce, Harper had written mean-spirited letters to the town's African American citizens, trying to break civil rights–related boycotts in the late 1960s. It was difficult for me to reconcile the hateful man I saw in those documents with the generous man I knew from the courthouse, but I came to see Harper's personal history as something of an ideological journey. Harper's biography helped me understand many of the changes that have taken place in Sunflower County over the past half-century.

Harper's parents had been sharecroppers who lived for most of his youth just outside of Indianola. "We did our own labor," he told a news-paper reporter in 1983. "The blacks didn't suffer for me [as a farmer], I suffered with them." His experiences during the Great Depression turned him into a staunch Democrat. "The Democratic party was generous with the people of the South [during the New Deal], and in those days the people of the South were in turn generous with their votes for the Demo-crats," he recalled. Harper's parents pushed him to obtain the best possible education available to him. He graduated from Indianola High School, Mississippi Delta Junior College, and the Ole Miss Law School (with finan-cial assistance from the New Deal's National Youth Administration), then returned to Indianola to practice law. When the United States entered World War II, he served for nearly three years as a Marine Corps officer. As a reservist, he fought again for a year in Korea.[5]

When he returned to Indianola, an entire way of life that he had never had reason to question came under attack. Though Harper refused to acknowledge it when I interviewed him in 1997, the black assault on Jim Crow that followed the *Brown* ruling must have thoroughly confused him. It was not difficult to imagine what must have gone through his mind at the time. Harper, the scrapping local-boy lawyer, was the archetype of the white men who formed the first Citizens' Councils, and the December 22, 1955, *Indianola Enterprise-Tocsin* identified Harper as a leader in the new movement. By 1997, this fact was a political liability for Harper and, it seemed to me, a personal embarrassment. He stated flatly in our oral history interview that he had nothing to tell me about the Citizens' Councils. But Harper also added somewhat cryptically, "I established the proposition, as sort of my trademark, that I don't consider myself responsible for anything that happened before I became a mature individual on the scene, but I do accept responsibility for what happened under my watch." By 1997, it appeared to me, Harper considered the council movement a youthful indiscretion, one that he wished could be forgotten, if not forgiven.

Following the Meredith crisis at Ole Miss, Harper said (in our 1997 interview) that he began to have serious doubts about what the Citizens' Councils stood for and about resistance to the Second Reconstruction in general. He kept returning to what he had been taught in his constitutional law classes in Oxford; with that in mind, he said, the neo-nullifiers' arguments against federal enforcement of desegregation laws seemed silly. "We studied the constitutional law that indicated that we were federated under the federal statutes," he said. "You can declare interposition or do whatever you want to do, but you're going to always be under federal laws." Harper began to think that the diehard segregationists were irrational and quixotic; besides, as Sunflower County's chancery court clerk, Harper had taken an oath in 1956 to uphold the U.S. Constitution, and he took that oath seriously.[6]

Or so he said in 1997. Harper remained a member of the Citizens' Council after the Meredith crisis at Oxford. The September 19, 1963, *Enterprise-Tocsin* once again identified Harper as a leader in the organization, this some three months after Byron de la Beckwith, an avowed white supremacist and a member of the Citizens' Council next door in Leflore County, had murdered Medgar Evers. Over the next several years, however, Harper began to push the county through several small steps toward wide-scale desegregation. He was all but invisible during Freedom Summer; the SNCC staffers and volunteers focused their attention on Cecil C. Campbell, the county circuit clerk whose responsibilities included registering voters. If Harper did anything to thwart their program, he did so only behind the scenes; his name does not even appear in the Sovereignty Commission investigators' reports from the Delta. Of course, Harper did nothing in public to promote voter registration during Freedom Summer, either.

Harper said that he could read the writing on the wall after the Civil Rights Act of 1964 and the Voting Rights Act of 1965 passed Congress, and he was convinced that the federal government was serious about its support for the desegregation of public life. There was precious little, Harper believed, that any white person in Sunflower County could do to stop it. This belief, Harper later said, cost him several white friends. In the 1970s, Harper worked with his political ally Aaron Henry to unify the loyalists and regulars of the Mississippi Democratic Party. In 1972, he chaired the county party convention that united the two factions in Sunflower County. In 1976, he served on the committee created by Governor Cliff Finch that finally united the factions on the state level. Harper's service was rewarded when the state party—now completely integrated—named him a state convention cochairman in 1980. This story of Harper's post–Voting Rights Act career seemed to trace a straight trajectory toward a full commitment to interracial democracy.[7]

There remained, however, the problem of the fliers Harper had mailed to African Americans in and around Indianola in the spring of 1968. Civil rights groups were trying to organize a boycott of Indianola merchants over the issues of African American employment and the use of courtesy titles. Harper, acting as the president of the Indianola chamber of commerce, responded to the boycott leaders with mailings that demanded, "Stand up For Freedom . . . BE A MAN." Harper portrayed the boycott organizers as dangerous radicals who were trampling the constitutional rights of both area merchants and African Americans who wanted to shop downtown. Harper urged local blacks to "DO YOUR PROPER DUTY AS AN AMERICAN CITIZEN—DO YOUR CHRISTIAN DUTY" and call the police if any of the boycott organizers tried to pressure them into participating.

The document reminded me that no biography is linear. Jack Harper may have evolved from a racist—or even from a small-town lawyer who wanted to do what his community thought best and was frightened by social change—into what I considered a dedicated public servant. He may have tried throughout his public career to do what he thought was best for his African American and white constituents alike. Whether he did or not is debatable, but his path from leadership in the Citizens' Council to being a supporter of the local chapter of the NAACP did not lead in a straight line.

So far as I know, Jack Harper never publicly disavowed the Citizens' Council program. (He passed away in 2003.) In our 1997 oral history interview, Harper did not issue a tearful mea culpa when I asked him directly about the council, but I did infer in his refusal to talk about the organization at least a vague regret. I believe that Harper privately acknowledged the terrible acts for which the council was responsible, whether he took an active part in those actions or not. As a politician and public servant who would have to serve and solicit the votes of a black majority, it is likely that he decided long ago that to bring attention to the councils' extralegal activities and fundamentally antidemocratic nature would be counterproductive. By 1997, a new generation of black Sunflower County voters knew Harper as a diligent public servant who was sensitive to their needs; indeed, Harper did not face an opponent in an election between 1965, when the Voting Rights Act was passed, and 2000, when he decided to retire from public office. If this is any guide, even those who remembered his service to the council must have thought that he had acted in good faith since he broke with that organization. There is much evidence on which to base this interpretation. By the late 1990s, Harper was buying one of the largest advertisements in the Sunflower County NAACP's banquet program every year. He had served for many years on the board of directors of Mississippi Delta Community College in Moorhead, which had benefited African Americans in the Delta at least as much as it had whites. Harper and the county board of commissioners had attracted several large employers to Indianola, accounting for millions of dollars in payroll for the county's black majority.

I found it difficult to argue with Harper's personal credo, "Either you go help make the deal, or one is made for you." In a hypothetical sense, it expressed an exemplary commitment to civic participation, but it was problematic when a white minority made the deals for a powerless black majority, as had been the case throughout most of Sunflower County's history. I suspect that Harper's need to be in rooms where decisions were being made forced him into a closer involvement with the council than he would otherwise have chosen. I also believe that what he told a reporter in 1983—that he lost old friends when he came to the realization that integration was inevitable and decided to make the best of it—is true. Harper received at least as much enmity from conservative whites after his transformation as he had ever caught from African Americans—and this was just the way he liked it. "Once you start catching it from both sides, you know you're in the right position," he told me. "I was not and am not an extremist or an activist."

White men in Sunflower County like Jack Harper did not get rich by cheating African Americans out of their settlements at harvest time. But by joining the Citizens' Council and supporting its actions, these men did support the dominance of planters who became rich and powerful by exploiting black labor, and they did work to maintain a society centered on the principle of white supremacy. Comparisons to the Ku Klux Klan are overblown, but the Citizens' Councils did do horrible things to African Americans in Sunflower County and throughout Mississippi.

In our conversations, Harper asserted that white small farmers and sharecroppers like himself grew up without animosity toward blacks. Abusing African Americans "was not on our record," he claimed. "We don't have to account for that. We made our own living." In one sense, he was right. Men like James Eastland, whose cotton empire literally rested on his father's proven ability to terrorize black labor, *do* have to answer for these sins—and the Eastland family's is but the most dramatic of many examples. They have not answered for it—they have tried to ignore it—and their decision continues to reverberate. African Americans in Sunflower County and elsewhere will find it difficult to trust their white neighbors until whites make an honest account of this troubling history, and civic life will suffer.

The whites of Sunflower County seem to have decided that it is better to let the sleeping dogs of the Citizens' Council lie, and they may have good reason to do so. As Senator Trent Lott learned much to his embarrassment in 2002, it is one thing to favor policies that undo the civil rights victories of the 1960s but quite another to advocate in public turning back the clock to the days of Jim Crow. In any case, I was unable to find whites in Indianola who were willing to talk openly about the council, even to set the historical record straight.

A cheap-grace consensus—that "the civil rights movement was a good thing"—has become conventional wisdom among whites and blacks in Sunflower County, as in the rest of the South and the nation. Nicholas Lemann has identified this phenomenon as "an excellent demonstration of the marvelous, and misleading, clarity of historical retrospection."[8] In reality, African Americans did not agree on the goals and tactics of the movements in the years this study covers, and if whites agreed on anything at the time, it was that the movements had to be stopped at all costs. By claiming now to embrace the ideals of the classical civil rights movement without doing the intellectual and emotional heavy lifting that a true conversion would require, Sunflower County's whites have managed to miss whatever lessons the movements might have taught them. Their neighbors and fellow citizens notice failures such as this, and they do not forget them.

W. Fitzhugh Brundage reminds us that the southern past is "raw and sensitive" and predicts, "For the foreseeable future, ongoing contests over the meanings of that history will ensure that the southern past remains an open wound."[9] If whites continue to conceive of the Jim Crow era not as a usable past but as an old time there that is best forgotten—which is, in some ways, the ultimate white privilege—the nasty culture wars south- erners have fought in recent years will fester and worsen. To move beyond the culture wars, the whites of Sunflower County would have to begin an open, honest, and self-critical examination of the Citizens' Council move- ment and violent reactions to the civil rights struggles of the 1960s. They might start by investigating the night riders who shot at, firebombed, and generally terrorized African Americans who tried to vote before 1965 and prosecuting those who are still living among them.

Charles McLaurin reminds his fellow citizens of their shared past by his mere presence in Sunflower County. After Freedom Summer, McLaurin went off to study at Mississippi Valley State College, got married, and stayed active in the SNCC wing of the movement.[10] He decided to remain in the Delta and chose to live in Indianola. Through the late 1960s and 1970s, he cobbled together what work he could for civil rights organizations, registering voters and planning strategy for the MFDP, managing the af- fairs of Freedom Farm, doing organizational work for the National Council of Negro Women. For a time in the 1980s, McLaurin gave up on the Delta and retreated to Jackson, where economic prospects were far better. But the Delta pulled him back. When a friend from the movement days was appointed Indianola's director of public works, he asked McLaurin to re- turn to Sunflower County and work as his assistant director. McLaurin agreed and upon his return found that the white power structure was much more accommodating than he had expected it would be. (A member of the structure later told me that he had always respected McLaurin's tenacity and was happy finally to have him on the same team.)

Outside observers might think it strange that McLaurin has been able to make his peace with Indianola. But McLaurin has no difficulty explaining why he finds the Delta attractive. The slow and easy pace of life in Indi- anola clearly suits him, allowing McLaurin to showcase his storytelling skills. He likes being able to own his home and a small piece of property. The landscape has grown on him, as it has on many visitors to the Delta. Most importantly, perhaps, the Delta is where McLaurin became a *man*. He can look around him and see evidence of concrete changes for the better that he helped bring about.

In the period since the Indianola superintendent crisis, McLaurin has seen African American political muscle in Sunflower County approach a level proportional to the black segment of the total population. By 1997, all of Sunflower County's representatives in the state legislature were African American. Bennie Thompson, an African American, had succeeded Mike Espy as the Delta's U.S. congressman after Espy joined the Clinton administration as the first black U.S. secretary of agriculture. Blacks held 40 to 60 percent of the seats on local school boards, town boards of aldermen, and the county board of supervisors.

Unfortunately, the rise in black political power in the Delta coincided with a new set of problems that were far beyond the control of local politicians. The families who migrated from Sunflower County to northern cities from the 1940s through the 1970s in search of better economic opportunity often times found blight and despair instead. In the 1980s and 1990s, when many of those families began to send children back to the Delta to live with relatives, they inadvertently imported gang activity and created new networks in the drug trade. The distribution and use of crack cocaine put a terrible strain on countless families in Sunflower County. Teenage pregnancy rates in the Delta were astounding. This sad fact literally hit home for me when I lived in Indianola and young teenagers came trick-or-treating on Halloween with their own children.

Few industries moved into the Delta to replace the jobs displaced by agricultural mechanization (though in the 1990s Indianola did begin to make up for lost time in this area), and another generation of African American men grew up without significant prospects of finding fulfilling, sustaining work. Concurrently, over the last two decades of the twentieth century the federal government abandoned its commitment to the social welfare of its citizens. I did much of the research for this project while Mississippi governor Kirk Fordice was racing to implement "welfare reform" in his state. The human results of these policies were, as local community leaders described them to me, Dickensian. Welfare "reform" was championed in the 1996 elections by a white southern Democratic president who owed his electoral success largely to African American voters. It placed the burden of welfare—the relief of society's most disadvantaged— back on the shoulders of overworked black churchwomen. Some of these leaders, who had withstood the Citizens' Councils' harassment, been spied on by the State Sovereignty Commission, and had their homes shot into by night riders, were ready to throw up their hands in the face of this assault.[11]

The people of Sunflower County have not solved the problems created by a society based on the institution of slavery, and they are not likely to solve them in the foreseeable future. If they *are* to find resolutions to these dilemmas, Sunflower County's two racial communities—now closer to

being equal than they have ever been, but in many ways no less separate—
will have to find creative ways to come together and discuss their common
problems.

In May 1998, Carver Randle proposed a novel approach for Sunflower
County that itself showed how entrenched the county's problems in race
relations had become. Randle was born in Indianola and educated in its
segregated school system. After excelling at Mississippi Valley State University in nearby Itta Bena, he became one of the first African Americans
trained in the law at Ole Miss. He returned to Indianola and established a
successful practice. Randle was a leader of Concerned Citizens and had
since won election to the county board of supervisors. By 1998, he was one
of the two or three most economically and politically powerful African
Americans in the county.

Randle suggested that the African American students of the public
schools and the white children of Indianola Academy embark on a student-
exchange program along the lines of those that send students from various
nations to distant corners of the globe to learn more about foreign cultures.
He wrote in a letter to the editor of the *Enterprise-Tocsin*:

> My main concern is that our White and African American youths who
> will run our city, county, education system, business and industry in the
> near future do not have enough opportunities to get to relate to each
> other and thus to get to know each other better. This has to be changed.
> They do not go to school together in large enough numbers. They do not
> go to church together and they only have other limited opportunities to
> associate with each other. . . .
>
> I think there is a remedy to this dilemma. . . . I would like to see five or
> so students from Gentry High School and the Indianola Academy, pre-
> ferably juniors, enter into an exchange program. This would be a begin-
> ning and if properly conducted could prove rewarding.[12]

Randle's observation struck me as spot-on, and, based on my own experience in Sunflower County, I considered his idea a great one. But I do not
expect to see it implemented any time soon. Students at Mississippi's segregation academies are still immersed in a curriculum that one historian
describes as "a heroic history of the white, Protestant South that empha-
size[s] the Lost Cause, the horrors of Reconstruction, and the essential
nobility of the southern white people."[13] It should go without saying that
their African American neighbors do not share this fundamental world-
view. Randle's warning should resonate, moreover, in communities far
beyond the borders of Sunflower County, reaching throughout the South

and indeed across the United States. A society that cannot manage to teach its children about each other—much less provide all of its children with the best possible education—will assuredly reap what it sows.

The people who created the civil rights movement in all of its incarnations have at least defined Sunflower County's problems and suggested solutions to them. Many movement participants recognize that in the future these solutions will have to be creative and homegrown, just as Sunflower County's civil rights movements have always been. If these problems persist, and if local people look to themselves and each other in an effort to solve them, Fannie Lou Hamer's struggle will continue.

Notes

Abbreviations

FLHP   Fannie Lou Hamer Papers, Amistad Research Collection, Tulane University, New Orleans, La. (microfilm)

LBJL   Lyndon B. Johnson Presidential Library, Austin, Tex.

MDAH   Mississippi Department of Archives and History, Jackson, Miss.

MLKL   Martin Luther King, Jr., Center for Nonviolent Social Change Library and Archives, Atlanta, Ga.

NAACPP   NAACP Papers, Library of Congress, Washington, D.C.

OHP   Oral History Program, University of Southern Mississippi, Hattiesburg, Miss.

RBC   Rare Books Collection, University of North Carolina, Chapel Hill, N.C.

SCEFP   Southern Conference Education Foundation Papers, Southern Labor Collection, Georgia State University Special Collections, Atlanta, Ga.

SHC   Southern Historical Collection, Wilson Library, University of North Carolina, Chapel Hill, N.C.

SLC   Southern Labor Collection, Georgia State University Special Collections, Atlanta, Ga.

SovCom   Mississippi Sovereignty Commission Collection, Mississippi Department of Archives and History, Jackson, Miss.

SRCP   Southern Regional Council Papers, Special Collections, Atlanta University Center, Atlanta, Ga.

USMSC   University of Southern Mississippi Special Collections, McCain Library, Hattiesburg, Miss.

VEPP   Voter Education Project Papers, Southern Regional Council Papers, Woodruff Library, Atlanta University Center, Atlanta, Ga. (microfilm)

Prologue

1. Charles McLaurin, "To Overcome Fear [report to SNCC headquarters]," ca. 1964, SNCC Papers, box 104, MLKL.

2. There is no accurate record of annual lynching statistics. See Waldrep, "War of Words," for a perceptive examination of this historical problem. I wish to thank Chris Waldrep for his helpful comments on this chapter after it was delivered as a paper at the 2002 Emory University Conference on Lynching and Racial Violence in America.

Neil McMillen reckons conservatively that there were nine lynchings in Sunflower

County between 1889 and 1945 and that 70 percent of the lynchings in the state took place in the Black Belt, which includes Sunflower County. See McMillen, *Dark Journey,* 229–37. Journalist Ralph Ginzburg found evidence of at least forty-four lynchings of blacks in the Delta counties between 1897 and 1910, with a wave of lynchings between 1898 and 1905. See Ginzburg, *100 Years of Lynchings,* 263–65. Historian Terrence Finnegan counts 137 lynching incidents in the Mississippi Delta between 1891 and 1900. See Finnegan, "Lynching and Political Power," 193. I agree with Leon Litwack that "even an accurate body count of black lynching victims could not possibly reveal how hate and fear transformed ordinary white men and women into mindless murderers" and cheapened black life. See Litwack, *Trouble in Mind,* 284.

3. Quote from the *Greenwood Enterprise,* February 12, 1904. Sources for the following are eyewitness accounts from this issue of the *Enterprise*; the *Greenwood Commonwealth,* February 13, 1904; the *Vicksburg Evening Post,* February 13, 1904; the *New York Herald,* February 8, 1904; "Doddsville Savagery," 81–82; and a related story in the *Greenville Times,* February 27, 1904. Idiosyncrasies in spelling and capitalization have been retained. Mississippi newspapers are courtesy of the MDAH. Only direct quotes have been footnoted.

4. See McMillen, *Dark Journey,* ch. 1, passim.

5. S. Davis, *Mississippi Negro Lore,* 21.

6. McMillen, *Dark Journey,* 202, 203.

7. Powdermaker, *After Freedom,* 173. Powdermaker based *After Freedom* on her observations in "Cottonville," a disguised small southern town. When he reviewed *After Freedom* in 1939, W. E. B. Du Bois "outed" Indianola, the seat of Sunflower County, as "Cottonville." See Du Bois, "Review of *After Freedom.*" See Dollard, *Caste and Class,* which was also based on fieldwork conducted in Indianola.

8. Attorneys quoted in McMillen, *Dark Journey,* 203.

9. Powdermaker, *After Freedom,* 173.

10. S. Davis, *Mississippi Negro Lore,* 27–28. Davis wrote this piece in 1914; it is possible that he used the Holbert incident as the evidence upon which he based this description of black law justice.

11. Figures from 1900 U.S. census data and Rowland, *Encyclopedia,* 2:754. According to the same data, less than 60 percent of the total land considered farmland in Sunflower County had been cleared by 1907.

12. Quotes from H. Davis, *Trials of the Earth,* 86, 98, 129–30. See also Hicks, *Song of the Delta.* The June 2, 1891, and September 25, 1886, issues of the *Sunflower Tocsin,* from the clippings file at the Sunflower County Library, report numerous panther and bear attacks.

13. Litwack titles his chapter on the wave of lynchings in the South at the turn of the century "Hellhounds" and quotes Johnson's lyrics in *Trouble in Mind,* 478–79.

14. See Oshinsky, *Worse Than Slavery.* Adam Gussow speculates that W. C. Handy, the "Father of the Blues," may have gotten caught up in the mob's whirlwind while on tour through the Delta. See Gussow, "Racial Violence," 56–77.

15. See Rowland, *Encyclopedia,* 2:660.

16. Quote from *Vicksburg Evening Post,* February 13, 1904.

17. Again, it is impossible to know how many lynchings took place in Mississippi

between 1890 and 1920, but the number would surely run into the hundreds. See note 2 above.

18. "Hopeful Signs in Mississippi," *Voice of the Negro* 1, no. 5 (May 1904): 173.

19. Kight, "'The State Is on Trial.'" See D. Crosby, "A Piece of Your Own," for a similar treatment of a Mississippi lynching.

20. No evidence of correspondence regarding the incident remains in either governor's correspondence or letterbook files in the MDAH. By 1907, Indianola had a "local military company"—a lynch mob on standby—composed entirely of whites that called itself the "Vardaman Rifles." See Rowland, *Encyclopedia*, 2:933.

21. *New York Herald*, February 8, 1904.

22. *Greenwood Enterprise*, February 12, 1904.

23. The 1900 U.S. census puts the total population of Sunflower County at just over 16,000. A crowd of 1,000 was certainly newsworthy for the time.

24. Quotes from *Greenwood Commonwealth*, February 13, 1904, and the *Vicksburg Evening Post*, February 13, 1904. The MDAH's microfilm copy of the *Commonwealth* is in poor condition. Words in brackets represent my best guess at parts of the text that have disintegrated.

25. *Vicksburg Evening Post*, February 13, 1904.

26. *Greenwood Commonwealth*, February 13, 1904.

27. *Vicksburg Evening Post*, February 13, 1904.

28. *Greenwood Commonwealth*, February 13, 1904.

29. *Greenwood Enterprise*, February 12, 1904.

30. *New York Herald*, February 8, 1904.

31. "Doddsville Savagery." See also the report in the *New York Tribune*, February 8, 1904, quoted in NAACP, *Thirty Years of Lynching*.

32. See Finnegan, "Lynching and Political Power," 189–218; and Holmes, "Whitecapping" and "Leflore County Massacre."

33. "Doddsville Savagery," 82. Of course, black Atlantans were not immune to "bare-faced humiliations" or outright savagery, either. See Bauerlein, *Negrophobia*, and Du Bois, "My Evolving Program for Negro Freedom," 53.

34. Hall, *Revolt against Chivalry*, 136.

35. Arcola, like Greenville, Mississippi (to Sunflower County's immediate west), is a Mississippi River town, so the likelihood that two businessmen from the same small midwestern town would have contacts in the Delta is not as slight as it may otherwise seem.

36. *Greenville Times*, February 27, 1904.

37. Booker T. Washington, letter to the editor, reprinted in Ginzburg, *100 Years of Lynchings*, 64.

38. Harris, *Exorcising Blackness*, 1–2, 79–80; Griggs, *Hindered Hand*, 299.

39. See reports in the *New York Times*, September 11, 18, and 23, 1904.

40. The definitive biography of James O. Eastland is yet to be written, in part because the senator's papers are still closed to researchers. Journalist Robert G. Sherrill did devote a great deal of attention to Eastland, and much of my biographical sketch here is drawn from Sherrill's "James Eastland: Child of Scorn" and his extended treatment of Eastland in *Gothic Politics in the Deep South*, ch. 7, passim.

41. For the culture of Mississippi politics and the importance of the Hills-Delta political divide, see Key, *Southern Politics*, ch. 11, passim, and Wilkie, *Dixie*.

42. Eastland 1942 campaign literature, James O. Eastland jumbo file, MDAH.

43. As Eastland's critics consistently pointed out, while he voted against food stamp bills for the poor, the senator unabashedly supported agricultural policies that paid his plantation huge subsidies (which annually ran into the six figures) not to plant cotton. See, for instance, the editorial in the *Delta Democrat-Times*, January 19, 1978.

44. Eastland quoted in *Jackson Daily News*, December 12, 1955, and *Memphis Press-Scimitar*, August 13, 1955, group III, box A70, NAACPP.

45. See "Vote Suit Scores Eastland County," *New York Times*, January 23, 1963.

Chapter One

1. Robinson and Sullivan, "Reassessing," 2. See also Eagles, "Toward New Histories."

2. See, for example, the movements middle-class blacks created in Greensboro, North Carolina, and Tuskegee, Alabama, which are the subjects of Chafe, *Civilities and Civil Rights*, and Norrell, *Reaping the Whirlwind*, respectively.

3. I use the term "paternalist" guardedly. The architects of the Delta's racialized socioeconomic system most certainly did not have the best interests of African Americans at heart, no matter what they told themselves and others, and African Americans throughout the period of this study found ways to register their disapproval of the system. White planters have, however, continually defined the Delta's sharecropping system in precisely the terms of paternalism. The best example of this mindset may be found in William Alexander Percy's autobiography, *Lanterns on the Levee: Recollections of a Planter's Son*, an excerpt of which begins this chapter. Because the planter LeRoy Percy ran for a U.S. Senate seat and campaigned on the theme that Delta-style "paternalism" was the best possible arrangement for blacks and whites alike, and because his son William Alexander Percy was a poet and memoirist who wrote voluminously about Delta race relations, the family has long been considered the personification of Delta paternalism. See also Wyatt-Brown, *House of Percy*; L. Baker, *Percys of Mississippi*; and Barry, *Rising Tide*. My own understanding of the concept of paternalism relies heavily on the works of Italian theorist Antonio Gramsci and sociologist Mary Jackman. Jackman defines the essence of paternalism as an unequal relationship in which one social group expropriates resources from another and then creates a persuasive ideology that enables the inferior group to rationalize and accept the inequality. See Hoare and Smith, *Selections from "The Prison Notebooks"*; Boggs, *Two Revolutions*; and Jackman, *Velvet Glove*. Clyde Woods has argued persuasively that any social order backed so clearly by violence and terrorism cannot reasonably be called paternalist. See Woods, *Development Arrested*, 7.

4. For the rise and spread of the Citizens' Council movement, see McMillen, *Citizens' Council*; Bartley, *Rise of Massive Resistance*; Martin, *Deep South Says "Never!"*; and Carter, *South Strikes Back*.

5. "As Sunflower County goes . . .": quote from Lamar Hooker (a Mississippi land appraiser), oral history interview with author.

6. Hemphill, *Fevers, Floods, and Faith*, 37–39, 53–54; Works Progress Administra-

tion Papers, Federal Writers Project source material for Mississippi History files, MDAH; Robertson and Conger, *Lehrton, Mississippi*.

7. H. Davis, *Trials of the Earth*; Robertson and Conger, *Ruleville, Mississippi*, 7, 28; newspaper stories from the Sunflower County Library's "Sunflower County History" clippings file.

8. Census data, from the Historical United States Census Browser, is available online (as of February 26, 2004) at <http://fisher.lib.virginia.edu/census/>. For this period of the Delta's history, see Willis, *Forgotten Time*.

9. Written sources and oral history interviewees from Sunflower County refer to "halving" so often that for all practical purposes, the term is synonymous with "share-cropping."

10. Lamar Hooker, oral history interview with author.

11. Daniel, *Breaking the Land*, 6.

12. For the development of cotton culture in the modern South, see Daniel, *Breaking the Land*.

13. For the contested effort to bring industry to Mississippi, see Woodruff, "Mississippi Delta Planters"; Clark, "Legislative Adoption"; Prince, "Balance Agriculture with Industry Program"; and Cobb, *Industrialization and Southern Society*.

14. For the causes and effects of this massive out-migration, see Lemann, *Promised Land*, and Grossman, *Land of Hope*.

15. Data from U.S. Department of Commerce, *County Data Book*, 222, and *Census of the Population*, 26–11, 26–24.

16. Pete Daniel has argued persuasively that resistance to desegregation had to be manufactured throughout the South. See Daniel, *Lost Revolutions*, ch. 10, passim. Sunflower County whites were at the forefront of this process.

17. For the development of this near-consensus, see Bartley, *Rise of Massive Resistance*.

18. *General Laws of the State of Mississippi*, 1956, ch. 365, 520–24. See also Katagiri, *Mississippi State Sovereignty Commission*.

19. Maass, "Secrets of Mississippi," 21. For more on the battle to open the Sovereignty Commission's files, see Trillin, "State Secrets"; and Kevin Sack, "The South's History Rises, Again and Again," *New York Times*, March 21, 1998.

20. See Goodwyn, *Democratic Promise*, particularly the author's introduction and ch. 17, passim.

21. Ibid., xi.

22. Ibid., xii.

23. Anonymous SNCC field secretary in the Mississippi Delta quoted by Bond in *Freedomways Reader*, 72.

24. Hamer, foreword to *Stranger at the Gates*, by Sugarman, vii, viii. For examinations of Hamer's understanding of Christian discipleship, see Marsh, *God's Long Summer*, ch. 1, passim, and Chappell, *Stone of Hope*.

25. The chicken comment comes from Charles Cobb, a SNCC worker in Ruleville, October 21, 1996, oral history interview with John Rachal, OHP.

26. Hamer's performance at the church is recounted in Sugarman, *Stranger at the Gates*, 120–21.

27. It is worth noting that Oscar Johnston, manager of the Delta and Pine Land Company, a massive plantation in neighboring Bolivar County, devised the Agricultural Adjustment Administration's cotton program almost single-handedly. For the impact of federal policies, see Cobb, "'Somebody Done Nailed Us on the Cross'" and *Most Southern Place on Earth*; Woodruff, "African-American Struggles for Citizenship" and "Mississippi Delta Planters"; Daniel, *Breaking the Land*; Wright, *Old South, New South*; C. Campbell, *Farm Bureau*; Conrad, *Forgotten Farmers*; Holley, *Uncle Sam's Farmers*; and Kirby, *Rural Worlds Lost*.

28. For African Americans and the New Deal, see Sitkoff, *New Deal for Blacks*; Weiss, *Farewell to the Party of Lincoln*; Sullivan, *Days of Hope*; and Bernstein, *Only One Place of Redress*.

29. Sillers quoted in Frederickson, *Dixiecrat Revolt*, 11. See also Sullivan, *Days of Hope*.

30. Cobb, "'Somebody Done Nailed Us on the Cross,'" 914.

31. See the issue of *Sojourners* magazine (December 1982) dedicated to Hamer. Hamer is the subject of two excellent biographies. See Kay Mills, *This Little Light of Mine*, and Chana Kai Lee, *For Freedom's Sake*.

Chapter Two

1. Key, *Southern Politics*, 229.

2. For the South's moderates in the pre–civil rights era, see Sullivan, *Days of Hope*, and Egerton, *Speak Now against the Day*. For Mississippi's equalization movement, see Bolton, "Mississippi's School Equalization Program."

3. For the "Mississippi Plan" of the 1890s, see Woodward, *Origins of the New South*; Wharton, *Negro in Mississippi*; and Kirwan, *Revolt of the Rednecks*.

4. Sitkoff, "African American Militancy," 79.

5. Henry, Moore, and Evers are the classic Mississippi examples of the "We return fighting" (the term comes from a W. E. B. Du Bois essay on black veterans returning from World War I) school of thought concerning veterans' civil rights activity. See Dittmer, *Local People*, ch. 1, passim; Payne, *I've Got the Light of Freedom,* ch. 2, passim; Daniel, *Lost Revolutions*, ch. 1, passim; and McMillen, "Fighting for What We Didn't Have." Sitkoff challenges the interpretation in "African American Militancy."

6. McMillen, *Remaking Dixie*, 105–6.

7. Jack Harper Jr., oral history interview with author. As subsequent chapters will demonstrate, Harper may have remembered his perceptions of black soldiers creatively and to his own advantage. After returning from Korea, Harper became a leader in the Indianola Citizens' Council. Yet his wartime experiences were almost certainly a deciding factor in Harper's later decision to enforce the laws of the United States. This particular statement should probably be read with some skepticism but cannot be dismissed outright.

8. Eastland quoted in *Jackson Daily News*, March 16, 1954.

9. Smith, *Congressman from Mississippi*, 101.

10. George Jordan, oral history interview with author; Sunflower County Voting Records, Office of the County Circuit Clerk, Indianola, Miss. These numbers do not

represent the people who tried to register but were denied, but there is no reason to think that a great number of blacks attempted to register in this particular period.

11. Obadiah 1:1–2 Revised Standard Version.

12. George Jordan, oral history interview with author.

13. David Matthews, oral history interview with author.

14. Sunflower County Voting Records, Office of the County Circuit Clerk, Indianola, Miss.

15. See the preface to University of Mississippi Bureau of Educational Research, "Study of the Education for Negroes," for names of committee members and pp. 1–4 for motivations behind improvement of black schools.

16. Bolton, "Mississippi's School Equalization Program," 781–86.

17. "Sunrise in Sunflower?" *Newsweek*, August 14, 1950, 80; Ashmore, *Negro and the Schools*, 187; University of Mississippi Bureau of Educational Research, "Study of the Education for Negroes," 120.

18. "Sunrise in Sunflower?" 80.

19. Many blacks did not enroll until after January 1, according to the report; the county estimated that the black student population would swell to over 10,000 after the new year began. (See University of Mississippi Bureau of Educational Research, "Study of the Education for Negroes," 31, 39–40.)

20. University of Mississippi Bureau of Educational Research, "Study of the Education for Negroes," 44.

21. To take one example, the average Sunflower County African American in the eighth grade was almost four years older than the average southern white eighth-grader and three years and three months older than the average southern African American eighth-grader. Even so, Sunflower County students scored more than three grade levels below southern whites in reading, more than four levels below in vocabulary, an average of three levels below in two mathematical categories, more than three levels below in English, and over two levels below in spelling. See University of Mississippi Bureau of Educational Research, "Study of the Education for Negroes," ch. 3, passim.

22. University of Mississippi Bureau of Educational Research, "Study of the Education for Negroes," 59. The figures do not include teachers in the Doddsville, Drew, and Indianola school districts; for Indianola, anecdotal evidence suggests that teachers had attained higher levels of education than these figures show.

23. "Sunrise in Sunflower?" 80; University of Mississippi Bureau of Educational Research, "Study of the Education for Negroes," 78.

24. See, for instance, W. W. Evans, "How We Equipped the Stephensville Vocational School," and B. B. Bailey, "Dwiggins Grammar School," appendices to University of Mississippi Bureau of Educational Research, "Study of the Education for Negroes," 143–45. Several African American adults who were interviewed for this project remembered picking cotton as children to raise money for their schools as late as 1964.

25. Hemphill, *Fevers, Floods, and Faith*, 544.

26. Carter, *South Strikes Back*, 12–13.

27. Hemphill, *Fevers, Floods, and Faith*, 544.

28. *Southern School News*, September 3, 1954, 8; *Indianola Enterprise*, January 5,

1954. For the situation in Mississippi and the South as a whole, see Ashmore, *Negro and the Schools*, 144–45. The book is based on the research of forty-five scholars under the auspices of a Ford Foundation–sponsored study; Ashmore edited their findings. *The Negro and the Schools* is probably the most reliable single source for education statistics in the South on the eve of the *Brown* decision.

29. Faulkner's letter, presumably to the *Memphis Commercial Appeal*, quoted in NAACP press release, June 30, 1954, group II, box A227, NAACPP.

30. Indianola branch charter, group II, box C242, NAACPP; Foster to NAACP National Headquarters, May 10, 1948, and March 14, 1949, W. A. Bender to Gloster Current, September 22, 1948, and NAACP press release, February 2, 1949, group II, box C96, NAACPP.

31. Foster to Gloster Current, April 18, 1950, group II, box C96, NAACPP.

32. Robert Love, oral history interview with author.

33. Ibid.; Bernice White, September 19, 1997, oral history interview with author; Gloster Current to Roy Wilkins, memo, December 13, 1954, group II, box C98, NAACPP; "Siamese Twins Who Survived," *Ebony Magazine*, February 1957, 39–45.

34. Robert Love, oral history interview with author; Walker to Lucille Black, November 1, 1954, group II, box C96, NAACPP; Keenan to Evers, December 9, 1955, group II, box A422, NAACPP.

35. Hurley to Current, memo, March 27, 1952, group II, box C98, NAACPP; Sunflower County Voting Records, Office of the County Circuit Clerk, Indianola, Miss. In contrast to the number of registrants during the pre-*Brown* period, only four Sunflower County blacks registered to vote in the eight years following *Brown*.

36. *Jackson Clarion-Ledger*, November 7, 1953, group II, box C98, NAACPP.

37. Ibid.; NAACP press release, November 12, 1953, group II, box A227, NAACPP.

38. Patterson quoted in Martin, *Deep South Says "Never!"* 1. Patterson recommended Martin's book to other segregationists even though it was critical of Patterson's movement—an indication that at the very least Patterson considered his quotations in the book accurate.

39. Patterson, undated letter, reprinted in ibid., 1–2.

40. Ibid.

41. *Indianola Enterprise*, December 8, 1953. Jim Abbott, present editor of the newspaper, was kind enough to make the newspaper's morgue available to me during an extended research trip. I am grateful for his and his staff's generous help.

42. *Indianola Enterprise*, December 8, 1953, to June 15, 1954.

43. Ibid., December 8, 1953.

44. *Jackson Daily News*, May 17, 1954; Wilma Sledge's column in *Indianola Enterprise*, May 25, 1954.

45. Kefauver quoted in McMillen, *Citizens' Council*, 9. For Smith, see his autobiography, *Congressman from Mississippi*. For national reaction to the verdict, see Kluger, *Simple Justice*, ch. 26, passim.

46. Carter, *South Strikes Back*, 16. Pete Daniel has written extensively on the deafening silence of southern moderates following *Brown*. See Daniel, *Lost Revolutions*, ch. 11, passim.

47. Thomas P. Brady, oral history interview, vol. 2, pt. 1 (1972), 26, OHP.

48. Brady, *Black Monday*, foreword.

49. Ibid., 10–11.

50. Ibid., 12, 45, 78.

51. *Congressional Record*, 83rd Cong., 2d sess., 1954, 100, pt. 6:7252. See also "Eastland Scores Supreme Court," *New York Times*, May 28, 1954; "Inquiry on Court Asked," *New York Times*, May 26, 1955; and "Decision Pleases Many in Congress," *New York Times*, June 1, 1955.

52. *Congressional Record*, 83rd Cong., 2d sess., 1954, 100, pt. 6:7252–53; Thomas P. Brady, oral history interview, 23, OHP.

53. *Congressional Record*, 83rd Cong., 2d sess., 1954, 100, pt. 6:7253, 7257.

54. Brady, *Black Monday*, 39.

Chapter Three

1. This account of the original Indianola meeting is based on Stan Opotowsky's investigative series "Dixie Dynamite: The Inside Story of the White Citizens Councils," which was published in the *New York Post* from January 7 to January 20, 1957, and reprinted by the NAACP under the same title, presumably in the same year, 5–6; and Carter, *South Strikes Back*, 34–35. Moore's quote appears in "Dixie Dynamite." Opotowsky based his version of events at the original mass meeting on materials he was able to squirrel away from an official Citizens' Council file marked "Confidential," and Carter based his chronicle on an audio recording of the Indianola meeting. The two versions corroborate one another, though the two authors attribute nearly identical statements to different speakers in at least one case. "Integration Foes Arise in the New South," an article in the November 21, 1954, *New York Times*, reported that the Indianola meeting had been taped and transcribed and that copies of each had gone out to a select mailing list in Mississippi. For black organizing in the period Moore references, see Woodruff, *American Congo*.

2. Clark quoted in Opotowsky, "Dixie Dynamite," 5.

3. Opotowsky, "Dixie Dynamite," 5; Carter, *South Strikes Back*, 32–33.

4. Thomas P. Brady, oral history interview, vol. 2, pt. 1 (1972), 25, OHP.

5. See group II, boxes A423 and A424, NAACPP. As of April 1955, the special fund had made over $250,000 available to victims of council intimidation.

6. Robert Love, oral history interview with author. For an example of the practice of copying license numbers, then tracing owners, see SovCom document 2-38-1-9-1-1-1, MDAH, a roster of the vehicles parked at Jackson's Masonic Temple during a May 17, 1959, speech by Roy Wilkins.

7. Sledge quoted in *Southern School News*, October 1, 1954, 9. Carter editorial in *Delta Democrat-Times*, September 6, 1954.

8. Sledge quoted in *Southern School News*, October 1, 1954, 9.

9. Carter and the editor of the *Montgomery Advertiser* quoted in Elizabeth Geyer, "The 'New' Ku Klux Klan," *Crisis*, March 1956, 147, in Citizens' Councils Collection, USMSC. Patterson, "The Citizens' Council" (pamphlet) November 1954, RBC.

10. Frederickson, *Dixiecrat Revolt*, 234.

11. Association of Citizens' Councils of Mississippi, "The Citizens' Council," and

"Second Annual Report," August 1956 (pamphlets), RBC. Official Citizens' Councils existed in Mississippi, Alabama, Louisiana, South Carolina, Texas, Florida, Arkansas, Tennessee, and Virginia, and related organizations such as the Patriots of North Carolina and the States Rights Council of Georgia were similar enough to the councils that they may be considered virtually synonymous.

Bartley argues convincingly that if anything, the councils and related groups were most responsible for crystallizing "sentiment in the white community . . . into stone-like unanimity" in the face of perceived forced integration. Bartley names this ideological unanimity in the face of danger "the neobourbon rationale," linking the "Never!" men of the 1950s with their predecessors who "redeemed" the South from Reconstruction. At the heart of this rationale, which is far from dead among white conservatives, is a belief in white supremacy and the truism that society is naturally hierarchical—a belief that places "high value upon order and status as the natural way of things." See Bartley, *Rise of Massive Resistance*, 237.

12. Brady, "Review of Black Monday."

13. "Letters to the Editor," *Time*, June 14, 1954, 8–10.

14. Brady, "Review of Black Monday," 14.

15. Council of Federated Organizations workers in the 1964 Freedom Summer found a brochure written and circulated by the White Knights of the Ku Klux Klan of Mississippi, which the civil rights workers copied and saved. The Klan's rhetoric nearly matched public pronouncements from Citizens' Council leaders. See "The Most Awful Disease of Our Time," MFDP Papers, box 23, MLKL.

16. Large farmers, comfortable bankers, and established merchants formed the backbone of the Indianola council. Conventional wisdom holds that the Klans were dominated by poor whites, and conventional wisdom almost certainly held true in the instance of Mississippi. Klan activity was surprisingly muted in the state until at least 1963 (alas, it was not muted thereafter)—arguably, because traditional elites in the form of the councils did such a good job to that point of maintaining the racial status quo. The United Klans of America and White Knights of the Ku Klux Klan wreaked havoc in other parts of the state, especially in 1964, but did not establish footholds in the Delta, where there were fewer poor whites and more established hierarchies. Perhaps ironically, the best source on Klan activity in the state may be the House Un-American Activities Committee. See Committee on Un-American Activities, *Activities of Ku Klux Klan Organizations*, and Whitehead, *Attack on Terror*.

17. Quotes from Bartley, *Rise of Massive Resistance*, 190, 211. See Bartley, chs. 11 and 12, "The Quest for Conformity, Parts I and II," passim.

18. "The Mississippi Bombings—Who Is Responsible?" *MFDP Newsletter*, November 27, 1967 (Jackson: Freedom Information Service), 5, box 7, reel 3, FLHP.

19. Chamber of commerce statement in *Indianola Enterprise-Tocsin*, March 21, 1957. Patterson quoted in Martin, *Deep South Says "Never!"* 133. I am indebted to Joe Crespino for helping me develop my thinking on this issue.

20. Patterson quoted in Martin, *Deep South Says "Never!"* 2.

21. Ibid.

22. Bartley, *Rise of Massive Resistance*, 99.

23. Martin, *Deep South Says "Never!"* 13; Robert Patterson, oral history interview with Howell Raines, in Raines, *My Soul Is Rested*, 297.

24. The December 22, 1955, and September 19, 1963, issues of the *Indianola Enterprise-Tocsin* report the names of council leaders.

25. Jack Harper Jr., oral history interview with author.

26. Dittmer, *Local People*, 38.

27. *Southern School News*, September 3, 1954, 8.

28. *Jackson Clarion-Ledger*, November 7, 1953, group II, box C98, NAACPP.

29. White quoted in *Southern School News*, September 3, 1954, 8.

30. Dittmer, *Local People*, 32–33; T. R. M. Howard, "The Mississippi Negro's Stand on Segregation in the Public Schools of Mississippi" (speech at the governor's conference, July 30, 1954), group II, box A227, NAACPP.

31. White quoted in *Southern School News*, September 3, 1954, 8; see also Dittmer, *Local People*, 38–40, and Carter, *South Strikes Back*, 35–36.

32. See Genovese, *Roll, Jordan, Roll*, 114, 128–33, 143–58.

33. Carter, *South Strikes Back*, 36.

34. White quoted in *Southern School News*, October 1, 1954, 9.

35. Patterson's baseball and fire readiness analogies can be found (among other places) in Martin, *Deep South Says "Never!"* 12. Thomas P. Brady, oral history interview, 27, OHP; Patterson, "The Citizens' Council," November 1954 (pamphlet), RBC; McMillen, *Citizens' Council*, 26.

36. Katagiri, *Mississippi State Sovereignty Commission*, xxxii.

37. Association of Citizens' Councils of Mississippi, "Second Annual Report," August 1956 (pamphlet), RBC.

38. Wilkie, *Dixie*, 61.

39. *Indianola Enterprise-Tocsin*, September 18, 1955.

40. Ibid., October 3, 1957.

41. Courts to NAACP headquarters, 1954, group II, box A422, NAACPP; "Report on Mississippi for Board and Staff Reference," group II, box C98, NAACPP. Courts identified his assailant as "Paul (Junior) Townes" of "Gundy" Bank, but the man was almost certainly Townsend of Guaranty Bank and Trust Co.

42. Ruby Hurley to Governor Hugh White, May 9, 1955, group II, box A422, NAACPP; Lapidary, "Belzoni, Mississippi," 12.

43. Alex Hudson, May 26, 1955, affidavit, Roy Wilkins to Herbert Brownell, May 19, 1955, and NAACP press release, May 13, 1955, group II, box A422, NAACPP.

44. Robert Love, oral history interview with author; Ruby Hurley to Governor Hugh White, May 19, 1955, group II, box A422, NAACPP.

45. Robert Love, oral history interview with author; Battle quoted in *Indianola Enterprise-Tocsin*, January 9, 1958.

46. NAACP press release, May 22, 1955, group II, box A422, NAACPP.

47. Lapidary, "Belzoni, Mississippi," 13; *New York Post*, December 1, 1955, and Gloster Current to Henry Lee Moon, memo, December 1, 1955, group II, box A422, NAACPP; Ruby Hurley to Gloster Current, memo, December 28, 1955, group II, box C224, NAACPP.

48. See Whitfield, *Death in the Delta*, and Metress, *Lynching of Emmett Till*. Studs Terkel includes a moving edited oral history interview with Mamie Till Mobley, Emmett's mother, in *Will the Circle Be Unbroken?* 393–96. See also Huie, "Shocking Story," 46–50, and "Emmett Till Killers," 63–68, for remarkable (if suspect) firsthand accounts and interviews with Milam and Bryant.

49. "The Lynching of Emmett Louis Till: Chronology of a Tragedy," group II, box A423, NAACPP; Whitfield, *Death in the Delta*, 39–40.

50. "Lynching of Emmett Louis Till"; Hurley to Gloster Current, memo, September 30, 1955, group II, box C224, NAACPP. See also the *New York Times*, September 23, 1955, and James L. Hicks, "White Reporters Doublecrossed Probers Seeking Lost Witnesses," *Cleveland Call and Post*, October 15, 1955. In an oral history interview with the author, November 14, 1997, Mae Bertha Carter identified a farm west of Drew as the site where Till was beaten. According to T. R. M. Howard in an interview with Hicks, Reed and Bradley identified the scene of the beating as the headquarters shed of the Clint Sheridan plantation, which was approximately three and a half miles west of Drew near the Bolivar County line.

51. Faulkner quoted in *Crisis*, October 1955, 481; Wilkins to U.S. Department of Justice, September 7, 1955, group II, box A422, NAACPP.

52. "Lynching of Emmett Louis Till."

53. Ibid.

54. Ruby Hurley to Gloster Current, memo, December 28, 1955, group II, box C224, NAACPP; and Mildred Bond to Roy Wilkins, memo, January 25, 1956, group III, box A228, NAACPP.

55. Bernice White, September 19, 1997, oral history interview with author.

56. *Indianola Enterprise-Tocsin*, September 20, 1956; group III, box A228, NAACPP.

57. Battle quoted in Carter, *South Strikes Back*, 126, and *Indianola Enterprise-Tocsin*, January 9, 1958.

Chapter Four

1. Clayborne Carson, *In Struggle*, 19. Carson's work is the definitive history of the Student Non-violent Coordinating Committee. See also Zinn, *SNCC*. For SNCC activities in Mississippi, see Dittmer, *Local People*, and Payne, *I've Got the Light of Freedom*, and the movement memoirs by Holland, *From the Mississippi Delta*, and Sellers with Terrell, *River of No Return*. For the importance of Baker's organizing style, see Payne, *I've Got the Light of Freedom*; Grant, *Ella Baker*; and Ransby, *Ella Baker*.

2. Lewis with D'Orso, *Walking with the Wind*, 114.

3. Farmer quoted in Williams, *Eyes on the Prize*, 147.

4. Southern Regional Council, "Negro Voter Registration for Selected Years and Voting Age Populations," reel 177, VEPP. According to the VEP, every other former state of the Confederacy allowed at least 15 percent of its African American citizens of voting age to register; Alabama and South Carolina had percentages of just over 15 percent, or more than three times that of Mississippi. The numbers for other states varied considerably upward, with Tennessee registering the highest percentage, 58.9, of its black citizens. In this light, Mississippi's statistics are even more damning.

5. Population total and percentage based on 1960 U.S. census figures from U.S. Department of Commerce, *County and City Data Book 1962*.

6. Charles McLaurin, November 1, 1997, oral history interview with author.

7. Ibid.

8. Ibid. Nash, James Bevel, and three other SNCC veterans from Nashville set up the Jackson SNCC office in 1961 after they had participated in the Freedom Ride, been arrested in Jackson, and spent time in Parchman Penitentiary. See Dittmer, *Local People*, 99, 116.

A note on sources: I do not consider oral history research a substitute for archival research, and I have weighed information gleaned from oral histories against other available evidence. In many cases, I have used information from oral histories to flesh out the framework of events that are described in contemporary written documents or secondary sources. In others, I have used oral history to tell stories that would otherwise go undocumented. I have not to my knowledge privileged information from an oral history over conflicting information from a contemporary written source, with this one exception.

The details of McLaurin's description of how he got involved in civil rights work from our 1997 interviews contradicted his description in Tracy Sugarman's *Stranger at the Gates*, published in 1966. I privileged McLaurin's 1997 version of the story because I considered it a more humanistic explanation. If McLaurin stretched the truth a bit in telling it, this version of the story at least portrayed a three-dimensional human being responding to a real-world situation. If McLaurin did not himself join the civil rights movement because it had already attracted comely coeds, moreover, we might name dozens of other men who did. Careful readers might wish in this case that I had let the "facts," or at least a more contemporary piece of autobiography, get in the way of a good story. So be it.

9. Charles McLaurin, November 1, 1997, oral history interview with author. For Moses' importance, see Dittmer, *Local People*, and Payne, *I've Got the Light of Freedom*, as well as Burner, *And Gently He Shall Lead Them*, and Branch, *Pillar of Fire*. Moses' memoirs of the Mississippi movement appear in Moses and Cobb, *Radical Equations*.

10. For the Greenwood movement, see Payne, *I've Got the Light of Freedom*, ch. 5, passim, and Holland, *From the Mississippi Delta*.

11. Charles Cobb, October 21, 1996, oral history interview with John Rachal, OHP; available online (as of February 26, 2004) at <http://www.lib.usm.edu/~spcol/crda/oh/cobbtrans.htm>. See also Cobb's oral history interview with Howell Raines, in Raines, *My Soul Is Rested*, 244–48.

12. Charles McLaurin, December 14, 1997, oral history interview with author. Shots were fired at the car Moses was driving from Greenwood toward Indianola almost exactly one year later. See Carson, *In Struggle*, 80–81.

13. In his October 5, 1961, Monthly Field Report (group III, box A115, NAACPP), Evers detailed exactly this problem and complained that CORE was stealing the NAACP's momentum in Jackson. NAACP director of branches Gloster Current and executive secretary Roy Wilkins bristled when the NAACP had to bail out the students who had become so critical of the NAACP's comparatively moderate approach to change.

14. Charles McLaurin, December 14, 1997, oral history interview with author.

15. Charles McLaurin, "Notes on Organizing," ca. 1963, Townsend Davis Personal Papers, copy in author's possession.

16. "Ruleville, Mississippi: A Background Report," SNCC Papers, box 104, MLKL.

17. Charles McLaurin, December 14, 1997, oral history interview with author.

18. "A Chronology of Violence and Intimidation in Mississippi since 1961," SNCC Papers, box 104, MLKL.

19. McLaurin, "To Overcome Fear."

20. McLaurin, "Notes on Organizing."

21. I have come across only one example of this type in Sunflower County. The local people I interviewed for this project who were associated with SNCC programs were, almost to an individual, grateful for SNCC's commitment. There are remarkably few instances in the historical record and in my own oral history interviews where an African American in the county accused a SNCC volunteer of trying to control or direct the community, although local whites often claimed that this was precisely SNCC's purpose.

22. Fannie Lou Hamer, oral history interview with Howell Raines, in Raines, *My Soul Is Rested*, 249.

23. Charles McLaurin, November 1 and December 14, 1997, oral history interviews with author.

24. Charles Cobb, October 21, 1996, oral history interview with John Rachal, OHP; Bernice White, September 9, 1997, oral history interview with author.

25. Charles Cobb, October 21, 1996, oral history interview with John Rachal, OHP; Charles McLaurin, November 1 and December 14, 1997, oral history interviews with author. The two best sources for Hamer's life and times are K. Mills, *This Little Light of Mine*, and Lee, *For Freedom's Sake*. See also Hamer's oral history interviews with Howell Raines in Raines, *My Soul Is Rested*; with Egerton in *A Mind to Stay Here*; and with McMillen in OHP, available online (as of February 26, 2004) at <http://www.lib.usm.edu/~spcol/crda/oh/hamertrans.htm>.

26. Lawrence Guyot, oral history interview, in Hampton and Fayer, *Voices of Freedom*, 178.

27. Chana Kai Lee disagrees, citing (in *For Freedom's Sake*) oral histories that portray Hamer as a leader among the would-be registrants from the outset of the trip. Cobb and McLaurin both claimed in separate oral history interviews years later not to have noticed Hamer before she began singing on the school bus, but the matter is largely academic.

28. K. Mills, *This Little Light of Mine*, 41. When I asked L. C. Dorsey, who grew up in a sharecropper family in Sunflower County and other parts of the Delta, how she had become involved with the movement, she explained, "We was waitin' on it!" The same could have been said of Hamer.

29. Reagon, "Civil Rights Movement," 15.

30. Fannie Lou Hamer, oral history interview with Howell Raines, in Raines, *My Soul Is Rested*, 250–51. In the same interview, Hamer describes a scene that may well be the classic snapshot of Delta society. Pap Hamer worked for the Marlows for thirty

years, and Fannie Lou Hamer worked for the family for the eighteen years between her marriage to Pap and her eviction. The couple and their two adopted children never once had a working toilet inside their house. They did have a commode—because they moved into a house that had previously been inhabited by a white sharecropping family—but it never worked while the Hamers lived there, and Marlow told them that an outdoor privy was good enough for them. One day Hamer was cleaning the Marlows' house to earn extra money, and W. D. Marlow's daughter told her not to waste too much time on one of the house's several bathrooms, because only "old Honey" used it. "Honey" was the Marlows' family dog.

31. "Ruleville, Mississippi: A Background Report," 2; "Chronology of Violence and Intimidation in Mississippi since 1961," 9–10.

32. Hamer's husband, Pap, had become alarmed when he saw shotgun shells in the Marlows' machinery shop; he knew that the rabbits and birds that one would normally hunt with shot were out of season and warned his wife to be careful. Several other Ruleville blacks had also heard mumbled threats against Hamer's life from their white employers, and they too passed them along to Hamer.

33. Tom Scarborough, memo, April 22, 1963, SovCom document 1-71-0-3-2-1-1. See also "Registration Efforts in Mississippi Continue Despite Violence and Terror," *Student Voice* 58 (October 1962). Editions of this newspaper, the official organ of SNCC, have been compiled and republished as *The Student Voice, 1960–1965: Periodical of the Student Nonviolent Coordinating Committee*, edited by Clayborne Carson, under the auspices of the MLKL.

34. Charles McLaurin, "Report on Activity in Ruleville and Sunflower County from August 19th to December 28th," reel 177, VEPP; Charles McLaurin, November 1 and December 14, 1997, oral history interviews with author; Charles Cobb, October 21, 1996, oral history interview with John Rachal, OHP; Tom Scarborough, memo, April 22, 1963; *Memphis Commercial-Appeal*, September 14, 1962, and *Jackson Daily News*, September 11, 1962 (SovCom documents 10-77-0-3-1-1-1 and 10-77-0-4-1-1-1, respectively). Through his own investigation, McLaurin learned several years later that black employees of a gas station owned by notoriously racist Ruleville whites had been hired to do the shooting.

35. I am grateful to my friend and colleague Worth Long, formerly the staff coordinator of SNCC, for his insights into the philosophical differences between nonviolence and "un-violence." The growing literature on black self-defense in civil movements includes Fairclough, *Race and Democracy*; Tyson, *Radio Free Dixie*; Umoja, "Eye for an Eye"; and especially Umoja, "1964." Kwame Ture quoted in Umoja, "1964," 214.

36. McLaurin, "Report on Activity in Ruleville and Sunflower County from August 19th to December 28th."

37. Charles McLaurin, December 14, 1997, oral history interview with author; McLaurin, "Report on Activity in Ruleville and Sunflower County from August 19th to December 28th."

38. Charles McLaurin, December 14, 1997, oral history interview with author.

39. Chapman's editorials in the *Indianola Enterprise-Tocsin*, September 20 and September 27, 1962; Barnett quoted in Dittmer, *Local People*, 139–40. Barnett's public

war of words was meant for Mississippi consumption only; Dittmer discovered that the governor was contemporaneously involved in secret negotiations with the Kennedys over the particulars of Meredith's entrance to the university.

40. *Indianola Enterprise-Tocsin*, October 18, 1962. The poem is apparently based on a popular song that probably spread via the vaudeville circuit. The traditional lyrics begin, "Ain't no use my workin' so hard / I got a gal in the white folks' yard." (Bob Dylan changed it to "Ain't no use in workin' so heavy / I got a woman who works on the levee.") I am indebted to Cliff Kuhn for this insight.

41. Charles McLaurin, December 14, 1997, oral history interview with author; Charles Cobb, oral history interview with Howell Raines, in Raines, *My Soul Is Rested*, 247.

42. James Jones and Charles McLaurin, "Voter Registration Activity in Ruleville and Sunflower County January 14, 1963, to January 19," reel 177, VEPP.

43. Charles Cobb, October 21, 1996, oral history interview with John Rachal, OHP. A white observer of Sunflower County wrote, "The women make up the lion's share of the movement [in Ruleville]. This may be partially because they aren't as vulnerable economically but I don't think that factor is very important. Too many women work and oftentimes a man will get fired for the sins of his wife. Perhaps the major reason is that the women seem to have the calm courage necessary for a nonviolent campaign." This observation comes from an anonymous, undated letter in Sutherland, *Letters from Mississippi* [a collection of letters written by Freedom Summer volunteers to friends and family members], 61.

44. Council of Federated Organizations, "The Sunflower County Project," ca. November 1964, 7–8 (Bernice White Personal Papers, copy in author's possession); Charles McLaurin, "Report from Charles McLaurin on Voter Registration Activities in Sunflower County From February 10–21, 1963," reel 177, VEPP.

45. L. C. Dorsey, oral history interview with author; Dorsey, "Harder Times Than These," 168.

46. McLaurin, "Report on Activity in Ruleville and Sunflower County from August 19th to December 28th."

47. Ibid.

48. Ibid.

49. Charles McLaurin, "Report on Progress in Voter Registration in Ruleville," October 11, 1962, reel 177, VEPP.

50. Charles Cobb and Charles McLaurin, "Preliminary Survey on the Condition of the Negro Farmers in Ruleville . . ." (emphasis in original) and Bob Moses to Wiley Branton, memo, "Mississippi Voter Education Project," ca. December 1962, reel 177, VEPP.

51. McLaurin, "Report on Activity in Ruleville and Sunflower County from August 19th to December 28th"; Bob Moses, "Mississippi Voter Education Project"; McLaurin, "[Report on Activity in Sunflower County from December 11 to December 16, 1962]" and "Ruleville and Sunflower County Report January 4 thru 12, 1963," reel 177, VEPP.

52. Audiotape 6403.12 program 4, Johnson-Eastland telephone conversation, March 18, 1964, LBJL.

53. "Friends Send Food, Clothes" and "Registration Up Since Food, Clothes Arrive," *Student Voice*, 118, 126 (February 11 and 25, 1964); Tom Scarborough, "Sunflower County–Ruleville, Mississippi," February 21, 1964, Sovereignty Commission report, Paul B. Johnson Jr. Papers, box 135, USMSC.

54. Scarborough, "Sunflower County–Ruleville, Mississippi"; DeMuth, "Tired of Being Sick and Tired," 551.

55. In 1970, for instance, Dorrough wrote Hamer, "Many people have been publicly commended and decorated for battles won, where they actually were not exposed to the real dangers and rath [*sic*] of the enemy. This is not the case with you, for you have carried your fight straight into the camp of the opposition. . . . If more Americans gave of themselves as you have for the things they believe in, ours would be a better nation." See box 4, reel 2, FLHP.

56. Charles Cobb, October 21, 1996, oral history interview with John Rachal, OHP.

57. Ibid.

58. See Branch, *Parting the Waters*, 716–17. According to Branch, Branton of the Southern Regional Council was very interested in the Mississippi project and spent a good deal of time worrying about the safety of canvassers and the local people who attempted to register. Branton's practical side simply got the better of him.

59. COFO was founded in 1961. Aaron Henry and Medgar Evers of the NAACP, Moses of SNCC, and Dave Dennis of CORE were the main players of the group, which they organized in order to coordinate civil rights activity and to minimize conflicts between national civil rights organizations in the state. As Dittmer points out, COFO has traditionally been described as an "umbrella agency," but Moses and Dennis have always maintained that COFO was an important institution in its own right for black Mississippians who needed to feel that they were working in tandem. See Dittmer, *Local People*, 118–19.

60. See Sinsheimer, "Freedom Vote of 1963," 217–44, and Dittmer, *Local People*, 200–207.

61. "Chronology of Violence and Intimidation in Mississippi since 1961."

62. Henry/King campaign literature in Allard Lowenstein Papers, box 32, SHC. Emphasis in original.

63. Dittmer, *Local People*, 201; Lawrence Guyot, oral history interview with Howell Raines, in Raines, *My Soul Is Rested*, 287; Moses quoted in Dittmer, *Local People*, 206.

64. Telegram in Allard Lowenstein Papers, box 32, SHC.

65. "Chronology of Violence and Intimidation in Mississippi since 1961," 14.

66. Lawrence Guyot, oral history interview with Howell Raines, in Raines, *My Soul Is Rested*, 286.

67. Charles Cobb, oral history interview with Howell Raines, in Raines, *My Soul Is Rested*, 286 n.

68. Peacock quoted in Dittmer, *Local People*, 207–9.

69. Hamer quoted in Dittmer, *Local People*, 209.

70. The great majority of the volunteers came from northeastern and California colleges. See McAdam, *Freedom Summer*, and Belfrage, *Freedom Summer*.

71. James Charles Black, June 9, 1964, affidavit, MFDP Papers, box 25, MLKL; Charles McLaurin, undated affidavit reprinted in Holt, *Summer That Didn't End*, 257–60.

72. James Charles Black, June 9, 1964, affidavit, MFDP Papers, box 25, MLKL; Charles McLaurin, undated affidavit reprinted in Holt, *Summer That Didn't End*, 257–60; see also Sugarman, *Stranger at the Gates*, ch. 1, passim.

Chapter Five

1. "Workers Arrested on Syndicalism Charge," *Student Voice*, 197 (October 28, 1964); Erle Johnston Jr., Special Report to Paul B. Johnson Jr., May 1, 1964, Paul B. Johnson Jr. Papers, USMSC.

2. Umoja has argued that the federal government's refusal to protect civil rights workers in the state drove the final nail in the coffin of a completely nonviolent Mississippi movement. Without federal protection to counteract the violence of white terrorists, nonviolence could not work in Mississippi as a strategy. See Umoja, "1964," 222.

3. Anonymous, undated letter, in Sutherland, *Letters from Mississippi*, 38–39, 46.

4. Audiotape 6406.14 program 3, Johnson-Eastland telephone conversation, June 23, 1964, LBJL. Eastland later made the same claim publicly. See "Eastland Labels Rights Drive 'Red,'" *New York Times*, July 23, 1964.

5. See Dittmer, *Local People*, 247–52; Sellers with Terrell, *River of No Return*, 84–93; Holt, *Summer That Didn't End*, 17–30; and Cagin and Dray, *We Are Not Afraid*.

6. Audiotape 6406.16 program 1, Johnson-Johnson telephone conversation, June 23, 1964, LBJL.

7. Sutherland, *Letters from Mississippi*, 150–51.

8. Ibid., 52, 53, 59.

9. See Wren, "Mississippi: The Attack on Bigotry," *Look*, September 8, 1964, 20–28; and Sugarman, *Stranger at the Gates*, 54–59, for descriptions of the mass meetings.

10. Charlie Cobb, "Some Notes on Education," no date (ca. 1963), SNCC Papers, box 104, MLKL; Young and Long, "Movement Remembered."

11. Hamer quoted in "The Three Educations," no author, ca. 1964, MFDP Papers, box 17, MLKL. Cobb quoted in Dittmer, *Local People*, 259.

12. Cobb, "Some Notes on Education."

13. Eddie Laroy Johnson, July 30, 1964, affidavit and "Statement from Certain Teenagers in Ruleville, Mississippi," MFDP Papers, box 11, MLKL. See also the affidavits from Irene Johnson and Earline King in the same collection.

14. Liz Fusco, "Freedom Schools in Mississippi, 1964," ca. 1964, Bernice White Personal Papers, copy in author's possession.

15. Cobb, "Some Notes on Education."

16. Fusco, "Freedom Schools in Mississippi, 1964."

17. Ibid. Predictably, most Freedom School students sided with Du Bois. Rennie Williams of Ruleville wrote in a Freedom School composition, "What the Summer School Ment to Me," "We have learn about B. T. Washington and DuBois which one ment most for the Negro race that is DuBois." MFDP Papers, box 17, MLKL.

18. Zinn, "Schools in Context," 371.

19. Jerry Shields, Willie Shields, and Flozell Shields, "How It Feels to Be a Negro in Mississippi," July 29, 1964, Freedom School assignment, MFDP Papers, box 17, MLKL.

20. Bettye Butler, Charles Evans, Willie Shields, and Willie Hatchett, "How It Feels to Be a Negro in Mississippi," July 29, 1964, Freedom School assignment, MFDP Papers, box 17, MLKL. See also "Rights Plan Hit by Southern Bloc," *New York Times*, June 20, 1963.

21. Bessie Mae Herring, Gertrude Beverly, and R. Williams, "What the Freedom School Meant to Me," undated Freedom School essays, MFDP Papers, box 17, MLKL.

22. Kirsty Powell, "What the Freedom School Meant to Me," undated Freedom School essays, MFDP Papers, box 17, MLKL. Powell was much more critical of the school program in a later report for the SNCC. See "A Report, Mainly on Ruleville Freedom School, Summer Project, 1964," MFDP Papers, box 17, MLKL.

23. Sutherland, *Letters from Mississippi*, 97.

24. See Hamer, "To Praise Our Bridges," 322–23.

25. Mae Bertha Carter, November 14, 1997, oral history interview with author.

26. David Halberstam, "Negroes Meet Nightly Despite Tension in the Delta," *New York Times*, June 29, 1964.

27. See Sugarman, *Stranger at the Gates*, 86–93, 127–28; Council of Federated Organizations, "Mississippi Project: Running Summary of Incidents," reprinted in Holt, *Summer That Didn't End*, 208.

28. Sugarman, *Stranger at the Gates*, 86, 128–32; Council of Federated Organizations, "Mississippi Project," reprinted in Holt, *Summer That Didn't End*, 217.

29. The clergymen do not deserve all of the blame for this caution. In Ruleville, the pastor of Williams Chapel was reluctant to allow the use of his building until his congregation embraced the Freedom Riders and forced him to open the doors of the chapel to the civil rights movement. The same thing could have happened in Indianola had there been enough of a groundswell among congregants.

30. Sugarman, *Stranger at the Gates*, 172–73.

31. David Matthews, oral history interview with author; Bernice White, September 19, 1997, oral history interview with author; Sugarman, *Stranger at the Gates*, 173.

32. Sugarman, *Stranger at the Gates*, 177–80.

33. Charles McLaurin, December 14, 1997, oral history interview with author.

34. Willie Spurlock, oral history interview with author; Alice Giles, oral history interview with author; Bernice White, September 19, 1997, oral history interview with author; and Charles McLaurin, November 1, 1997, oral history interview with author.

35. Charles McLaurin, "Washington and Sunflower Counties, Mississippi Voter Registration 6/11/63 to 6/16/63," reel 178, VEPP.

36. Ibid.

37. Mike Yarrow, undated letter, in Sutherland, *Letters from Mississippi*, 163–64.

38. Ibid.

39. The MFDP has already received a great deal of scholarly attention. See Dittmer, "Transformation of the Mississippi Movement" and *Local People*, ch. 12, passim; Payne, *I've Got the Light of Freedom*; N. Mills, *Like a Holy Crusade*; K. Mills, *This Little Light of Mine*, ch. 6, passim; Lee, *For Freedom's Sake*, chs. 4 and 5, passim; Holt, *Summer That Didn't End*, ch. 8, passim; Ransby, *Ella Baker*, ch. 11, passim; and Bass, "Johnson and the MFDP Controversy," among others. William Scott's words come

from the minutes of the Sunflower County precinct meeting of the MFDP, August 1, 1964, MFDP Papers, box 20, MLKL.

40. K. Mills, *This Little Light of Mine*, 90.

41. Ibid., 92.

42. Charles McLaurin, December 14, 1997, oral history interview with author.

43. Hamer campaign literature, MFDP Papers, box 18, MLKL.

44. Bob Moses, "Emergency Memorandum to All Field Staff and Voter Registration Volunteers," July 19, 1964, Paul B. Johnson Jr. Papers, box 136, USMSC.

45. "Minutes of the Mississippi State Democratic Convention," July 28, 1964, MFDP Papers, box 22, MLKL; Joseph L. Rauh, Eleanor K. Norton, and H. Miles Jaffe, "Brief Submitted by the Mississippi Freedom Democratic Party," Allard Lowenstein Papers, box 32, SHC.

46. Campaign literature in Allard Lowenstein Papers, box 32, SHC.

47. For a fine history of the Dixiecrat movement, see Frederickson, *Dixiecrat Revolt*.

48. "Brief Submitted by the Mississippi Freedom Democratic Party."

49. Erle Johnston Jr. to Ruble Griffin, memo, August 18, 1964, Paul B. Johnson Jr. Papers, box 136, USMSC. The Sovereignty Commission's case rested on the arguments that the MFDP had been organized in the first place by non-Mississippians, some of whom were Communists, and that the delegation was chosen haphazardly by COFO leaders.

50. Hamer quoted in K. Mills, *This Little Light of Mine*, 119–21.

51. Johnson quoted in Branch, *Pillar of Fire*, 448.

52. See Dittmer, "Transformation of the Mississippi Movement," 18, and Branch, *Pillar of Fire*, ch. 34, passim.

53. Charles McLaurin, December 14, 1997, oral history interview with author; Fannie Lou Hamer, November 1966, oral history interview with Anne Romaine, Anne Romaine Papers, box 1, MLKL.

54. Charles McLaurin, December 14, 1997, oral history interview with author.

55. Ibid.

56. Alice Giles, oral history interview with author. I am indebted to John Dittmer for reminding me of the fact that while the Atlantic City experience may have soured many MFDP delegates on interracial politics, it did not prevent most of them from supporting national Democrats.

57. "The Civil Rights Bill in Sunflower County," an undated COFO report authored by James Dann or Charles Scattergood, Bernice White Personal Papers, copy in author's possession.

58. Ibid.

59. Ibid.

60. Ibid.

61. Stories about Hough and the Police Auxiliary appear in the *Indianola Enterprise-Tocsin*, July 19, 1956, June 16, 1960, and May 15, 1986; "Sunflower County Project," 6.

62. John Harris, "Sunflower County Report," October 17, 1964, SNCC Papers, box 104, MLKL; unknown author, "COFO Program (Winter 1964–Spring 1965)," Paul B. Johnson Jr. Papers, box 141, USMSC.

63. Undated memorandum from SNCC headquarters to Project Directors, box 4,

SCEFP. Anecdotal evidence suggests that the number of volunteers who remained in the county was far higher.

64. October 1964 Incident Summaries, SNCC Papers, box 103, MLKL. See also the *New York Times*, March 6, 1965.

65. November 1964 Incident Summaries, SNCC Papers, box 103, MLKL; Harris, "Sunflower County Report."

66. Harris, "Sunflower County Report."

67. Ibid.

68. John Harris, "Report on Sunflower County," ca. November/December 1964, SNCC Papers, box 104, MLKL.

69. Linda Davis, "Sunflower County—Activity Report, Monday, January 12, 1965," SNCC Papers, box 104, MLKL.

70. Tom Scarborough, "Sunflower County," September 15, 1965, SovCom document 2-38-1-98-1-1-1; U.S. Justice Department Voting Statistics, MFDP Papers, box 18, MLKL.

Chapter Six

1. Anonymous letter from a Ruleville volunteer, August 30, 1964, in Sutherland, *Letters from Mississippi*, 222.

2. Ibid.

3. "Mississippi Freedom Primer No. 1: The Convention Challenge and the Freedom Vote," ca. October 1964, MFDP Papers, box 20, MLKL.

4. Minutes of the Executive Committee of the MFDP, September 13, 1964, MFDP Papers, box 20, MLKL.

5. Viorst, *Fire in the Streets*, 236–37; Sellers quoted in Dittmer, "Transformation of the Mississippi Movement," 20–21.

6. Lawrence Guyot to John Bailey, telegram, October 30, 1964, reprinted in Holt, *Summer That Didn't End*, 179–81.

7. Moses quoted in Dittmer, *Local People*, 318.

8. *Congressional Record*, November 3, 1967, MFDP Subject File, MDAH.

9. MFDP Subject File, MDAH; March 11, 1969, MFDP press release, box 7, reel 3, FLHP.

10. Minutes of the Executive Committee of the MFDP, box 7, reel 3, FLHP.

11. Claude Ramsay, "A Report on the Delta Farm Strike," August 16, 1965, AFL-CIO Civil Rights Department Papers, box 1602, SLC.

12. George Shelton, "Dear Friends" letter, "Report," and "Financial Report," ca. 1965, Paul B. Johnson Jr. Papers, box 142, USMSC.

13. Transcript of McKenna Mack conversation with KZSU (the Stanford University radio station), *Project South, 1965* (microform) (Stanford University Libraries, 1976), 0302–3; George Shelton, "Dear Friends" letter, "Report," and "Financial Report"; *National Guardian*, June 12, 1965, SovCom document 2-153-0-2-1-1-1; "A New Alliance Shapes Up in Dixie," *Business Week*, July 10, 1965, 124–28, AFL-CIO Civil Rights Department Papers, box 1602, SLC. See also Woodruff, "African American Struggles for Citizenship."

14. Transcript of unidentified organizer conversation with KZSU, *Project South*, 0302-11-12.

15. "New Alliance Shapes Up in Dixie," 126.

16. Ramsay, "Report on the Delta Farm Strike"; transcript of Bob Williams conversation with KZSU, *Project South*, 0302–12. See also Draper, *Conflict of Interests*, ch. 6, passim. For a history of the Delta Ministry, see Mark Newman, *Divine Agitators*.

17. Ramsay, "Report on the Delta Farm Strike"; Draper, *Conflict of Interests*, 148.

18. Carter, "Negro Exodus," 26.

19. Correspondence with Hamer, 1967–77, box 1, reel 1, FLHP.

20. Hamer quotes from K. Mills, *This Little Light of Mine*, 274, and box 1, reel 1, FLHP.

21. K. Mills, *This Little Light of Mine*, 144; Douglas to Hamer, March 19, 1974, box 1, reel 1, FLHP. Ironically, at the same time, SNCC radicals were disassociating themselves from the integrationist Hamer. See Payne, *I've Got the Light of Freedom*, ch. 13, passim; and Carson, *In Struggle*, ch. 13, passim.

22. Freedom Farm financial documents, box 7, reel 3, and box 10, reel 4, FLHP.

23. "Brief Historical Background of Freedom Farm Corporation," no author, no date, box 11, reel 5, FLHP. See also Peterson, "Sunflowers Don't Grow in Sunflower County," 9–21 and "Pig Banks Reap Dividends," *Dallas Morning News*, January 31, 1973.

24. Freedom Farm financial documents, box 7, reel 3, and box 10, reel 4, FLHP.

25. Hamer, "Status Report and Request for Funds," July 1973, box 11, reel 5, FLHP.

26. Joe Harris, "Economic and Training Needs, Mississippi Delta," ca. 1967, box 5, reel 2, FLHP.

27. Freedom Farm financial documents, box 3, reel 2, FLHP.

28. K. Mills, *This Little Light of Mine*, 259–60. Senate liberals rejected Townsend anyway.

29. Campbell to Harris, May 11, 1973, box 10, reel 4, FLHP.

30. Delta Ministry Newsletter, October 1965, box 26, reel 11, FLHP.

31. Untitled document on the history of Freedom Farm, no author, no date, box 11, reel 5, FLHP.

32. The Twenty-fourth Amendment to the U.S. Constitution, ratified in 1964, outlawed the poll tax but applied only to elections for national office.

33. "Special Elections in the Towns of Sunflower and Moorhead to be Held May 2, 1967," no author, no date, box 9, reel 4, FLHP.

34. Committee for Free Elections for Sunflower County Literature, ca. 1967, box 3, reel 2, FLHP.

35. Committee for Free Elections in Sunflower County press release, August 19, 1966, box 7, reel 3, FLHP.

36. The battles over Head Start and the administration of Office of Economic Opportunity funds were byzantine in most of Mississippi, nowhere more so than in Sunflower County. See K. Mills, ch. 11, passim, and P. Greenberg, *Devil Has Slippery Shoes*.

37. Barry campaign literature, box 9, reel 4, FLHP.

38. Davis campaign literature, ibid.

39. Green campaign literature, ibid.

40. Lewis campaign literature, ibid.

41. The tamale has an interesting history as a favorite food among black Deltans. John T. Edge, a food writer based in Oxford, Mississippi, has given more thought to the phenomenon than anyone else; he concludes that black farm workers gleaned the tamale from migrant Mexican farm workers in the early 1900s. Craig Claiborne, who grew up in Indianola and went on to become the food editor of the *New York Times*, fondly remembered a Mexican American who peddled "the most tempting, mouth-watering hot tamales you could hope to sample" around the county seat during the Great Depression. Unfortunately, according to Claiborne, the tamale vendor was unceremoniously escorted out of town after authorities found more than 100 cat skeletons under his cabin. See the *Atlanta Journal-Constitution*, February 7, 1999, and Claiborne, *Feast Made for Laughter*.

42. Brown campaign literature, box 9, reel 4, FLHP. See also *New York Times*, April 30, 1967.

43. "Citizens of Sunflower," author unknown, ca. 1967, box 9, reel 4, FLHP.

44. Mayor and Board of Alderman of Sunflower, "Important Notice to Citizens of Sunflower," ca. 1967, ibid.

45. "Delta Ministry Reports," April 1967, box 26, reel 11, FLHP.

46. "Sunflower in the Spring," *New Republic*, April 5, 1967, box 3, reel 1, FLHP; Charles Kerns, "Miss. Leader Tells of Plans to Win Historic Poll," *UE News*, March 20, 1967, box 3, reel 1, FLHP.

47. Kerns, "Miss. Leader Tells of Plans to Win Historic Poll."

48. "Delta Ministry Reports," May 1967, box 26, reel 11, FLHP; *New York Times*, May 3, 1967.

49. Romine and Patterson quoted in the *New York Times*, May 3, 1967. Voting statistics from 1967 from Mississippi AFL-CIO records, box 2186, SLC. Beckwith easily distanced Paul B. Johnson and Charles Sullivan in Sunflower County, but Johnson and Sullivan dwarfed De La Beckwith's total statewide vote.

50. Draper, *Conflict of Interests*, 152.

51. See ibid., 156, and Wilkie, *Dixie*, 249–55.

52. *Indianola Enterprise-Tocsin*, December 28, 1967, and January 25, 1968.

53. Carver Randle, oral history interview with author; *Indianola Enterprise-Tocsin*, April 11, 1968.

54. *Indianola Enterprise-Tocsin*, April 11, May 23, May 30, and June 20, 1968.

55. Carver Randle, oral history interview with author; *Indianola Enterprise-Tocsin*, June 20, 1968; Cobb, *Most Southern Place on Earth*, 251.

56. Joseph S. Clark, Gaylord Nelson, Jannings Randolph, Robert F. Kennedy, Claiborne Pell, Winston L. Prouty, Edward M. Kennedy, Jacob K. Javits, and George Murphy to Johnson, April 27, 1967, box 26, reel 11, FLHP.

57. Transcript of Bob Williams conversation with KZSU, *Project South*, 0302–12.

58. Figures from box 8, reel 4, FLHP; and Joe Harris, "Sunflower County Progress Report 1968," box 26, reel 11, FLHP.

59. Office of Economic Opportunity Information Center, "Community Profile," 1968, box 3, SCEFP (unprocessed); Cobb, " 'Somebody Done Nailed Us on the Cross,' " 919; Kotz, *Let Them Eat Promises*, 5.

60. For the effects of federal welfare policy in the Delta, see Cobb, "'Somebody Done Nailed Us on the Cross,'" 919; and Kotz, *Let Them Eat Promises*, 4, 25, 84–85, 91–93.

61. Census figures from the U.S. Department of Commerce, *1970 Census of Population*, 26-16, 26-309, and 26-316, and *1980 Census of Population*, 26-11, 26-24.

62. Dunbar, *Delta Time*, 85, 13; Cobb, *Most Southern Place on Earth*, 333.

63. The human toll that the civil rights struggle took on Hamer is a central theme of Lee's excellent *For Freedom's Sake*.

64. Fannie Lou Hamer, November 1966, oral history interview with Anne Romaine, Anne Romaine Papers, box 1, MLKL; Lee, "Passionate Pursuit of Justice," 146, 436–38.

Chapter Seven

1. According to the *Indianola Enterprise-Tocsin*, July 31, 1986, the 1985 Sunflower County cotton crop was worth $47.9 million and county farmers raised $44 million worth of catfish. Sunflower County was the state's leading producer of agricultural products, to the tune of $142.7 million.

2. Activist Bayard Rustin dubbed the years between 1955 and 1965 the "classical" period of the American civil rights movement. See Rustin, "From Protest to Politics," 296.

3. Salomone, *Equal Education under Law*, 46. For "freedom of choice" and other statewide efforts to block desegregation, see Charles C. Bolton, "Last Stand of Massive Resistance."

4. Marian Wright to Barbara Brandt, January 5, 1966, MFDP Papers, box 11, MLKL; Prathia Hall Wynn to Jean Fairfax and other AFSC staff, memo, September 23, 1965, Constance Curry Personal Papers, copy in author's possession.

5. Mae Bertha Carter, November 14, 1997, oral history interview with author; Prathia Hall Wynn memo. See also Curry's superb *Silver Rights*, which tells the Carters' story in vivid detail. Curry herself worked as an AFSC staffer in the mid-1960s, when she befriended the family. For the importance of Amzie Moore's life and example, see Payne, *I've Got the Light of Freedom*.

6. Prathia Hall Wynn memo.

7. Mae Bertha Carter, November 14, 1997, oral history interview with author.

8. Ibid.

9. Curry, *Silver Rights*, 11.

10. Prathia Hall Wynn memo; Mae Bertha Carter, October 17, 1997, oral history interview with author.

11. Prathia Hall Wynn memo.

12. All quotes from Prathia Hall Wynn memo.

13. Erle Johnston Jr. to J. L. Sanders, March 7, 1967, SovCom document 2-38-1-110-1-1-1.

14. Tom Scarborough, "Sunflower County (Drew, Mississippi)" report, March 22, 1967, SovCom document 2-38-1-111-1-1-1.

15. Scarborough, "Sunflower County (Drew, Mississippi)."

16. Salomone, *Equal Education under Law*, 46.

17. *Indianola Enterprise-Tocsin*, February 6, 1986.

18. Council leaders listed in the *Indianola Enterprise-Tocsin*, December 22, 1955.

19. Salomone, *Equal Education under Law*, 47. Emphasis in original.

20. Ruling in *U.S. v. Indianola Municipal Separate School District*. Copy in author's possession, courtesy of Isabel Lee.

21. *Indianola Enterprise-Tocsin*, August 27, 1964.

22. Ibid., March 25, 1965.

23. Ibid., November 30, 1967; Hemphill, *Fevers, Floods, and Faith*, 549.

24. Fuquay, "Private School Movement," 160, 164.

25. Joseph Harris, "Economic and Training Needs, Mississippi Delta," ca. 1967, box 5, reel 2, FLHP.

26. Eastland and Brady, fund-raising letter for the Council Schools, May 7, 1970, Paul B. Johnson Jr. Papers, box 135, USMSC.

27. Hemphill, *Fevers, Floods, and Faith*, 551.

28. Isabel Lee, oral history interview with author. Sunflower County's two other segregation academies—North Sunflower Academy, between Drew and Ruleville, and Central Delta Academy in Inverness—both sprouted in a similar fashion.

29. Dudley Clendinen, "White Grip on Southern Schools: Keeping Control," *New York Times*, June 23, 1986.

30. Kinsey quoted in *Jackson Clarion-Ledger*, November 12, 1985. Jackson-area newspapers courtesy the "Indianola-Education" subject file, MDAH.

31. *Washington Post*, April 21, 1986; Jim Abbott, October 4, 1997, oral history interview with author.

32. Isabel Lee, oral history interview with author.

33. *Jackson Clarion-Ledger*, March 6, 1986; Jim Abbott, October 4, 1997, oral history interview with author.

34. Spurlock quoted in *Jackson Clarion-Ledger*, March 6, 1986.

35. Letters to the editor, *Indianola Enterprise-Tocsin*, February 6, 1986.

36. *Indianola Enterprise-Tocsin*, March 27, 1986.

37. Jim Abbott, October 4, 1997, oral history interview with author.

38. Spurlock quoted in *Jackson Clarion-Ledger*, March 26, 1986; see also *Indianola Enterprise-Tocsin*, March 27, 1986.

39. *Jackson Clarion-Ledger*, March 27, 1986.

40. See SovCom document 6-70-0-78-3-1-1, which lists residents and businesses of Sunflower County who donated money through the Sovereignty Commission to the Coordinating Committee for Fundamental American Freedoms, a lobby formed to oppose the Civil Rights Bill in 1963. The *Indianola Enterprise-Tocsin*, September 19, 1963, identifies Bill Gresham as a Citizens' Council member.

41. Steve Rosenthal, oral history interview with author.

42. Johnson and Lewis quoted in *Washington Post*, April 21, 1986.

43. Steve Rosenthal, oral history interview with author; Moll and Coleman quoted in *Indianola Enterprise-Tocsin*, March 27, 1986.

44. Smith quoted in *Jackson Clarion-Ledger*, March 28, 1986.

45. Fratesi quoted in *Indianola Enterprise-Tocsin*, March 27, 1986.

46. *Indianola Enterprise-Tocsin*, April 24, 1986; Steve Rosenthal, oral history interview with author.

47. Spurlock quoted in *Indianola Enterprise-Tocsin*, April 3, 1986, and *Jackson Daily News*, March 30, 1986.

48. Spurlock quoted in *Indianola Enterprise-Tocsin*, April 3, 1986.

49. *Washington Post*, April 21, 1986.

50. *Indianola Enterprise-Tocsin*, April 24, 1986; Willie Spurlock, oral history interview with author, and Jim Abbott, October 4, 1997, oral history interview with author. According to Spurlock and others, Jackson actually contacted Concerned Citizens and offered to come to Indianola to lead protests and/or organize statewide or nationwide boycotts of Delta products. He was politely refused.

51. Powdermaker, *After Freedom*, 362.

52. Willie Spurlock, oral history interview with author.

53. *Jackson Clarion-Ledger*, March 27 and April 1, 1986.

54. *Indianola Enterprise-Tocsin*, April 3, 1986; *Jackson Clarion-Ledger*, April 15, 1986.

55. *Indianola Enterprise-Tocsin*, April 17, 1986.

56. Spurlock and Freeman quoted in *Jackson Clarion-Ledger*, April 13, 1986.

57. *Jackson Clarion-Ledger*, April 13, 1986.

58. Paris quoted in *Indianola Enterprise-Tocsin*, March 27, 1986.

59. David Matthews, oral history interview with author.

60. Jack Harper Jr., oral history interview with author.

61. McWilliams quoted in *Indianola Enterprise-Tocsin*, April 24, 1986.

62. McWilliams's family ran a grocery store in Holly Ridge and was considered friendly and fair by the blacks on the nearby Robinson plantation. Tommy McWilliams's first job out of Ole Miss was with a law firm in Drew that represented Freedom Farm. He was arguably the only man in Sunflower County with such strong ties to both communities.

63. Group of sixteen named in *Indianola Enterprise-Tocsin*, April 24, 1986.

64. For Mississippi's official industrialization program, see Clark, "Legislative Adoption"; and Prince, "Balance Agriculture with Industry Program." For the effort to industrialize Mississippi and the South, see Cobb, *Industrialization and Southern Society*. The debate over the social benefits of industrial development is of course not limited to the state of Mississippi nor the South but is a long and continuing one in the fields of political economy and economic history. One of the best summarizations of the debate may be found in S. Greenberg, *Race and State in Capitalist Development*, 5–28. Greenberg compares the experiences of several racial orders, including that of Birmingham, Alabama, as they undergo modernization and concludes that "whether the racial order persists and in what form depends [in large part but not entirely] on the strength of the business challenge to the traditional racial hegemony" (28).

65. Clark, "Legislative Adoption," 285.

66. For an example of later theorists' belief that the Mississippi Delta needed more industry, see Joseph Harris, "Economic and Training Needs, Mississippi Delta," ca. 1967, box 5, reel 2, FLHP.

67. Steve Rosenthal, oral history interview with author.

68. For the Birmingham movement, see Eskew, *But for Birmingham*. For Port Gibson, see E. Crosby, "Common Courtesy."

69. Hortense Powdermaker, writing in the late 1930s, placed all professionals, including teachers, in Indianola's black upper class. She placed vagrants, prostitutes, and welfare cases in the black lower class. The rest of the black community, roughly 90 percent of it, she placed in an upper- and lower-middle class. Thus, according to Powdermaker, any black who labored on a farm was "middle class." Farm owners who worked for themselves were upper-middle class, and sharecroppers were lower-middle class. Powdermaker's classifications were not, of course, based on occupation or income but on behavior she observed during her fieldwork. I define professionals—lawyers, doctors, teachers, business owners, undertakers, etc.—and black farm owners as the members of a black middle class in Sunflower County.

70. After Fannie Lou Hamer and others organized on civil rights grounds, I believe one can speak of a "class consciousness," as E. P. Thompson and others have used the term, among black Sunflower County farmworkers.

71. For "scared teachers," see Sugarman, *Stranger at the Gates*, 48, 58. Bob Cableton, a black civil rights worker from Indianola, used the latter, particularly descriptive term, to describe middle-class blacks who waited until the coast was clear to align themselves with the civil rights movement. Bob Cableton, oral history interview with author.

72. *Indianola Enterprise-Tocsin*, May 8, 1986.

73. Letters to the editor, *Indianola Enterprise-Tocsin*, April 24, 1986.

74. Steve Rosenthal, oral history interview with author.

75. Jim Abbott, October 4, 1997, oral history interview with author. The latter interviewee asked not to be identified.

76. *Indianola Enterprise-Tocsin*, May 8, 1986.

77. Fratesi quoted in *Jackson Daily News*, May 8, 1986.

78. Duease and Rosenthal quoted in *Indianola Enterprise-Tocsin*, May 8, 1986.

79. Merritt quoted in *Indianola Enterprise-Tocsin*, May 8, 1986.

80. Harper and parents quoted in *Indianola Enterprise-Tocsin*, June 19, 1986.

81. Jim Abbott, "Robert Merritt Leaves Legacy of Accomplishment," *Indianola Enterprise-Tocsin*, June 9, 1994.

82. Grissom quoted in *Jackson Clarion-Ledger*, May 19, 1986.

83. Richard Schweid, *Catfish and the Delta*, 116.

84. The catfish industry has aggressively marketed its product, effectively rehabilitating catfish's image from a "trash fish" that only poor (usually black) southerners ate into a gourmet delicacy. For an example of the marketing campaign, see *Indianola Enterprise-Tocsin*, June 26, 1997, for a photograph of Catfish Queen Shanna Bearden promoting catfish at a reception in New York's Central Park. By the late 1990s, the catfish had become the symbol of economic resurgence in Mississippi.

85. *Indianola Enterprise-Tocsin*, July 31, 1986.

86. Schweid, *Catfish and the Delta*, 117; *Indianola Enterprise-Tocsin*, May 15, 1986.

87. Schweid, *Catfish and the Delta*, 122–23.

88. "Catfish Plant Strikers Reach Tentative Pact," *New York Times*, December 14,

1990; Peter T. Kilborn, "Charges of Exploitation Roil a Catfish Plant," *New York Times*, December 10, 1990.

89. Walker and Young quoted in Schweid, *Catfish and the Delta*, 123, 124.

90. B. Campbell, *Your Blues Ain't Like Mine*, 377.

91. *Indianola Enterprise-Tocsin*, May 15, 1986.

92. Ibid.

93. Peter T. Kilborn, "Charges of Exploitation Roil a Catfish Plant," *New York Times*, December 10, 1990.

94. *Indianola Enterprise-Tocsin*, June 5, 1986.

95. Ibid., October 9, 1986.

96. Ibid., July 24, October 9, and October 16, 1986.

97. Ibid., July 24, 1986.

98. A year earlier, the federal Occupational Health and Safety Administration had fined Delta Pride $32,800 for violating health and safety standards and for refusing to work with the union to decrease the occurrence of repetitive-motion injuries at its Indianola facility. See Richard Schweid, "Delta Strike: Civil Rights or Just Plain Economics?" *Los Angeles Times*, November 18, 1990.

99. Jackson and Lowery quoted in Schweid, "Delta Strike."

100. Delta Pride president Larry Joiner quoted in Schweid, "Delta Strike."

101. See "Catfish Plant Strikers Reach Tentative Pact," *New York Times*, December 14, 1990, and "Pact Approved at Delta Pride," *New York Times*, December 16, 1990.

102. Dent, *Southern Journey*, 364–65.

103. Ibid.

Epilogue

1. The diversification of Sunflower County's economy and its effect on a growing black middle class can surely be exaggerated, however. By one estimate, Sunflower County's per capita income remained at $7,885 in 1990, and more than a third of all Sunflower County families lived below the federal poverty line. See CACI Marketing Systems, *Sourcebook of County Demographics*, 34A–34D.

2. For the Mississippi Delta Empowerment Zone Alliance, see the *Atlanta Journal-Constitution*, April 13, 1997, and the *Indianola Enterprise-Tocsin*, June 26, 1997. The Delta region has the lowest average wage in Mississippi, which in 1996 had the lowest average wage of any southern state, at $21,822. See the *Jackson Clarion-Ledger*, November 2, 1997.

3. Dent, *Southern Journey*, 365.

4. This fact need not have puzzled me. Henry himself was effusive in his praise of the senator when Eastland died in 1986 and even claimed that Big Jim had experienced a road-to-Damascus conversion on racial matters sometime in the 1980s. If Eastland really did change his colors as drastically as Henry claimed, it must be said that he kept that change mostly to himself.

5. Harper quoted in the *Jackson Clarion-Ledger*, June 19, 1983, Indianola subject file, MDAH; Jack Harper Jr., oral history interview with author.

6. Jack Harper Jr., oral history interview with author.

7. Jack Harper Jr. campaign materials, in author's possession.

8. Lemann, "Long March."

9. Brundage, *Where These Memories Grow*, 2.

10. See the later chapters of Sugarman, *Strangers at the Gates*, for McLaurin's activities immediately after Freedom Summer.

11. For the social consequences of Fordice's policies, see Peter Applebome, *Dixie Rising*, chs. 10 and 11, passim. Fordice and President Clinton especially disappointed Mae Bertha Carter; several of our conversations included her comparisons of welfare "reform" with Mississippi's draconian social policies of the 1950s.

12. Carver Randle, "Letter to the Editor," *Indianola Enterprise-Tocsin*, May 7, 1998.

13. Fuquay, "Private School Movement," 179.

Bibliography

Manuscript Collections

Center for American History, Austin, Tex.
  Natchez Trace Collection
Constance Curry Personal Papers, Atlanta, Ga.
Townsend Davis Personal Papers, New York, N.Y.
Fisk University Special Collections, Nashville, Tenn.
  Charles Johnson Papers
Lyndon B. Johnson Presidential Library, Austin, Tex.
  Audio recordings of Johnson telephone conversations
  John Bailey Papers
  Democratic National Committee Records
  Harry C. McPherson Papers
  Bill Moyers Papers
  Charles Roche Papers
  Marvin Watson Papers
  Lee C. White Papers
  White House Central File Diary Backup
Martin Luther King, Jr., Center for Nonviolent Social Change Library and Archives,
  Atlanta, Ga.
  Delta Ministry Papers
  MFDP Papers
  Anne Romaine Papers
  SCLC Papers
  SNCC Papers
Library of Congress, Washington, D.C.
  NAACP Papers
Worth Long Personal Papers, Atlanta, Ga.
Mississippi Department of Archives and History, Jackson, Miss.
  Letterbooks of Governors Andrew Longino and James Vardaman
  Mississippi Sovereignty Commission Collection
  Name Files
  Newspaper Files
  Subject Files
  Works Progress Administration Papers

National Archives and Records Administration, Southeastern Regional Office, Atlanta, Ga.
  Selective Service Records
  U.S. Census Records
  War Manpower Commission Files
Southern Historical Collection, Wilson Library, University of North Carolina, Chapel Hill, N.C.
  Allard Lowenstein Papers
  Southern Tenant Farmers' Union Papers
Southern Labor Collection, Georgia State University Special Collections, Atlanta, Ga.
  AFL-CIO Civil Rights Department Papers
  Mississippi AFL-CIO Records
  Southern Conference Education Foundation Papers
Sunflower County Library, Indianola, Miss.
  Clippings Files
Sunflower County Voting Records, Office of the County Circuit Clerk, Indianola, Miss.
University of Mississippi Special Collections, John Williams Library, Oxford, Miss.
University of Southern Mississippi Special Collections, McCain Library, Hattiesburg, Miss.
  Citizens' Councils Collection
  Paul B. Johnson Jr. Papers
Bernice White Personal Papers, Indianola, Miss.

Microfilm Collections

Facts on Film, Race Relations Information Center, Nashville, Tenn.
Fannie Lou Hamer Papers, Amistad Research Center, Tulane University, New Orleans, La.
Project South, KZSU and Stanford University Libraries, Stanford, Calif.
Voter Education Project Papers, Southern Regional Council Papers, Woodruff Library, Atlanta University Center, Atlanta, Ga.

Oral History Interviews

Conducted by the Author

All interviews, unless otherwise noted, have been placed in the archives of the Oral History Program, University of Southern Mississippi, Hattiesburg, Miss.
Jim Abbott, October 4, 1997, and March 22, 1998, Indianola, Miss.
Owen Brooks, January 13, 1998, Indianola and Greenville, Miss.
Bob Cableton, January 26, 1998, Indianola, Miss.
Mae Bertha Carter, October 17, 1997, Drew, Miss.; November 14, 1997, Drew and Marigold, Miss.

Ed Cole, November 26, 1997, Jackson, Miss.
L. A. Davidson, December 9, 1997, Indianola, Miss.
L. C. Dorsey, January 13, 1995, Mound Bayou, Miss.
Alice Giles, November 4, 1997, Indianola, Miss.
Jack Harper Jr., September 30, 1997, Indianola, Miss.
Lamar Hooker, September 21, 1997, Kosciusko, Miss.
George Jordan, October 29, 1997, Ruleville, Miss.
Elisha Langdon, October 23, 1997, Ruleville, Miss.
Jimmy Langdon, November 14, 1997, Drew, Miss.
Isabel Lee, December 15, 1997, Indianola, Miss.
Marie Lee, December 12, 1997, Indianola, Miss.
Robert Love, October 16, 1997, Indianola, Miss.
David Matthews, December 12, 1997, Indianola, Miss.
Charles McLaurin, November 1, 1997, and December 14, 1997, Indianola, Miss.
Matt McWilliams, September 18, 1997, Indianola and Holly Ridge, Miss.
Anice Powell, September 17, 1997, Indianola, Miss.
Carver Randle, October 22, 1997, Indianola, Miss. (unrecorded)
Steve Rosenthal, January 12, 1998, Indianola, Miss.
Bobby Rushing, November 18, 1997, Indianola, Miss.
Willie Spurlock, January 24, 1998, Indianola, Miss.
Bernice White, September 19, 1997, and December 10, 1997, Indianola, Miss.

Collections

Lyndon B. Johnson Presidential Library, Austin, Tex.
  Ramsey Clark
  Aaron Henry
  Nicholas deB. Katzenbach
  Joseph L. Rauh Jr.
  Lee C. White
Martin Luther King, Jr., Center for Nonviolent Social Change Library and Archives, Atlanta, Ga.
  Fannie Lou Hamer
Oral History Program, University of Southern Mississippi, Hattiesburg, Miss.
  Thomas P. Brady
  A. E. Britt
  Charles Cobb
  Fannie Lou Hamer
  Aaron Henry
  Amzie Moore
Sunflower County Library, Indianola, Miss.
  James Corder
  Mary Dotson
  Les and Bubba Fletcher
  Jack Harper Jr.

Morris Lewis
David Matthews
Lois McMurtry
Arch Pierson
Anice Powell
Ed Scott Jr.
Ivory Strong
Christine Swartz and Jessie Lee
Clifton Taulbert
Tommy Taylor
Viola Tillman
Ida Walker

Newspapers

Atlanta Journal-Constitution
Cleveland Call and Post
(Greenville, Miss.) Delta Democrat-Times
Greenville Times
Greenwood (Miss.) Commonwealth
Greenwood Enterprise
Indianola (Miss.) Enterprise
Indianola Enterprise-Tocsin
Jackson (Miss.) Clarion-Ledger
Jackson Daily News
Los Angeles Times
New York Herald
New York Times
Southern School News
Student Voice
Sunflower (Miss.) Tocsin
Vicksburg (Miss.) Evening Post
Washington Post

Books

Abbott, Dorothy, ed. *Mississippi Writers: Reflections of Childhood and Youth*, vol. 2, *Non-Fiction*. Jackson: University of Mississippi Press, 1986.

Applebome, Peter. *Dixie Rising: How the South Is Shaping American Values, Politics, and Culture*. New York: Times Books, 1996.

Archer, Chalmers, Jr. *Growing Up Black in Rural Mississippi: Memories of a Family, Heritage of a Place*. New York: Walker and Company, 1992.

Ashmore, Harry S. *Civil Rights and Wrongs: A Memoir of Race and Politics, 1944–1994*. New York: Pantheon Books, 1994.

——. *The Negro and the Schools*. Chapel Hill: University of North Carolina Press, 1954.

Ayers, Edward L. *The Promise of the New South: Life after Reconstruction*. New York: Oxford University Press, 1992.

Baker, Lewis. *The Percys of Mississippi: Politics and Literature in the New South*. Baton Rouge: Louisiana State University Press, 1983.

Ball, Howard, Dale Krane, and Thomas Lauth. *Compromised Compliance: Implementation of the 1965 Voting Rights Act*. Westport, Conn.: Greenwood Press, 1982.

Barry, John M. *Rising Tide: The Great Mississippi Flood of 1927 and How It Changed America*. New York: Simon and Schuster, 1997.

Bartley, Numan V. *The Rise of Massive Resistance: Race and Politics in the South during the 1950s*. Baton Rouge: Louisiana State University Press, 1969.

Bauerlein, Mark. *Negrophobia: A Race Riot in Atlanta, 1906*. San Francisco: Encounter Books, 2001.

Belfrage, Sally. *Freedom Summer*. New York: Viking, 1965.

Belknap, Michael. *Federal Law and Southern Order: Racial Violence and Constitutional Conflict in the Post-Brown Era*. Athens: University of Georgia Press, 1987.

Bernstein, David E. *Only One Place of Redress: African Americans, Labor Regulations, and the Courts from Reconstruction to the New Deal*. Durham, N.C.: Duke University Press, 2001.

Boggs, Carl. *The Two Revolutions: Gramsci and the Dilemmas of Western Marxism*. Boston: South End Press, 1984.

Brady, Thomas. *Black Monday: Segregation or Amalgamation, America Has Its Choice*. Winona, Miss.: Association of Citizens' Councils, 1955.

Branch, Taylor. *Parting the Waters: America in the King Years, 1954–63*. New York: Touchstone, 1988.

——. *Pillar of Fire: America in the King Years, 1963–65*. New York: Simon and Schuster, 1998.

Brauer, Carl. *John F. Kennedy and the Second Reconstruction*. New York: Columbia University Press, 1977.

Brundage, W. Fitzhugh, ed. *Under Sentence of Death: Lynching in the South*. Chapel Hill: University of North Carolina Press, 1997.

——. *Where These Memories Grow: History, Memory, and Southern Identity*. Chapel Hill: University of North Carolina Press, 2000.

Bunche, Ralph J. *The Political Status of the Negro in the Age of FDR*. Chicago: University of Chicago Press, 1973.

Burner, Eric. *And Gently He Shall Lead Them: Robert Parris Moses and Civil Rights in Mississippi*. New York: New York University Press, 1994.

Burns, Stewart. *Social Movements of the 1960s: Searching for Democracy*. Boston: Twayne Publishers, 1990.

Button, James W. *Blacks and Social Change: Impact of the Civil Rights Movement in Southern Communities*. Princeton, N.J.: Princeton University Press, 1989.

CACI Marketing Systems. *The Sourcebook of County Demographics*. 6th ed. Arlington, Va.: CACI Marketing Systems, 1993.

Cagin, Seth, and Philip Dray. *We Are Not Afraid: The Story of Goodman, Schwerner, and Chaney, and the Civil Rights Campaign for Mississippi.* New York: Macmillan, 1988.

Califano, Joseph A. *The Triumph and Tragedy of Lyndon Johnson.* New York: Simon and Schuster, 1991.

Calt, Stephen, and Gayle Wardlow. *King of the Delta Blues: The Life and Music of Charlie Patton.* Newton, N.J.: Rock Chapel Press, 1988.

Campbell, Bebe Moore. *Your Blues Ain't Like Mine.* New York: Ballantine Books, 1992.

Campbell, Christiana M. *The Farm Bureau and the New Deal: A Study of the Making of National Farm Policy, 1933–40.* Urbana: University of Illinois Press, 1962.

Carson, Clayborne. *In Struggle: SNCC and the Black Awakening of the 1960s.* Cambridge: Harvard University Press, 1981.

——, ed. *The Autobiography of Martin Luther King, Jr.* New York: Intellectual Properties Management in association with Warner Books, 1998.

Carter, Hodding, III. *The South Strikes Back.* Garden City, N.Y.: Doubleday, 1959.

Cash, W. J. *The Mind of the South.* 1941. Reprint, New York: Vintage, 1991.

Cell, John W. *The Highest Stage of White Supremacy: The Origins of Segregation in South Africa and the American South.* New York: Cambridge University Press, 1982.

Chafe, William. *Civilities and Civil Rights: Greensboro, North Carolina, and the Black Struggle for Freedom.* New York: Oxford University Press, 1980.

——. *Never Stop Running: Allard Lowenstein and the Struggle to Save American Liberalism.* New York: Basic Books, 1993.

Chappell, David L. *Inside Agitators: White Southerners in the Civil Rights Movement.* Baltimore: Johns Hopkins University Press, 1994.

——. *A Stone of Hope: Prophetic Religion and the Death of Jim Crow.* Chapel Hill: University of North Carolina Press, 2004.

Claiborne, Craig. *A Feast Made for Laughter.* New York: Holt, Rinehart, and Winston, 1982.

Cobb, James C. *Industrialization and Southern Society, 1877–1984.* Chicago: Dorsey Press, 1988.

——. *The Most Southern Place on Earth: The Mississippi Delta and the Roots of Regional Identity.* New York: Oxford University Press, 1992.

Cohn, David. *Where I Was Born and Raised.* 1935. Reprint, South Bend: Notre Dame Press, 1967.

Colburn, David R. *Racial Change and Community Crisis: Saint Augustine, Florida, 1877–1980.* New York: Columbia University Press, 1985.

Cone, James. *Martin and Malcolm and America: A Dream or a Nightmare?* Maryknoll, N.Y.: Orbis, 1991.

Congressional Record. 83rd Cong., 2d sess., 1954. Vol. 100, pt. 6. Washington, D.C.

Conrad, David E. *The Forgotten Farmers: The Story of Sharecroppers in the New Deal.* Urbana: University of Illinois Press, 1965.

Couto, Richard A. *Ain't Gonna Let Nobody Turn Me Around: The Pursuit of Racial Justice in the Rural South.* Philadelphia: Temple University Press, 1991.

Crawford, Vicky L., Jacqueline Anne Rouse, and Barbara Woods, eds. *Women in the Civil Rights Movement: Trailblazers and Torchbearers, 1941–1965*. Brooklyn: Carlson Publishing, 1990.

Crotty, William J. *Decision for the Democrats: Reforming the Party Structure*. Baltimore: Johns Hopkins University Press, 1978.

Curry, Constance. *Silver Rights*. Chapel Hill: Algonquin Books, 1995.

Curry, Constance, et al. *Deep in Our Hearts: Nine White Women in the Civil Rights Movement*. Athens: University of Georgia Press, 2000.

Daniel, Pete. *Breaking the Land: The Transformation of Cotton, Tobacco, and Rice Cultures since 1800*. Urbana: University of Illinois Press, 1985.

———. *Deep'n as It Come: The 1927 Mississippi River Flood*. New York: Oxford University Press, 1977.

———. *Lost Revolutions: The South in the 1950s*. Chapel Hill: University of North Carolina Press, 2000.

Davis, Helen Dick, ed. *Trials of the Earth: The Autobiography of Mary Hamilton*. Jackson: University Press of Mississippi, 1992.

Davis, Sidney Fant. *Mississippi Negro Lore*. Jackson, Tenn.: McCowat-Mercer, 1914.

Dent, Thomas C. *Southern Journey: A Return to the Civil Rights Movement*. New York: William Morrow, 1997.

Dittmer, John. *Local People: The Struggle for Civil Rights in Mississippi*. Urbana: University of Illinois Press, 1994.

Dollard, John. *Caste and Class in a Southern Town*. New York: Doubleday, 1949.

Draper, Alan. *Conflict of Interests: Organized Labor and Civil Rights in the South*. Ithaca: Cornell University Press, 1994.

Dray, Philip. *At the Hands of Parties Unknown: The Lynching of Black America*. New York: Random House, 2002.

Dunbar, Tony. *Delta Time: A Journey through Mississippi*. New York: Pantheon Books, 1990.

Eagles, Charles, ed. *The Civil Rights Movement in America*. Jackson: University Press of Mississippi, 1986.

Egerton, John. *A Mind to Stay Here: Profiles from the South*. New York: Macmillan, 1970.

———. *Speak Now against the Day: The Generation before the Civil Rights Movement*. Chapel Hill: University of North Carolina Press, 1995.

Eskew, Glenn T. *But for Birmingham: The Local and National Movements in the Civil Rights Struggle*. Chapel Hill: University of North Carolina Press, 1997.

Evans, David. *Big Road Blues: Tradition and Creativity in the Folk Blues*. 1982. Reprint, New York: Da Capo, 1987.

Fairclough, Adam. *Martin Luther King, Jr.* Athens: University of Georgia Press, 1990.

———. *Race and Democracy: The Civil Rights Struggle in Louisiana, 1915–1972*. Athens: University of Georgia Press, 1996.

———. *To Redeem the Soul of America: The Southern Christian Leadership Conference and Martin Luther King, Jr.* Athens: University of Georgia Press, 1987.

Ferris, William. *Blues from the Delta*. New York: Da Capo, 1978.

Finegold, Kenneth, and Theda Skocpol. *State and Party in America's New Deal*. Madison: University of Wisconsin Press, 1995.

Frederickson, Kari. *The Dixiecrat Revolt and the End of the Segregated South, 1932–1968*. Chapel Hill: University of North Carolina Press, 2001.

Fredrickson, George. *Black Liberation: A Comparative History of Black Ideologies in the United States and South Africa*. New York: Oxford University Press, 1995.

——. *White Supremacy: A Comparative Study in American and South African History*. New York: Oxford University Press, 1981.

Garrow, David J. *Bearing the Cross: Martin Luther King, Jr., and the Southern Christian Leadership Conference*. New York: William Morrow, 1986.

——. *The FBI and Martin Luther King, Jr.* New York: Norton, 1981.

Genovese, Eugene. *Roll, Jordan, Roll: The World the Slaves Made*. 1972. Reprint, New York: Vintage, 1976.

Ginzburg, Ralph. *100 Years of Lynchings*. 1962. Reprint, Baltimore: Black Classic Press, 1988.

Gitlin, Todd. *The Sixties: Years of Hope, Days of Rage*. New York: Bantam Books, 1987.

Goodwyn, Lawrence. *Democratic Promise: The Populist Moment in America*. New York: Oxford University Press, 1976.

Gould, Lewis L. *1968: The Election That Changed America*. Chicago: Ivan R. Dee, 1993.

Graham, Hugh Davis. *The Civil Rights Era: Origins and Development of National Policy, 1960–1972*. New York: Oxford University Press, 1998.

Grant, Joanne. *Ella Baker: Freedom Bound*. New York: Wiley, 1998.

Greenberg, Polly. *The Devil Has Slippery Shoes: A Biased Biography of the Child Development Group of Mississippi*. New York: Macmillan, 1969.

Greenberg, Stanley B. *Race and State in Capitalist Development: Comparative Perspectives*. New Haven: Yale University Press, 1980.

Greene, Melissa Fay. *Praying for Sheetrock*. New York: Fawcett Columbine, 1991.

Griggs, Sutton. *The Hindered Hand: Or, the Reign of the Repressionist*. Nashville: Orion Publishing, 1905.

Grossman, James. *Land of Hope: Chicago, Black Southerners, and the Great Migration*. Chicago: University of Chicago Press, 1989.

Haines, Herbert H. *Black Radicals and the Civil Rights Mainstream, 1954–1970*. Knoxville: University of Tennessee Press, 1988.

Haley, Alex. *The Autobiography of Malcolm X as Told to Alex Haley*. New York: Ballantine Books, 1974.

Hall, Jacquelyn Dowd. *Revolt against Chivalry: Jesse Daniel Ames and the Women's Campaign against Lynching*. New York: Columbia University Press, 1979.

Hampton, Henry, and Steve Fayer, eds. *Voices of Freedom: An Oral History of the Civil Rights Movement from the 1950s through the 1980s*. New York: Bantam Books, 1990.

Harris, Trudier. *Exorcising Blackness: Historical and Literary Lynching and Burning Rituals*. Bloomington: Indiana University Press, 1984.

Hemphill, Marie M. *Fevers, Floods, and Faith: A History of Sunflower County, Mississippi, 1844–1976*. Indianola, Miss.: Sunflower County Historical Society, 1980.

Henry, Aaron, and Constance Curry. *Aaron Henry: The Fire Ever Burning*. Jackson: University Press of Mississippi, 2000.

Hicks, Ruby Sheppeard. *The Song of the Delta*. Jackson: Howich House, 1976.

Hoare, Quintin, and Geoffrey Nowell Smith, eds. *Selections from "The Prison Notebooks" of Antonio Gramsci*. New York: International Publishers, 1971.

Holland, Endesha Ida Mae. *From the Mississippi Delta: A Memoir*. New York: Simon and Schuster, 1997.

Holley, Donald. *Uncle Sam's Farmers: The New Deal Communities in the Lower Mississippi Valley*. Urbana: University of Illinois Press, 1975.

Holt, Len. *The Summer That Didn't End*. New York: William Morrow, 1965.

Hudson, Winson, and Constance Curry. *Mississippi Harmony: Memoirs of a Freedom Fighter*. New York: Palgrave, 2002.

Humphrey, Hubert H. *The Education of a Public Man: My Life and Politics*. Edited by Norman Sherman. Garden City, N.Y.: Doubleday and Company, 1976.

Jackman, Mary. *The Velvet Glove: Paternalism and Conflict in Gender, Class, and Race Relations*. Berkeley: University of California Press, 1994.

Jacoway, Elizabeth, and David R. Colburn. *Southern Businessmen and Desegregation*. Baton Rouge: Louisiana State University Press, 1982.

Johnston, Erle. *Mississippi's Defiant Years, 1953–1973: An Interpretive Documentary with Personal Experiences*. Forest, Miss.: Lake Harbor Publishers, 1990.

Joint Center for Political and Economic Studies. *Black Elected Officials: A Statistical Summary, 2000*. Washington, D.C.: Joint Center for Political and Economic Studies, 2002.

Jones, Jacqueline. *Labor of Love, Labor of Sorrow: Black Women, Work, and the Family, from Slavery to the Present*. New York: Basic Books, 1985.

Katagiri, Yasuhiro. *The Mississippi State Sovereignty Commission: Civil Rights and States' Rights*. Jackson: University Press of Mississippi, 2001.

Kennedy, Stetson. *Jim Crow Guide: The Way It Was*. 1959. Reprint, Boca Raton: Florida Atlantic University Press, 1992.

Key, V. O. *Southern Politics in State and Nation*. 1949. Reprint, Knoxville: University of Tennessee Press, 1984.

King, B. B., with David Ritz. *Blues All around Me: The Autobiography of B. B. King*. New York: Avon, 1996.

Kirby, Jack Temple. *Rural Worlds Lost: The American South, 1920–1960*. Baton Rouge: Louisiana State University Press, 1987.

Kirwan, Albert D. *Revolt of the Rednecks: Mississippi Politics, 1876–1925*. Lexington: University of Kentucky Press, 1951.

Kluger, Richard. *Simple Justice: The History of Brown v. Board of Education and Black America's Struggle for Equality*. New York: Knopf, 1976.

Kotz, Nick. *Let Them Eat Promises: The Politics of Hunger in America*. Englewood Cliffs, N.J.: Prentice-Hall, 1969.

Lawson, Steven F. *Black Ballots: Voting Rights in the South, 1944–1969*. New York: Columbia University Press, 1976.

——. *In Pursuit of Power: Southern Blacks and Electoral Politics, 1965–1982*. New York: Columbia University Press, 1985.

Lawson, Steven F., and Charles Payne. *Debating the Civil Rights Movement, 1945–1968*. Lanham, Md.: Rowan and Littlefield, 1998.

Lee, Chana Kai. *For Freedom's Sake: The Life of Fannie Lou Hamer*. Urbana: University of Illinois Press, 1999.

Lemann, Nicholas. *The Promised Land: The Great Black Migration and How It Changed America*. New York: Vintage, 1991.

Levy, Peter B., ed. *Documentary History of the Civil Rights Movement*. New York: Greenwood Press, 1992.

Lewis, John, with Michael D'Orso. *Walking with the Wind: A Memoir of the Movement*. New York: Simon and Schuster, 1998.

Lipsitz, George. *A Life in the Struggle: Ivory Perry and the Culture of Opposition*. Philadelphia: Temple University Press, 1988.

Litwack, Leon F. *Been in the Storm So Long: The Aftermath of Slavery*. New York: Vintage, 1980.

———. *Trouble in Mind: Black Southerners in the Age of Jim Crow*. New York: Vintage, 1999.

Loewen, James W. *The Mississippi Chinese: Between Black and White*. 1971. Reprint, Prospect Heights, Ill.: Waveland, 1988.

Loewen, James W., and Charles Sallis, eds. *Mississippi: Conflict and Change*. New York: Pantheon Books, 1974.

MacLean, Nancy. *Behind the Mask of Chivalry: The Making of the Second Ku Klux Klan*. New York: Oxford University Press, 1994.

Marable, Manning. *Race, Reform, and Rebellion: The Second Reconstruction in Black America, 1945–1990*. 2d ed. Jackson: University Press of Mississippi, 1991.

Marsh, Charles. *God's Long Summer: Stories of Faith and Civil Rights*. Princeton, N.J.: Princeton University Press, 1997.

Martin, John Bartlow. *The Deep South Says "Never!"* New York: Ballantine Books, 1957.

Matusow, Allen J. *The Unraveling of America: A History of Liberalism in the 1960s*. New York: Harper and Row, 1984.

McAdam, Doug. *Freedom Summer*. New York: Oxford University Press, 1988.

McGill, Ralph. *The South and the Southerner*. 1959. Reprint, New York: Little, Brown, and Company, 1964.

McMillen, Neil. *The Citizens' Council: Organized Resistance to the Second Reconstruction, 1954–1964*. 1971. Reprint, Urbana: University of Illinois Press, 1994.

———. *Dark Journey: Black Mississippians in the Age of Jim Crow*. Urbana: University of Illinois Press, 1989.

———, ed. *Remaking Dixie: The Impact of World War II on the American South*. Jackson: University Press of Mississippi, 1997.

Meier, August, and Elliot Rudwick. *CORE: A Study of the Civil Rights Movement, 1942–1968*. New York: Oxford University Press, 1973.

Metress, Christopher, ed. *The Lynching of Emmett Till: A Documentary Narrative*. Charlottesville: University of Virginia Press, 2002.

Mills, Kay. *This Little Light of Mine: The Life of Fannie Lou Hamer*. New York: Plume, 1993.

Mills, Nicolaus. *Like a Holy Crusade: Mississippi 1964—The Turning of the Civil Rights Movement in America*. Chicago: Ivan R. Dee, 1992.

Moody, Anne. *Coming of Age in Mississippi*. New York: Laurel Books, 1968.

Moore, Barrington. *Social Origins of Dictatorship and Democracy: Lord and Peasant in the Making of the New World*. Boston: Beacon Press, 1966.

Morris, Aldon D. *The Origins of the Civil Rights Movement: Black Communities Organizing for Change*. New York: Free Press, 1984.

Moses, Robert, and Charles E. Cobb Jr. *Radical Equations: Math Literacy and Civil Rights*. Boston: Beacon Press, 2001.

National Association for the Advancement of Colored People. *Thirty Years of Lynching in the United States, 1889–1918*. New York: Arno Press, 1969.

Newman, Mark. *Divine Agitators: The Delta Ministry and Civil Rights in Mississippi*. Athens: University of Georgia Press, 2004.

Norrell, Robert. *Reaping the Whirlwind: The Civil Rights Movement in Tuskegee*. New York: Vintage, 1985.

Oshinsky, David M. *Worse Than Slavery: Parchman Farm and the Ordeal of Jim Crow Justice*. New York: Free Press, 1996.

Palmer, Robert. *Deep Blues: A Musical and Cultural History of the Mississippi Delta*. New York: Penguin Books, 1981.

Parker, Frank M. *Black Votes Count: Political Empowerment in Mississippi after 1965*. Chapel Hill: University of North Carolina Press, 1990.

Payne, Charles M. *I've Got the Light of Freedom: The Organizing Tradition and the Mississippi Freedom Struggle*. Berkeley: University of California Press, 1995.

Percy, William Alexander. *Lanterns on the Levee: Recollections of a Planter's Son*. New York: Knopf, 1941.

Piven, Frances Fox, and Richard A. Cloward. *Poor People's Movements: Why They Succeed, How They Fail*. New York: Pantheon Books, 1977.

Powdermaker, Hortense. *After Freedom: A Cultural Study in the Deep South*. 1939. Reprint, Madison: University of Wisconsin Press, 1993.

Raines, Howell. *My Soul Is Rested: Movement Days in the Deep South Remembered*. New York: Penguin Books, 1977.

Ransby, Barbara. *Ella Baker and the Black Freedom Movement: A Radical Democratic Vision*. Chapel Hill: University of North Carolina Press, 2003.

Robertson, John A., and Tom W. Conger Jr. *Early History of the Town of Ruleville, Mississippi, in the Heart of the Mississippi Delta*. Parchman, Miss.: Parchman Enterprises, 1993.

——. *Lehrton, Mississippi, 1850–1900: Supplement to Early History of the Town of Ruleville*. Parchman, Miss.: Parchman Enterprises, 1993.

Robnett, Belinda. *How Long? How Long? African-American Women in the Struggle for Civil Rights*. New York: Oxford University Press, 1997.

Rosengarten, Theodore. *All God's Dangers: The Life of Nate Shaw*. New York: Avon, 1974.

Rowland, Dunbar, ed. *Encyclopedia of Mississippi History, Comprising Sketches of Counties, Towns, Events, Institutions, and Persons*. Vol. 2. Madison, Wis.: Selwyn A. Brant, 1907.

Royce, Edward. *The Origins of Southern Sharecropping*. Philadelphia: Temple University Press, 1993.

Salomone, Rosemary C. *Equal Education under Law: Legal Rights and Federal Policy in the Post-Brown Era*. New York: St. Martin's Press, 1986.

Schweid, Richard. *Catfish and the Delta: Confederate Fish Farming in the Mississippi Delta*. Berkeley, Calif.: Ten Speed Press, 1992.

Sellers, Cleveland, with Robert Terrell. *The River of No Return: The Autobiography of a Black Militant and the Life and Death of SNCC*. Jackson: University Press of Mississippi, 1990.

Sherrill, Robert. *Gothic Politics in the Deep South*. New York: Ballantine Books, 1968.

Silver, James. *Mississippi: The Closed Society*. New York: Harcourt, Brace and World, 1964.

Sitkoff, Harvard. *A New Deal for Blacks: The Emergence of Civil Rights as a National Issue*. New York: Oxford University Press, 1978.

———. *The Struggle for Black Equality, 1954–1980*. New York: Hill and Wang, 1981.

Smead, Howard. *Blood Justice: The Lynching of Mack Charles Parker*. New York: Oxford University Press, 1986.

Smith, Frank. *Congressman from Mississippi*. New York: Pantheon Books, 1964.

Southern, Eileen. *The Music of Black Americans: A History*. 2d ed. New York: W. W. Norton and Company, 1983.

Stack, Carol. *Call to Home: African Americans Reclaim the Rural South*. New York: Basic Books, 1996.

Sugarman, Tracy. *Stranger at the Gates: A Summer in Mississippi*. New York: Hill and Wang, 1966.

Sullivan, Patricia. *Days of Hope: Race and Democracy in the New Deal Era*. Chapel Hill: University of North Carolina Press, 1996.

Sutherland, Elizabeth, ed. *Letters from Mississippi*. New York: McGraw-Hill, 1965.

Taulbert, Clifton. *When We Were Colored*. New York: Penguin Books, 1995.

Terkel, Studs. *Race: How Blacks and Whites Think and Feel about the American Obsession*. New York: New Press, 1992.

———. *Will the Circle Be Unbroken? Reflections on Death, Rebirth, and Hunger for a Faith*. New York: Ballantine Books, 2002.

Theoharis, Athan, ed. *From the Secret Files of J. Edgar Hoover*. Chicago: Ivan R. Dee, 1991.

Tyson, Timothy B. *Radio Free Dixie: Robert F. Williams and the Roots of Black Power*. Chapel Hill: University of North Carolina Press, 1999.

U.S. Commission on Civil Rights. *Political Participation*. Washington, D.C.: Government Printing Office, 1968.

U.S. Department of Commerce. *1970 Census of Population: Characteristics of the Population, Part 26: Mississippi*. Washington, D.C.: Government Printing Office, 1973.

———. *1980 Census of Population: General Social and Economic Characteristics, Mississippi*. Washington, D.C.: Government Printing Office, 1983.

———. *County and City Data Book 1962: A Statistical Abstract Supplement*. Washington, D.C.: Government Printing Office, 1962.

———. *County Data Book: A Supplement to the Statistical Abstract of the United States*. Washington, D.C.: Government Printing Office, 1947.

U.S. House Committee on Un-American Activities. *Activities of Ku Klux Klan Organizations in the United States*. 89th Cong. Washington, D.C.: Government Printing Office, 1968.

Viorst, Milton. *Fire in the Streets: America in the 1960s*. New York: Simon and Schuster, 1979.

Waldrep, Christopher. *The Many Faces of Judge Lynch: Extralegal Violence and Punishment in America*. New York: Palgrave, 2002.

Walton, Anthony. *Mississippi: An American Journey*. New York: Vintage, 1996.

Weiss, Nancy J. *Farewell to the Party of Lincoln: Black Politics in the Age of FDR*. Princeton, N.J.: Princeton University Press, 1983.

West, Cornel. *Race Matters*. Boston: Beacon Press, 1993.

Whalen, Charles, and Barbara Whalen. *The Longest Debate: A Legislative History of the 1964 Civil Rights Act*. New York: Mentor, 1985.

Wharton, Vernon Lane. *The Negro in Mississippi, 1865–1890*. 1947. Reprint, Westport, Conn.: Greenwood Press, 1984.

Whayne, Jeannie M. *A New Plantation South: Land, Labor, and Federal Favor in Twentieth-Century Arkansas*. Charlottesville: University Press of Virginia, 1996.

Whitehead, Don. *Attack on Terror: The FBI against the Ku Klux Klan in Mississippi*. New York: Funk and Wagnalls, 1970.

Whitfield, Stephen J. *A Death in the Delta: The Story of Emmett Till*. Baltimore: Johns Hopkins University Press, 1988.

Wilkie, Curtis. *Dixie: A Personal Odyssey through Events That Shaped the Modern South*. New York: Simon and Schuster, 2001.

Williams, Juan. *Eyes on the Prize: America's Civil Rights Years, 1954–1965*. New York: Penguin Books, 1987.

Willis, John C. *Forgotten Time: The Yazoo-Mississippi Delta after the Civil War*. Charlottesville: University Press of Virginia, 2000.

Wilson, August. *The Piano Lesson*. New York: Plume, 1990.

Wirt, Frederick M. *We Ain't What We Was: Civil Rights in the New South*. Durham, N.C.: Duke University Press, 1997.

Woodruff, Nan Elizabeth. *American Congo: The African American Freedom Struggle in the Delta*. Cambridge: Harvard University Press, 2003.

Woods, Clyde. *Development Arrested: The Blues and Plantation Power in the Mississippi Delta*. London: Verso, 1998.

Woodward, C. Vann. *Origins of the New South, 1877–1913*. Baton Rouge: Louisiana State University Press, 1951.

Wright, Gavin. *Old South, New South: Revolutions in the Southern Economy since the Civil War*. New York: Basic Books, 1986.

Wyatt-Brown, Bertram. *The House of Percy: Honor, Melancholy, and Imagination in a Southern Family*. New York: Oxford University Press, 1994.

——. *Southern Honor: Ethics and Behavior of the Old South*. New York: Oxford University Press, 1982.

Yarborough, Steve. *The Oxygen Man: A Novel*. New York: Simon and Schuster, 1999.

Youth of the Rural Organizing and Cultural Center. *Minds Stayed on Freedom: The Civil Rights Movement in the Rural South, an Oral History*. Boulder, Colo.: Westview Press, 1991.

Zinn, Howard. *A People's History of the United States*. New York: Harper and Row, 1980.

——. *SNCC: The New Abolitionists*. Boston: Beacon Press, 1965.

Articles, Essays, Dissertations, Theses, and Papers

Aiken, Charles S. "A New Type of Black Ghetto in the Plantation South." *Annals of the Association of American Geographers* 80 (1990): 223–46.

American Friends Service Committee, Delta Ministry of the National Council of Churches, et al. "The Status of School Desegregation in the South, 1970." Unpublished paper.

Baker, Ella. "Bigger than a Hamburger." *Southern Patriot* 18, no. 4 (May 1960): 4.

Bass, Harold F., Jr. "Lyndon B. Johnson and the MFDP Controversy." *Presidential Studies Quarterly* (Winter 1991): 85–101.

Behel, Sandra K. "The Mississippi Home Front during World War II: Tradition and Change." Ph.D. diss., Mississippi State University, 1989.

Bolton, Charles C. "The Last Stand of Massive Resistance: Mississippi Public School Integration, 1970." *Journal of Mississippi History* 41 (1999): 329–50.

——. "Mississippi's School Equalization Program, 1945–1954: 'A Last Gasp to Try to Maintain a Segregated Educational System.'" *Journal of Southern History* 66, no. 4 (November 2000): 781–814.

Bond, Julian. "Nonviolence: An Interpretation, No. 1, 1963." In *The Freedomways Reader: Prophets in Their Own Country*, edited by Esther Cooper Jackson and Constance Pohl, 72–76. Boulder, Colo.: Westview Press, 2000.

Brady, Thomas. "A Review of Black Monday, in an Address Made to the Indianola Citizens' Council, October 28, 1954." Winona, Miss.: Association of Citizens' Councils of Mississippi (Rare Books Collection, University of North Carolina, Chapel Hill).

Carley, Paul S., and Marshall C. Balfour. "Prevalence of Malaria in Humphreys and Sunflower Counties, Mississippi, in 1927–28." *Southern Medical Journal* 22, no. 4 (April 1929): 379.

Carson, Clayborne. "Martin Luther King, Jr.: Charismatic Leadership in a Mass Struggle." *Journal of American History* 74, no. 2 (September 1987): 448–54.

Carter, Hodding, III. "Negro Exodus from the Delta Continues." *New York Times Magazine*, March 10, 1968, 26–30.

Clark, Eric C. "Legislative Adoption of BAWI, 1936." *Journal of Mississippi History* 52, no. 4 (November 1990): 283–99.

Cobb, James C. "Beyond Planters and Industrialists: A New Perspective on the New South." *Journal of Southern History* 54, no. 1 (February 1988): 45–79.

———. "'Somebody Done Nailed Us on the Cross': Federal Farm and Welfare Policy and the Civil Rights Movement in the Mississippi Delta." *Journal of American History* 77, no. 3 (December 1990): 912–36.

———. "The South's South: The Enigma of Creativity in the Mississippi Delta." *Southern Review* 25, no. 1 (Winter 1989): 72–86.

Crespino, Joseph. "Strategic Accommodation: Civil Rights Opponents in Mississippi and Their Impact on American Racial Politics, 1953–1972." Ph.D. diss., Stanford University, 2002.

Crosby, David. "A Piece of Your Own: The Tenant Purchase Program in Claiborne County." *Southern Cultures* 5, no. 2 (Summer 1999): 46–63.

Crosby, Emilye. "Common Courtesy: The Civil Rights Movement in Claiborne County, Mississippi." Ph.D. diss., University of Indiana, 1995.

Cunningen, Donald. "The Mississippi State Advisory Committee to the United States Commission on Civil Rights, 1960–1965." *Journal of Mississippi History* 53, no. 1 (February 1991): 1–17.

Dallek, Robert. "The President We Love to Blame." *Wilson Quarterly* 15 (Winter 1991): 100–107.

Daniel, Pete. "Going among Strangers: Southern Reactions to World War II." *Journal of American History* 77, no. 3 (December 1990): 886–911.

———. "The Transformation of the Rural South, 1930 to the Present." *Agricultural History* 55, no. 3 (1981): 231–48.

DeMuth, Jerry. "Summer in Mississippi: Freedom Moves in to Stay." *The Nation*, September 14, 1964, 104–10.

———. "Tired of Being Sick and Tired." *The Nation*, June 1, 1964, 548–51.

Dittmer, John. "The Transformation of the Mississippi Movement, 1964–1968: The Rise and Fall of the Freedom Democratic Party." In *The Walter Prescott Webb Lectures, Number 26: Essays on the American Civil Rights Movement*, edited by W. Marvin Dulaney and Kathleen Underwood, 9–43. College Station: Texas A&M University Press, 1993.

"The Doddsville Savagery." *Voice of the Negro* 1, no. 3 (March 1904): 81–82.

Dorsey, L. C. "Harder Times Than These." In *Mississippi Writers: Reflections of Childhood and Youth*, vol. 2, *Non-Fiction*, edited by Dorothy Abbott, 165–74. Jackson: University of Mississippi Press, 1986.

———. "A Prophet Who Believed." *Sojourners* 11 (December 1982): 21.

Draper, Alan. "Claude Ramsey, the Mississippi AFL-CIO, and the Civil Rights Movement." *Labor's Heritage* 4, no. 4 (1992): 4–19.

Du Bois, W. E. B. "My Evolving Program for Negro Freedom." In *What the Negro Wants*, edited by Rayford W. Logan, 53. Chapel Hill: University of North Carolina Press, 1944.

———. "Review of *After Freedom*." *Social Forces* 18, no. 1 (October 1939): 137–39.

Eagles, Charles W. "Toward New Histories of the Civil Rights Era." *Journal of Southern History* 66, no. 4 (November 2000): 815–48.

Evans, Sara. "Women's Consciousness and the Southern Black Movement." *Southern Exposure* 4, no. 4 (1977): 10–18.

Finnegan, Terrence. "Lynching and Political Power in Mississippi and South Carolina." In *Under Sentence of Death: Lynching in the South*, edited by W. Fitzhugh Brundage, 189–218. Chapel Hill: University of North Carolina Press, 1997.

Fuquay, Michael W. "Civil Rights and the Private School Movement in Mississippi, 1964–1971." *History of Education Quarterly* 42, no. 2 (Summer 2002): 159–80.

Gould, Lewis L. " 'Never a Deep Partisan': Lyndon Johnson and the Democratic Party, 1963–1969." In *The Johnson Years*, vol. 3, *LBJ at Home and Abroad*, edited by Robert A. Divine, 21–52. Lawrence: University Press of Kansas, 1994.

Greenfield, Meg. "LBJ and the Democrats." *The Reporter*, June 2, 1966, 8–13.

Gussow, Adam. "Racial Violence, 'Primitive' Music, and the Blues Entrepreneur: W. C. Handy's Mississippi Problem." *Southern Cultures* 8, no. 3 (Fall 2002): 56–77.

Hamer, Fannie Lou. Foreword to *Stranger at the Gates: A Summer in Mississippi*, by Tracy Sugarman. New York: Hill and Wang, 1966.

——. "To Praise Our Bridges." In *Mississippi Writers: Reflections of Childhood and Youth*, vol. 2, *Non-Fiction*, edited by Dorothy Abbott, 322–23. Jackson: University of Mississippi Press, 1986.

Hathorn, Clay. "Poverty along the Mississippi: Down and Out in the Delta." *The Nation*, July 9, 1990, 50–53.

Holmes, William F. "The Leflore County Massacre and the Demise of the Colored Farmers' Alliance." *Phylon* 34, no. 3 (September 1973): 267–74.

——. "Whitecapping: Agrarian Violence in Mississippi, 1902–06." *Journal of Southern History* 35, no. 2 (May 1969): 165–85.

Honey, Michael. "Operation Dixie: Labor and Civil Rights in the Postwar South." *Mississippi Quarterly* 45, no. 4 (Fall 1992): 439–52.

"Hopeful Signs in Mississippi." *Voice of the Negro* 1, no. 5 (May 1904): 173.

Huie, William Bradford. "The Shocking Story of Approved Killings in Mississippi." *Look*, January 24, 1956, 46–50.

——. "What's Happened to the Emmett Till Killers?" *Look*, January 22, 1957, 63–68

" 'I Want to Focus on People Problems': Interview with HEW Secretary Richardson." *U.S. News and World Report*, December 7, 1970, 35–39.

Jetter, Alexis. "We Shall Overcome, This Time with Algebra." *New York Times Magazine*, February 21, 1993, 28–72.

Johnson, Phillip J. "The Limits of Interracial Compromise: Louisiana, 1941." *Journal of Southern History* 69, no. 2 (May 2003): 319–48.

Kelley, Robin D. G. " 'We Are Not What We Seem': Rethinking Black Working-Class Opposition in the Jim Crow South." *Journal of American History* 80, no. 1 (June 1993): 75–112.

Kight, Lawrence E. " 'The State Is on Trial': Governor Edmund F. Noel and the Defense of Mississippi's Legal Institutions against Mob Violence." *Journal of Mississippi History* 60, no. 3 (Fall 1998): 191–222.

King, Ed. "Prophet of Hope for the Sick and Tired." *Sojourners* 11 (December 1982): 18–21.

Kopkind, Andrew. "New Radicals in Dixie: Those 'Subversive' Civil Rights Workers." *New Republic*, April 10, 1965, 13–16.

Lapidary, Charles J. "Belzoni, Mississippi." *New Republic*, May 7, 1956, 12.

———. "Ol' Massa Jim Eastland." *Nation*, February 9, 1957, 121.

Lawson, Steven F. "Freedom Then, Freedom Now: The Historiography of the Civil Rights Movement." *American Historical Review* 96, no. 2 (April 1991): 456–71.

Lee, Chana Kai. "A Passionate Pursuit of Justice: The Life and Leadership of Fannie Lou Hamer." Ph.D. diss., University of California, Los Angeles, 1993.

Lemann, Nicholas. "The Long March." *New Yorker*, February 10, 2003, 86–91.

Locke, Mamie E. "The Role of African-American Women in the Civil Rights and Women's Movements in Hinds County and Sunflower County, Mississippi." *Journal of Mississippi History* 53 (1991): 229–39.

Lynd, Staughton. "The Freedom Schools: Concept and Organization." In *The Freedomways Reader: Prophets in Their Own Country*, edited by Esther Cooper Jackson and Constance Pohl, 94–96. Boulder, Colo.: Westview Press, 2000.

Maass, Peter. "The Secrets of Mississippi." *New Republic*, December 21, 1998, 21–25.

Madison, Isaiah. "The Freedom Movement Lives On." *Southern Exposure* 21, no. 3 (Fall 1993): 43–45.

Marable, Manning. "Black Politics and the Challenge for the Left." *Monthly Review* 41, no. 11 (April 1990): 22–31.

———. "The Paradox of Reform: Black Politics and the Democratic Party." *Southern Exposure* 12, no. 1 (February 1984): 20–25.

McKnight, Laura Lynn. "Lessons in Freedom: Race, Education, and Progress in a Mississippi Delta Community since 1965." Master's thesis, University of Mississippi, 1996.

McLaurin, Charles. "Voice of Calm." *Sojourners* 11 (December 1982): 12–13.

McLemore, Leslie. "The Mississippi Freedom Democratic Party." Ph.D. diss., University of Massachusetts, Amherst, 1971.

McMillen, Neil. "Black Enfranchisement in Mississippi: Federal Enforcement and Black Protest in the 1960s." *Journal of Southern History* 43, no. 3 (August 1977): 351–72.

———. "Fighting for What We Didn't Have: How Mississippi's Black Veterans Remember World War II." In *Remaking Dixie: The Impact of World War II on the American South*, edited by Neil McMillen, 93–110. Jackson: University Press of Mississippi, 1997.

Miroff, Bruce. "Presidential Leverage over Social Movements: The Johnson White House and Civil Rights." *Journal of Politics* 43, no. 1 (February 1981): 2–23.

Moye, J. Todd. " 'If We Don't Get Seated This Time, We'll Probably Never Attend Another Convention': Lyndon Johnson and Mississippi Democrats." Master's report, University of Texas, 1995.

O'Dell, J. H. "Life in Mississippi: An Interview with Fannie Lou Hamer." In *The Freedomways Reader: Prophets in Their Own Country*, edited by Esther Cooper Jackson and Constance Pohl, 97–99. Boulder, Colo.: Westview Press, 2000.

Oshinsky, David. "Should the Mississippi Files Have Been Reopened?" *New York Times Magazine*, August 30, 1998, 30–34.

Peterson, Franklynn. "Sunflowers Don't Grow in Sunflower County." *Sepia* (February 1970): 9–21.

Prince, Jack E. "History and Development of the Mississippi Balance Agriculture with Industry Program, 1936–1958." Ph.D. diss., Ohio State University, 1961.

Reagon, Bernice Johnson. "The Civil Rights Movement." Liner notes to *Voices of the Civil Rights Movement: Black American Freedom Songs, 1960–1966* (audio recording). Washington, D.C.: Smithsonian Institution, 1980.

Robinson, Armstead, and Patricia Sullivan. "Reassessing the History of the Civil Rights Movement." In *New Directions in Civil Rights Studies*, edited by Armstead Robinson and Patricia Sullivan, 1–7. Charlottesville: University Press of Virginia, 1991.

Romaine, Anne. "The Mississippi Freedom Democratic Party through 1964." Master's thesis, University of Virginia, 1971.

Rowe-Simms, Sarah. "The Mississippi State Sovereignty Commission: An Agency History." *Journal of Mississippi History* 61 (1999): 29–58.

Rustin, Bayard. "From Protest to Politics: The Future of the Civil Rights Movement." In *The New Radicals: A Report with Documents*, edited by Paul Jacobs and Saul Landau, 295–310. New York: Random House, 1967.

Sherrill, Robert G. "James Eastland: Child of Scorn." *Nation* 201 (October 4, 1965): 184–95.

"Siamese Twins Who Survived." *Ebony Magazine*, February 1957, 39–45.

Sidey, Hugh. "Sad Song of the Delta (Many Afro-Americans in the Mississippi Delta Still Live an Impoverished Lifestyle)." *Time*, June 24, 1991, 14–19.

Simpson, William. "The Birth of the Mississippi 'Loyalist Democrats.'" *Journal of Mississippi History* 44, no. 1 (February 1982): 27–45.

Sinsheimer, Joseph A. "The Freedom Vote of 1963: New Strategies of Racial Protest in Mississippi." *Journal of Southern History* 55, no. 2 (May 1989): 217–44.

Sitkoff, Harvard. "African American Militancy in the World War II South: Another Perspective." In *Remaking Dixie: The Impact of World War II on the American South*, edited by Neil McMillen, 70–92. Jackson: University Press of Mississippi, 1997.

Skates, John R. "World War II as a Watershed in Mississippi History." *Journal of Mississippi History* 37 (1975): 131–42.

Sneed, Don, Daniel Riffe, and Roger Van Ommeren. "The Role of a Mississippi Weekly Newspaper in Defusing Racially Volatile Political News: A Case Study." *Western Journal of Black Studies* 20, no. 3 (Fall 1996): 151–57.

"Sunrise in Sunflower?" *Newsweek*, August 14, 1950, 80.

Swartz, Benjamin, and Christina Swartz. "Mississippi Monte Carlo." *Atlantic Monthly* 277, no. 1 (January 1996): 67–82.

Trillin, Calvin. "State Secrets." *New Yorker*, May 29, 1995, 54–64.

Umoja, Akinyele K. "Eye for an Eye: The Role of Armed Resistance in the Mississippi Freedom Movement." Ph.D. diss., Emory University, 1996.

——. "1964: The Beginning of the End of Nonviolence in the Mississippi Freedom Movement." *Radical History Review* 85 (Winter 2003): 201–26.

University of Mississippi Bureau of Educational Research. "The Report of a Study of the Education for Negroes in Sunflower County, Mississippi." Oxford: University of Mississippi, 1950, University of Mississippi Special Collections.

Waldrep, Christopher. "War of Words: The Controversy over the Definition of Lynching, 1899–1940." *Journal of Southern History* 66, no. 1 (February 2000): 75–100.

Webster, Donovan. "Heart of the Delta." *New Yorker*, July 8, 1991, 46–63.

Woodruff, Nan Elizabeth. "African-American Struggles for Citizenship in the Arkansas and Mississippi Deltas in the Age of Jim Crow." *Radical History Review* 55 (Winter 1993): 33–51.

——. "Mississippi Delta Planters and Debates over Mechanization, Labor and Civil Rights in the 1940s." *Journal of Southern History* 60, no. 2 (1994): 263–84.

Wren, Christopher S. "Mississippi: The Attack on Bigotry." *Look*, September 8, 1964, 20–28.

Young, Aurelia Norris, and Worth Long. "The Movement Remembered: 'Like a Banked Fire.'" *Southern Changes* 5, no. 6 (December 1983): 8–13.

Zinn, Howard. "Schools in Context: The Mississippi Idea." *The Nation*, November 23, 1964, 371–75.

Acknowledgments

This project began one day around 1993 when I learned that Fannie Lou Hamer, at that time an underappreciated heroine of the southern civil rights movement (she has since received much of her just due), and Jim Eastland had lived within spitting distance of each other in a region of the country whose rich blues culture I was just beginning to appreciate. I must first acknowledge Kay Mills and Robert Palmer, whose books—*This Little Light of Mine* and *Deep Blues*, respectively—showed me the way in the first place.

John Dittmer, David Montejano, Jim Sidbury, Davis Bowman, Byron Hulsey, Sean Kelley, Christopher Waldrep, Fitzhugh Brundage, Connie Curry, John Egerton, Bob Blythe, Cliff Kuhn, Pete Daniel, and Jim Abbott all read at least parts of this manuscript in one form or another and made valuable suggestions for improvement. I am grateful to all of them. Joe Crespino read several chapters on short notice, improved my prose, and helped me think through some important issues; I cannot thank him enough. I hope I have not neglected to thank anyone else whose work helped improve this book—but I almost certainly have, in which case I beg forgiveness. I cannot possibly repay all of the people whose ideas about the civil rights movement, themes in southern history, the practice of oral history, and other issues have found their way into *Let the People Decide*. Librarians and archivists from Austin, Texas, to Washington, D.C., and dozens of points in between offered valuable assistance that I wish I could return.

A fellowship and travel grants from the University of Texas history department facilitated the research behind the dissertation that was the origin of this book. A postdoctoral fellowship from the Avery Research Center for African-American History and Culture at the College of Charleston afforded the time to begin revisions to the manuscript, though my boss, Marvin Dulaney, assigned me such interesting work there that I found ample reason to put it off. I am grateful to him. My colleagues at the National Park Service's Tuskegee Airmen Oral History Project—Worth Long, Lisa Bratton, Bill Mansfield, and Judith Brown—have influenced me in ways that I am sure I haven't even begun to realize, and I am obliged to each of them. I enjoy their collegiality and am proud of the work we have done together.

In the paperback edition to his classic study of "Southerntown"—which was really Indianola—John Dollard wrote, "I expected to lose my friends in Southerntown when this book was published . . . [and] the matter turned out as I expected." My friends in Southerntown and its environs—among them Jim and Cynthia Abbott, Matt and Wendy McWilliams, Charles McLaurin, Owen and Lescener Brooks, Bernice White, and Mae Bertha Carter—made this book possible, and I hope they enjoy it. Even if they don't, I hope they remain my friends. Countless people in Sunflower County opened their homes and their personal histories to me during the course of this work, and I cannot possibly thank them enough. I owe a special debt to Mae Bertha Carter, who was generous with her time and her knowledge. She may be the savviest person I have ever met. I miss her. I want to thank Jim and Cynthia Abbott for their hospitality, friendship, and generosity. Indianola would be a much poorer place—in many ways—if not for the Abbotts and their stewardship of the town's newspaper.

My most heartfelt thanks go to Rachel Feit. Rachel allowed me to run off from Austin to Mississippi for several months at a time to do research and record oral history interviews, and she accepted me upon return. When I left again to take a job in Charleston, she tolerated it. When we married and I dragged her away from Austin to live in Atlanta, she . . . endured it (or has so far, anyway). I owe her everything.

I thank Luke Moye for giving me the best excuses an author ever had for not working on a book.

My grandfather Tom Davis, a lifelong southerner who ministered to a procession of Presbyterian congregations throughout Dixie, seemed to think it funny that a grandson of his would want to write a book about Mississippi. I am still not entirely sure why. In any case, I wish he had lived to see it published. I hope that the Davis, Moye, and Feit families can be proud of this book. They have given me so many gifts and so much support. To say "Thanks" to all of them seems profoundly inadequate, but I'll say it here anyway in the hope that they all know how deeply I mean it. The same goes for the dozens of friends along the way whose (seemingly) innocent question, "How is your book coming?," eventually shamed me into finishing it.

A final note: if you are at all interested in the ideals that Fannie Lou Hamer and her colleagues espoused and lived by, you should be aware of the fine work being done by the Sunflower County Freedom Project. As you read this, the Freedom Project is helping Sunflower County students overcome some of the same obstacles that their parents and grandparents faced. Inspired by the ideals of the original Freedom Schools and the area's particular movement heritage, Chris Myers and the other founders of the Freedom Project set out to raise expectations for children in Sunflower County. They are succeeding, and they deserve your support. For more information on the Freedom Project, point your browser to <www.sunflowerfreedom.org>.

Index